RÁBI'A

RÁBI'A OF BAṢRA has long been known to students of mysticism as a woman of unique personality among early Ṣúfís and a true mystic. This work by Margaret Smith is the first complete biography of the early Muslim saint, who died in the year 801. Dr Smith, a distinguished scholar of Ṣúfism, also offers in this fascinating book a rare survey of the other women mystics of Islám.

Henry D. Kashoutz

Henry David Kashoutz

RÁBI'A

THE LIFE & WORK OF RÁBI'A AND OTHER WOMEN MYSTICS IN ISLÁM

MARGARET SMITH

ONEWORLD

OXFORD

RÁBI'A

Oneworld Publications
(Sales and Editorial)
185 Banbury Road
Oxford OX2 7AR
England

Oneworld Publications
(U.S. Sales Office)
42 Broadway
Rockport
MA 01966, U.S.A.

A CIP record for this book is available
from the British Library

ISBN 1-85168-085-3

Printed and bound by WSOY, Finland

CONTENTS

PREFACE

RÁBI'A OF BAṢRA, the subject of this memoir, has long been known to students of Ṣúfism, and to a lesser extent to those interested in mysticism generally, as a unique personality among the early Ṣúfís, one who, in spite of her early date – she died in AD 801 – was a true mystic. The material for this account of her life and teachings is derived from one or two short biographical notices and from scattered references to be found in Arab and Persian writers on Ṣúfism and is the first biography of this early Muslim saint to appear, which aims at being complete, so far as the sources at present available make this possible.

In the compiling of this biography, originally undertaken for the degree of Doctor of Philosophy in the University of London, I have been indebted for valuable references to Professor L. Massignon, of the Collège de France, and to Prof. Ritter of Constantinople, and I take this opportunity of offering my thanks to both of these distinguished scholars.

My grateful thanks are due also to Sir Thomas Arnold, from whom I have had constant help and advice in the writing of this memoir, and to Professor Nicholson of Cambridge, whose writings first inspired me to study Ṣúfism, and whose unrivalled knowledge of the subject has been most generously placed at my disposal for the purposes of this book.

MARGARET SMITH

SURVEY OF SOURCES

The sources from which information is to be derived about the life and teachings of Rábi'a al-'Adawiyya al-Qaysiyya give us evidence which at the best is fragmentary and in many cases unreliable, chiefly because her biographers lived at a considerable distance of time after her death, and legend has played at least as great a part as history in the account given of the story of her life. This, however, is no uncommon thing where saints are concerned, be they Muslim or Christian, and the accounts given show us at least the estimation in which Rábi'a was held by those who came after her, and are a clear indication that she had a great reputation during her lifetime. Belonging to the sex to which Muslim theologians commonly attributed little capacity for thought, and less for religion,[1] only a woman of outstanding character and gifts could have won a place among the greatest of the Ṣúfí teachers, renowned as much for her teaching as for the blameless sanctity of her life.

A small point, but one of great significance, is that she is constantly referred to by later writers as "Rábi'a" pure and simple, proving that both to the writers and to those for whom they wrote, she was a personality too well known to need further description.

The earliest writer who mentions her is *al-Jáḥiz* (the Goggle-eyed) of Baṣra (*ob.* AD 869), a well-known thinker, who gave his name to a sect of the Mu'tazilites. He wrote the *Kitáb al-Ḥayawán* (The Book of Animals) and the *Kitáb al-Bayán wa al-Tabyín*, a popular book on rhetoric. In both of these he mentions Rábi'a al-Qaysiyya. His references to her are of the first importance, because of his early date, and the fact that he may have known Rábi'a in his early childhood and in any case is likely to have known those who were personally acquainted with her. As a native of Baṣra, her own city, he would be in close touch with all types of religious thought and religious thinkers in that place.

Abú Naṣr al-Sarráj (*ob.* AD 988), who was born at Ṭús, and was surnamed the "Peacock of the Poor",[2] mentions Rábi'a once in his

Kitáb al-Luma', one of the earliest treatises on Ṣúfism, which it was the author's intention to justify as being in accordance with the Qur'án and the Traditions, and as the knowledge directly revealed by God to His saints.[3] Al-Sarráj is concerned to give the views of Ṣúfí thinkers, not his own theories. He quotes from both books and oral traditions and in most cases states his authorities. Because of his early date and also because of his method of dealing with his subject, al-Sarráj's work is of great importance, though not so complete or so clear a statement of Ṣúfí doctrine as the *Qút al-Qulúb* of his contemporary Abú Ṭálib, nor so concise and readable as the *Risála* of al-Qushayrí.[4]

Abú Ṭálib al-Makkí (*ob.* AD 996), an ascetic who lived and taught in Mecca, Baṣra and Baghdád, was the author of the *Qút al-Qulúb* (The Food of the Hearts), another very early treatise on Ṣúfism, and in it he mentions Rábi'a al-'Adawiyya several times, giving incidents from her life, referring to her associates and, most valuable of all, quoting her well-known verses on the "two loves",[5] and giving his own comments on these verses at considerable length. Abú Ṭálib is a Ṣúfí author of great authority, and he is also a careful writer, for we note that he admits that different authors have been suggested for the verses above mentioned, but he himself believes that Rábi'a was responsible for them.

Another Ṣúfí writer contemporary with these two was *M. b. I. al-Kalábádhí* (*ob. c.* AD 1000), the author of the "Kitáb al-Ta'arruf li-Madhab ahl al-Taṣawwuf" (Book of Enquiry as to the Religion of the Ṣúfís) and the "Ma'ání al-Akhbár" (The Hidden Meanings of the Traditions), which are to be found only in MS. Both of these contain references to Rábi'a, and the former includes a version of her poem on love, which gives a slightly different reading from that of Abú Ṭálib.

Al-Hamádhání (*ob.* AD 1007), surnamed the "Wonder of the Age", a native of Ecbatána, in his "Shakwa al-Gharíb" (Complaint of the Stranger), of which only MSS. are available, speaks of Rábi'a's engagement to 'Abd al-Wáḥid b. Zayd, who was her contemporary and one of the same school of thought.

Abú Nu'aym al-Isfahání (*ob.* AD 1038) was one of the earliest to write a biography of the saints and his "Ḥilya al-Awliyá", known also as the "Ḥilya al-Abrár", is an authority of the greatest importance. There are several references to Rábi'a in Abú Nu'aym's accounts of other early Ṣúfís and there is said to be a complete biography of her in one of the MSS. of this work in Constantinople, but I have not yet been able to obtain a copy of it. If it could be found, it would probably throw much light on Rábi'a's life and teachings, as being the earliest biography of her available.

A very important authority is *Abú al-Qásim al-Qushayrí* (*ob.* AD 1074), who was born at Naysábúr in AD 986. He made a study of Islamic mysticism and was also a teacher of the Traditions at Baghdád towards the end of his life. His *Risála* (Treatise) is one of the most valuable books of reference on Ṣúfism written in Arabic and that he is a conscientious and reliable writer is proved by the fact that he is careful to quote his authorities and in the case of a traditional statement to give the chain of witnesses back to the original speaker. In the *Risála* he mentions Rábi'a frequently, quoting her teaching or some anecdote illustrating her practice, in connection with most of the stages of the mystic Way. As we have noted, she is accepted by these leading writers as a Ṣúfí teacher of recognised authority.

Among the minor authorities who mention Rábi'a is *al-Sarráj al-Qárí* (ob. AD 1106) of Baghdád, the writer of the *Maṣári' al-Ushsháq* (Poems about Lovers), including an account of a dream of Rábi'a's not given by any earlier writer and an anecdote found also in Abú Nu'aym's "Ḥilya".

Al-Ghazálí (*ob.* AD 1111), surnamed the "Proof of Islám", was born at Ṭús in AD 1059 and is such an outstanding figure in Islamic literature that his testimony to Rábi'a is of the greatest value. He was a lecturer at Naysábúr and later a professor at Baghdád. Having turned from orthodox Islám to the study of Ṣúfism, which he made it his business to reconcile, so far as he could, with the traditional faith, he went to live in Damascus, and after visiting Jerusalem and Alexandria, returned to his native town and died there. His greatest work is the *Iḥyá 'Ulúm al-Dín* (The Revivification of the Religious Sciences), in which he sets forth the Ṣúfí doctrine as he conceived it, quoting in all cases the early Ṣúfí teachers as his authorities. His work is scholarly and critical in the highest degree and he is too careful a writer for his conclusions not to be accepted as representing all the sources and knowledge to be obtained in his time, while his wide learning and also his extensive travels put a great deal of material at his disposal. He refers to Rábi'a (without any further distinguishing title)[6] among the leading teachers of Ṣúfism and accepts her teaching and her views as of at least equal authority with those of the great mystic *shaykhs*. He quotes the verses already referred to,[7] and gives his own interpretation of them. It is on the stage of love (on the mystic Way) that he considers her views as most important, and this is of great interest as an indication of her special contribution to this doctrine.[8]

The Persian writer *M. b. al-Munawwar* (*ob.* AD 1203) mentions Rábi'a in his *Asrár al-Tawḥíd* (The Secrets of Unification), which is an account of the life and sayings of his great-grandfather, the mystic Abú Sa'íd b. Abí al-Khayr, a very well-known Ṣúfí teacher who died in AD 1049, and whose quatrains represent some of the most exquisite Persian mystical poetry that is known. The *Asrár al-Tawḥíd* sets forth very clearly the mystical doctrines of the Ṣúfís of this period, based upon the teaching of those earlier Ṣúfís of Rábi'a's time.

I. A. A. b. Ghánim al-Maqdísí (*ob. c.* AD 1279) wrote a considerable number of works on mysticism, amongst them the "Kashf al-Asrár wa manáqib al Abrár" (The Unveiling of Mysteries and the Merits of the Righteous) in which he devotes a page to Rábi'a, giving some verses of hers not found in any other writer, but found in a very corrupt form in a MS. without title or author, under the heading "Tawba Rábi'a al-'Adawiyya" (The Conversion of Rábi'a al-'Adawiyya).[9] The lines as given by Maqdísí are quite characteristic of Rábi'a and it seems probable that both these and the whole poem quoted in a corrupt form by this unnamed writer, are derived from some older source, now missing. The "Kashf al-Asrár" and the "Tawba" are found only in MS.

By far the most extensive and complete biography of Rábi'a extant is that of the Persian poet *Faríd al-Dín 'Aṭṭár* (*ob.* AD 1230), who was born near Níshápúr about AD 1120. He followed the calling of a druggist when young, hence his surname of 'Aṭṭár, but later became a contemplative and gained a deep knowledge of Ṣúfism. His *Tadhkirat al-Awliyá* (The Memoirs of the Saints) is the oldest book in Persian dealing exclusively with the lives of the saints. He gives no precise indication of the sources upon which he drew for his information, but no doubt he used earlier biographies or treatises on Ṣúfism available to him, such as the "Ḥilya al-Awliyá" of Abú Nu'aym and the Risála of al-Qushayrí already referred to. He is at pains to make his biographies as complete as possible, giving a full account not only of the lives of his subjects, but of their reputed miracles and their sayings and teachings, so that we may assume that he searched all possible sources in pursuit of information and doubtless he had access to documents long since destroyed. Obviously, legends had grown up around the memory of the saints he portrayed and he has not hesitated to insert them, and probably to add considerably to them, along with what may well rest on historical facts and, for the modern student of his work, it is no easy task to disentangle the two. Yet by inference we may find corroboration for many of his statements, apart from any documentary confirmation. For example, he speaks of Rábi'a as having been a slave in her youth and gives a circumstantial account of the events which led to her being sold into slavery and what brought about her manumission. Other writers describe her as a freed woman. Now, it is a curious fact that Rábi'a, though given a tribal surname, is never called by the name of her father, as every unmarried Muslim woman is, to the present day. Her namesake, Rábi'a of Syria,[10] who died fifty years before our Rábi'a, is always called Rábi'a bint Ismá'íl (daughter of Ishmael) and details are given of her parentage. The fact that Rábi'a has no patronymic and is called only by the name of her tribe, is strong evidence of her having been a slave and therefore of no known parentage. The same would be the case today, in countries where slavery is prevalent or has prevailed up to recent years.

Again, a Muslim freewoman in practice is always under the guardianship of a male relative, father, husband, brother or uncle, and this guardian has the right to marry his ward to whom he will, and though technically, according to Muslim law, her consent is necessary, actually she will not be allowed to remain unmarried. There is no suggestion in any of the biographies that Rábi'a was under any such guardianship, and on the contrary it is plain that she was free to refuse the offers of marriage made to her,[11] and that she could – and did – live the celibate life is again strong proof that she had no known relatives, in her youth at least, to oblige her to follow the invariable custom for Muslim womanhood. A freed slave would be able to choose for herself and none would have the right to coerce her. So in this respect 'Aṭṭár's account is supported by other circumstances.

A Ṣúfí writer of considerable importance was *Shiháb al-Dín 'Umar b. A. al-Suhrawardí* (*ob.* AD 1234), who studied Ṣúfism in Baṣra, and was later known as a preacher and teacher in Baghdád. His best known work is the *'Awárif al-Ma'árif* (The Bounties of Knowledge) and in this he mentions Rábi'a and quotes her teaching several times.

J. Ṣibt Ibn al-Jawzí (*ob.* AD 1257) was the author of the "Mir'át al-Zamán" (The Mirror of the Age), containing a biography of Rábi'a of considerable length, which is of importance because it is most probably derived from the "Ṣafwa al-Ṣafwa" (The Cream of the Cream) by his grandfather Ibn al-Jawzí, which is a résumé of the "Ḥilya" of Abú Nu'aym. No available MS. of the "Ṣafwa al-Ṣafwa" contains the biography of Rábi'a which is known to form part of the complete work, and therefore this account, though at second-hand, is of interest.

One of the most famous of Rábi'a's biographers is *Ibn Khallikán* (*ob.* AD 1282), who was born at Arbela in AD 1211. After living for a time at Aleppo and Damascus, he went to Cairo and there began his great biographical dictionary, the *Wafayát al-A'yán* (Obituaries of Eminent Men). In his preface he explains clearly his motive and his method. He says that he adopted the alphabetical order, because he judged it to be more convenient than the chronological (which is the order we usually find employed by Oriental biographers). He says further:

> I have spoken of all these whose names are familiar to the public and about whom questions are frequently asked. . . . I have fixed, with all possible exactness, the dates of their birth and death; I have traced up their genealogy is high as I could . . . and I have cited the traits which may best serve to characterize each individual, such as noble actions, singular anecdotes, verses and letters, so that the reader may derive amusement from my work.[12]

Unfortunately, in his account of Rábi'a, he has confused her to some extent with Rábi'a, sometimes spelt Rá íy'a, bint Ismá'íl of Syria. At the same time, his notice of her is very valuable, because he gives his sources and it is possible therefore to fall back on earlier authorities to supplement his statements. Ibn Khallikán has put posterity under a great obligation to him for his invaluable work.

A well-known chronicler who mentions Rábi'a is *al-Dhahabí* (*ob.* AD 1348), who in his *Mizán al-I'tidál* (The Balance of the Equilibrium) quotes the opinion of her held by the traditionist Abú Dáwúd (*ob.* AD 889).

The Ṣúfí writer *M. b. al-Ḥ. b. 'Alí al-Isnawí Imád al-Dín* (*ob.* AD 1363), who studied in Cairo and Damascus and was also for some time a professor at Hamat, was the author of the *Ḥayát al-Qulúb* (The Life of the Hearts) in which Rábi'a's eschatological teaching is referred to.

Another of these later Ṣúfí writers was *Yáfi'í al-Sháfi'í* (*ob.* AD 1367), who was born in Yemen and travelled to Jerusalem, Damascus and Cairo, and died in Mecca. He wrote extensively and in his *Rawḍ al-Riyáḥín fí ḥikáyát al-Ṣáliḥín* (The Garden of the Perfumes in the Lives of the Virtuous) he gives several of Rábi'a's sayings.

Among the Persian biographers who mention Rábi'a is *Aflákí*, contemporary with these two last mentioned. He was a Mevlevi dervish, who wrote a history of Jalál al-Dín Rúmí and his successors called "Manáqib al-'Árifín" (The Merits of the Gnostics) which is not very exact chronologically, but contains some interesting anecdotes, including one of Rábi'a not found elsewhere. Aflákí spent the years from AD 1310 to 1353 in compiling this history, but though he claims to have obtained his information from trustworthy witnesses, much of what he writes is plainly incredible.

A writer who has a good deal to say of Rábi'a and quotes as hers verses not given elsewhere is *al-Ḥurayfísh* (*ob.* AD 1398), an Egyptian. He wrote *Al-Rawḍ al-Fá'iq* (The Super-Excellent Garden), a collection of anecdotes about famous men and women, and apart from his specific account of Rábi'a, his personal opinion which prefaces it is interesting because in it he takes pains to prove that God had bestowed His favours and promises upon women, equally with men. He makes at least one mistake in regard to Rábi'a, but there is little evidence for or against his credibility as a whole.

A late writer *Taqí al-Dín al-Ḥisní* (*ob.* AD 1426), of Damascus, has written a whole book on the virtuous women of Islám called the "Siyar al-Ṣáliḥát" (Lives of Good Women), which contains an account of Rábi'a, but not very much that is original. He has evidently derived his information from both al-Jahiz and Ibn Khallikán, but his book is interesting because he has thought it worthwhile to devote a whole volume to the women saints and has found no lack of material.

The Persian *'Abd al-Raḥmán*, surnamed *Jámí* from his birthplace in Khorasán (*ob.* AD 1492), was a man of great learning and a poet, and among his books wrote a history of famous saints entitled *Nafaḥát al-Uns* (The Breaths of Fellowship) which includes a section devoted to women, the first of whom is Rábi'a al-'Adawiyya. This history is a recension of an earlier work, the "Ṭabaqát al-Ṣúfiyya" (The Classes of the Ṣúfís) by 'Abd Allah b. Muḥammad al-Anṣárí (*ob.* AD 1088) which Jámí originally intended to re-edit,[13] but actually he limits himself to only the most prominent personalities among the Ṣúfís. These "Ṭabaqát" exist in MS. in Calcutta, but there is no copy available in Europe. Another still earlier source, which he mentions in connection with the women saints, is the "Ṭabaqát al-Ṣúfiyya" of Abú 'Abd al-Raḥmán al-Sulamí (*ob.* AD 1021), which is extant in MS. but not in a complete form. Jámí also made use of Yáfi'í[14] and Hujwírí[15] and a number of other Ṣúfí authors, including Ibn al-'Arabí.[16] Jámí is undoubtedly a reputable authority and his wide learning and great ability would enable him to make the fullest use of all sources available in his time.

A writer, who has been described as the "last great Muḥammadan theosophist", *'Abd al-Wahháb al-Sha'rání* (*ob.* AD 1565), though a weaver by trade, living in Old Cairo, yet became a man of great learning.[17] He has devoted some space in his *Lawáqiḥ al-Anwár* (The Manifestation of the Luminous Truths), otherwise called the *al-Ṭabaqát al-Kubrá* (The Great Classes), to women saints, including Rábi'a, but he gives more details concerning women of Egypt, which is natural enough, since he was in a position to gain first-hand information about them, and their shrines, in many cases, were still in existence and were places of pilgrimage in his time. He derived some of his information from the "Futúḥát al-Makkiyya" (The Meccan Revelations) of Ibn al-'Arabí (*ob.* AD 1240).

Dáwúd al-Antákí (*ob.* AD 1599), a late writer, who was born in Antioch and died at Mecca, wrote the *Tazyín al-Aswáq* (The Adorning of the Markets) for which he made use of al-Sarráj's *Maṣári'* already mentioned,[18] but obviously he had other sources as well. He does not mention Rábi'a by name, but gives some verses by an unnamed woman which he links up with Rábi'a's well-known lines on the "two loves", attributing all to one unnamed author. His testimony is therefore very uncertain and, in the absence of confirmation from more reliable sources, cannot be accepted without qualification.

An authority who is important, though so late as to be classed among modern writers, is *'Abd al-Rá'úf al-Munáwí* (*ob.* AD 1622) of Cairo, who was a prolific writer. Among his works is "Al-Kawákib al-Durríya" (The Glittering Stars), in which he gives an account at length of several women saints, including Rábi'a al-'Adawiyya. Munáwí is a careful writer, and takes pains to avoid the confusion between the two Rábi'as, into which several writers have fallen. He mentions Ibn al-Jawzí as a source for Rábi'a's biography and has evidently consulted al-Jáḥiẓ and al-Qushayrí; his account is valuable, including much that is not found elsewhere, and it is probable that he had access to sources now lost and unavailable. Since his method is definitely critical, we may suppose that he took pains to consult sources which he believed to be authentic.

The above represent the chief sources for Rábi'a's life and teachings, and for the accounts of other women saints included in this book. With regard to Ṣúfí doctrine, in addition to the works of Abú Ṭálib, al-Kalábádhí, Abú Nu'aym, al-Qushayrí and al-Ghazálí and others already mentioned, another early writer, who does not mention Rábi'a, is quoted, namely *al-Hujwírí* (*ob. c.* AD 1079). He was born at Ghazna and was contemporary with al-Qushayrí. He died at Lahore. In his great work, the *Kashf al-Maḥjub* (The Unveiling of the Veiled), his aim is not, like that of al-Sarráj in the *Kitáb al-Luma'*,[19] merely to report the opinions of previous Ṣúfí thinkers, but to set forth an exhaustive treatise on Ṣúfí doctrine, including his own personal views. He was already acquainted with the *Kitáb al-Luma'* and he also quotes from the "Ṭabaqát" of al-Sulamí,[20] and the *Risála* of al-Qushayrí. As the oldest treatise in Persian on Ṣúfism the *Kashf al-Maḥjúb* is a work of the greatest value to all interested in the early development of mysticism in Islám.[21]

There are certain sources for the life and teachings of Rábi'a which at present are unavailable and which might be of the greatest value if they could be discovered.

The first of these is the "Manáqib Rábi'a" (Biography [lit. Merits] of Rábi'a), which has been heard of and presumably is in existence, but so far has baffled all efforts for its discovery. If this work is early or by a writer who has the critical faculty and states the sources of his information, it is probable that it would throw much light upon Rábi'a's personal history, for which so little really authentic material is available at present.

Another missing authority which would undoubtedly be of great value is the section on women devotees and gnostics at the end of the "Ṭabaqát al-Ṣúfiyya" of Abú 'Abd al-Raḥmán al-Sulamí, to which Jámí refers[22] and to which there is also a reference in al-Munawwar's book, especially referring to Rábi'a.[23] Al-Sulamí was born in Naysábúr in AD 941 and died in AD 1021. The MSS. of the "Ṭabaqát" which are extant do not appear to include this section on the women saints, and as al-Sulamí is one of the earliest biographers of the Ṣúfís, his account would be of great interest. Yet another missing authority is the complete MS. of the "Ṣafwa al-Ṣafwa", already mentioned,[24] of Ibn al-Jawzí, who was born at Baghdád, and who died in AD 1200. His book is derived from Abú Nu'aym's "Ḥilya" and contains a biography of Rábi'a to which Ibn Khallikán refers in his *Wafayát al-A'yán*[25] and to which al-Munáwí also refers.[26]

For the third part of this book, the sources above mentioned have been used, and also some authorities dealing with History and Geography and subjects of general interest, rather than with Ṣúfís and Ṣúfism.

The "Chronicles of Mecca" are a collection of writings by authors of the ninth and tenth centuries, the first of whom was *Al-Azráqí* (*ob.* AD 858). From these Chronicles information has been derived concerning the convents of Muslim women.

Al-Baládhurí (*ob.* AD 892) was a Persian, but wrote in Arabic. His

Kitáb al-Futúḥ al-Buldán gives an account of the early Muḥammadan conquests and mentions the earliest Muslim saints, including some women.

A source of much information concerning the women of pre-Islamic and early Islamic times is the celebrated *Kitáb al-Aghání* (The Book of Songs) of *Abú al-Faraj al-Isfahání* (*ob.* AD 967), who was born at Isfahán. This work is a mine of invaluable information on early Islamic times and the writer frequently mentions the celebrated women of Islám. Though his book is primarily a collection of songs, he introduces a great many traditions and stories, and was near enough to the events he describes to be able to obtain authentic information.

Al-Maqdísí, born in AD 946 at Jerusalem, was a great traveller who set down an account of his travels in his "Aḥsan ul-Taqásím fí ma'rifat al-Aqálím" (The Best of the Divisions in Knowledge of the Climes), which is edited in the *Bibliotheca Geographorum Arabicorum*.

Another famous geographer to whom reference is made is *Yáqút* (*ob.* AD 1229), who was by birth a Greek but was enslaved and became a Muslim. He travelled a good deal and wrote the *Mu'jam al-Buldán* (Account of the Lands), a great geographical dictionary, which is full of valuable information.

A theological writer to whom reference is made in this part of the book is *M. b. M. al-'Abdárí* (*ob.* AD 1336) who has some strong comments to make on women in his *Madkhal al-Shari' al-Sharíf* (Introduction to the Sacred Law), which he writes from the point of view of an orthodox theologian.

A very celebrated traveller to whom several references are made is *Ibn Baṭṭúṭa* (*ob.* AD 1377), a native of Tangier, who travelled in Europe, going as far as India and China, and also to East Africa and the Sudan, and making copious notes of all he observed, which he set down in his delightful and entertaining book of travels called *Tuḥfa al-Nuzzár fí Ghará' ib al-amṣár wa 'ajá' ib al-asfár* (Rarities seen among the curiosities of cities and the marvels of travel), in which he notes especially the position and customs of women in foreign countries.

Among the writers referred to is *Ibn Khaldún* (*ob.* AD 1406), described as "the greatest historical thinker of Islám". He was born at Tunis. The most famous of his writings is the *Muqaddima* (Prolegomena), which forms the first volume of a large general history.[27]

A writer of considerable importance where places and shrines are concerned is *al-Maqrízí* (*ob.* AD 1442), a native of Cairo, who wrote a great work known as the *Khiṭaṭ* (Sites), on the topography and history of Egypt. Although his work is incomplete and sometimes vague, he has preserved much valuable information for generations to come and is usually accurate and careful to use contemporary evidence when available.[28]

A history arranged chronologically, which is of great use for reference, is the *Iṣába fí tamyíz al-Ṣaḥába* (Setting forth of the Excellences of the Companions) of Ibn Ḥajar (*ob.* AD 1449), a native of Ascalon. He traces his history from the time of the Prophet, and includes the celebrated women of Islám in his account. The above include all the important native authorities used; some obscure and late writers have been omitted.

1 See pp. 161 ff.
2 Jámí, *Nafaḥát al-Uns*, p. 319. No reason is given for the title.
3 *Kitáb al-Luma'*, p. 203.
4 See p. 4.
5 See p. 125.
6 See p. 2.
7 See p. 3.
8 See Part Two, Chapter X.
9 Berlin, *Bibl. Wetzstein*, II, 230.
10 See pp. 170 ff.
11 See Part One, Chapter II.
12 Ibn Khallikán, ed. de Slane, I, p. 3.
13 *Nafaḥát al-Uns*, p. 2.

14 See p. 9.

15 See p. 11.

16 For a complete list of Jámí's sources, see W. Iranon, *J.A.S. Bengal*, xviii, pp. 386 ff.; xix, pp. 298 ff.

17 Cf. R. A. Nicholson, *Literary History of the Arabs*, p. 464.

18 See p. 4.

19 See p. 3.

20 See p. 12.

21 For an account of al-Hujwírí and his writings see *Kashf al-Maḥjúb*, Translator's Preface. This work is available in an English translation by a master-hand, that of Professor R. A. Nicholson of Cambridge.

22 *Nafaḥát al-Uns*, p. 716.

23 *Asrár al-Tawḥíd*, p. 410.

24 See p. 7.

25 Vol. I, p. 34, No. 230.

26 "Al-Kawákib al-Durríya", fol. 52 a.

27 Cf. R. A. Nicholson, *Literary History of the Arabs*, pp. 437 ff.

28 Cf. A. R. Guest, "List of Writers, Books and other Authorities mentioned by al-Maqrízí in his Khiṭaṭ", *J.R.A.S.* 1902, pp. 103 ff.

Part One

THE LIFE OF RÁBI'A

CHAPTER I

RÁBI'A AL-'ADAWIYYA: HER BIRTH AND EARLY YEARS

In the history of Islám, the woman saint made her appearance at a very early period, and in the evolution of the cult of saints by Muslims, the dignity of saintship was conferred on women as much as on men. As far as rank among the "friends of God" was concerned, there was complete equality between the sexes.

It was the development of mysticism (Ṣúfism) within Islám, which gave women their great opportunity to attain the rank of sainthood.[1] The goal of the Súfí's quest was union with the Divine, and the Ṣúfí seeker after God, having renounced this world and its attractions, being purged of self and its desires, inflamed with a passion of love to God, journeyed ever onward, looking towards his final purpose, through the life of illumination, with its ecstasies and raptures, and the higher life of contemplation, until at last he achieved the heavenly gnosis and attained to the vision of God, in which the lover might become one with the Beloved, and abide in Him for ever.

Such a conception of the relations between the saint and his Lord left no room for the distinction of sex. In the spiritual life there could be "neither male nor female".[2] All whom God had called to be saints could attain, by following the Path, to union with Himself, and all who attained, would have their royal rank, as spiritual beings, in the world to come.

'Aṭṭár, to prove that saintship may be found in woman as naturally as in a man, says:

> The holy prophets have laid it down that "God does not look upon your outward forms". It is not the outward form that matters, but the inner purpose of the heart, as the Prophet said, "The people are assembled

> (on the Day of Judgement) according to the purposes of their hearts". . . . So also 'Abbás of Ṭús said that when on the Day of Resurrection the summons goes forth, "O men", the first person to set foot in that class of men (*i.e.* those who are to enter Paradise) will be Mary,[3] upon whom be peace. . . . The true explanation of this fact (that women count for as much as men among the saints) is that wherever these people, the Ṣúfís, are, they have no separate existence in the Unity of God. In the Unity, what remains of the existence of "I" or "thou"? So how can "man" or "woman" continue to be? So too, Abú 'Ali Fármadhí said, "Prophecy is the essence, the very being, of power and sublimity. Superiority and inferiority do not exist in it. Undoubtedly saintship is of the same type".[4]

So the title of saint was bestowed upon women equally with men, and since Islám has no order of priesthood and no priestly caste, there was nothing to prevent a woman from reaching the highest religious rank in the hierarchy of Muslim saints. Some theologians even name the Lady Fáṭima, daughter of the Prophet, as the first *Quṭb* or spiritual head of the Ṣúfí fellowship.[5] Below the *Quṭb* were four '*Awtád*', from whose ranks his successor was chosen, and below them, in the next rank of the hierarchy, were forty '*Abdál*' or substitutes, who are described as being the pivot of the world and the foundation and support of the affairs of men.[6] Jámí relates how someone was asked, "How many are the 'Abdál'?" and he answered, "Forty souls", and when asked why he did not say "Forty men", his reply was, " There have been women among them".[7] The biographies of the Muslim saints, such as those compiled by Abú Nu'aym,[8] Faríd al-Dín 'Aṭṭar,[9] Ibn' al-Jawzí,[10] Jámí[11] and Ibn Khallikán[12] and many others, are full of the mention of women Ṣúfís, their saintly lives, their good deeds, and their miracles. The influence which these women saints exercised both during their lives and after their deaths, is perhaps best proved by the fact that Muslim theologians, opposed to the Súfí movement, denounce also these women saints and the worship known to be given to them.[13]

The high position attained by the women Súfís is attested further by the fact that the Súfís themselves give to a woman the first place among the earliest Muḥammadan mystics and have chosen her to represent the first development of mysticism in Islám.[14]

This was the saintly Rábi'a, a freedwoman of the Ál-'Atík,[15] a tribe of Qays b. 'Adí, from which she was known as al-'Adawiyya or al-Qaysiyya, and also as al-Baṣriyya, from her birthplace: of whom a modern writer says, "Rábi'a is the saint par excellence of the Sunnite hagiography".[16] Her biographer 'Aṭṭár speaks of her as

> That one set apart in the seclusion of holiness, that woman veiled with the veil of religious sincerity, that one on fire with love and longing, that one enamoured of the desire to approach her Lord and be consumed in His glory, that woman who lost herself in union with the Divine,[17] that one accepted by men as a second spotless Mary – Rábi'a al-'Adawiyya, may God have mercy upon her. If anyone were to say, "Why have you made mention of her in the class of men?", I should say . . . "God does not look upon the outward forms. . . . If it is allowable to accept two thirds of our faith from 'Á'isha[18] the Trustworthy, it is also allowable to accept religious benefit from one of her handmaids [*i.e.* Rábi'a]. When a woman walks in the way of God like a man, she cannot be called a woman".[19]

A later biographer, al-Munáwí, says of her:

> Rábi'a al-'Adawiyya al-Qaysiyya of Baṣra, was at the head of the women disciples and the chief of the

> women ascetics, of those who observed the sacred law, who were God-fearing and zealous . . . and she was one of those who were pre-eminent and experienced in grace and goodness.

He gives the names of several well-known women saints and goes on to say, "She was the most famous among them, of great devotion and conspicuous in worship, and of perfect purity and asceticism".[20]

Unfortunately there is no writer very near her own time to give us her biography, and for an account of her early life we can find material only in the *Memoir of the Saints* of 'Aṭṭár, already mentioned, who lived more than four hundred years after Rábi'a. Much of what he tells of her must be regarded as purely legendary. Yet though the legends which surround Rábi'a's name may not, and in many cases certainly do not, correspond to historic facts, at least they give some idea of her personality and show the estimation in which she was held by those who lived after her and had heard of her fame.

She was born probably about AH 95 or 99 (AD 717)[21] in Baṣra, where she spent the greater part of her life.

Born into the poorest of homes, according to 'Aṭṭár (though a modern writer says she belonged to one of the noble families of Basra),[22] miraculous events were reputed to have taken place even at the time of her birth. 'Aṭṭár tells us that on the night of her birth there was no oil in the house, no lamp nor swaddling clothes in which to wrap the newborn child. Her father already had three daughters, and so she was called Rábi'a (the fourth). The mother asked her husband to go and ask for oil for the lamp from a neighbour, but he had made a vow that he would never ask anything of a creature (*i.e.* as a true Ṣúfí he would depend only upon God to supply his needs),[23] and so he came back without it. Having fallen asleep in great distress at the lack of provision for the child, he dreamt that the Prophet Muḥammad appeared to him in his sleep and said, "Do not be sorrowful, for this daughter who is born is a great saint, whose intercession will be desired by seventy thousand of my community". The Prophet said further:

> Tomorrow send a letter to 'Ísá Zádhán, Amír of Baṣra, reminding him that every night he is wont to pray one hundred prayers to me and on Friday night four hundred, but this Friday night he has neglected me, and as a penance (tell him) that he must give you four hundred *dínárs*, lawfully acquired.[24]

Rábi'a's father awoke, weeping; he rose up, wrote the letter as directed and sent it to the Amír through the latter's chamberlain. The Amír, when he had read the letter, said:

> Give two thousand *dínárs* to the poor as a thank-offering, because the prophet had me in mind, and four hundred *dínárs* to that Shaykh and say to him that I desire that he should come before me that I may see him, but it is not fitting that such a person as he is should come to me, but I will come and rub my beard on his threshold.[25]

But in spite of this event of good augury, 'Aṭṭár relates that misfortunes fell upon the family, and when Rábi'a was a little older, her mother and father died and she was left an orphan. A famine occurred in Baṣra and the sisters were scattered. One day, when Rábi'a was walking abroad, an evil-minded man saw her and seized upon her and sold her as a slave for six *dirhams* and the man who bought her made her work hard. One day a stranger (one who might not look at her unveiled) approached her. Rábi'a fled to avoid him and slipped on the road and dislocated her wrist. She bowed her face in the dust, and said, "O Lord, I am a stranger and without mother or father, an orphan and a slave and I have fallen into bondage and my wrist is injured, (yet) I am not grieved by this, only (I desire) to satisfy Thee. I would fain know if Thou art satisfied (with me) or not." She heard a voice saying, "Be not sorrowful, for on the day of Resurrection thy rank shall be such that those who are nearest to God in Heaven shall envy thee".[26]

After this Rábi'a returned to her master's house and continually fasted in the daytime and carried out her appointed tasks and in the service of God she was standing on her feet till the day. One night her master woke from sleep and looked down through a window of the house and saw Rábi'a, whose head was bowed in worship, and she was saying, "O my Lord, Thou knowest that the desire of my heart is to obey Thee, and that the light of my eye is in the service of Thy court. If the matter rested with me, I should not cease for one hour from Thy service, but Thou hast made me subject to a creature." While she was still praying, he saw a lamp above her head, suspended without a chain, and the whole house was illuminated by the rays from that light. This enveloping radiance or *sakína* (derived from the Hebrew Shekina, the cloud of glory indicating the presence of God) of the Muslim saint, corresponding to the halo of the Christian saint, is frequently mentioned in Ṣúfí biographies.[27]

Rábi'a's master, when he saw that strange sight, was afraid and rose up and returned to his own place and sat pondering until day came. When the day dawned he called Rábi'a and spoke kindly to her and set her free. Rábi'a asked for leave to go away; so he gave her leave, and she left that place and journeyed into the desert. Afterwards she left the desert and obtained for herself a cell and for a time was engaged in devotional worship there.[28] According to one account, Rábi'a at first followed the calling of a flute player, which would be consistent with a state of slavery. Then she became converted and built a place of retreat, where she occupied herself with works of piety.[29]

Among other stories related of this period of her life, is one telling how she purposed performing the pilgrimage to Mecca and set her face towards the desert; she had an ass with her to carry her baggage, and in the heart of the desert the ass died. Some people (in the caravan) said to her, "Let us carry thy baggage". She said, "Go on your way, for I am not dependent on you (for help)", *i.e.* she placed her trust in God and not in His creatures.

So the people went on and Rábi'a remained alone, and bowing her head, she said, "O my God, do kings deal thus with a woman, a stranger and weak? Thou art calling me to Thine own house (the Ka'ba), but in the midst of the way Thou hast suffered mine ass to die and Thou hast left me alone in the desert."

She had hardly completed her prayer, when the ass stirred and got up. Rábi'a put her baggage on it and went on her way. The narrator of this story said that some time afterwards he saw that same little ass being sold in the bazaar.[30]

Another story tells us how she went into the desert for a few days and prayed, "O my Lord, my heart is perplexed, whither shall I go? I am but a clod of earth and that house (the Ka'ba) is only a stone to me. Show Thyself (to me) in this very place." So she prayed until God Most High, without any medium, spoke directly within her heart, saying, "O Rábi'a . . . when Moses desired to see My Face, I cast a few particles of My Glory upon the mountain (Sinai) and it was rent into forty pieces. Be content here with My Name."[30]

It is told how another time she was on her way to Mecca, and when half-way there she saw the Ka'ba coming to meet her and she said, "It is the Lord of the house whom I need, what have I to do with the house? I need to meet with Him Who said, 'Whoso approaches Me by a span's length I will approach him by the length of a cubit'. The Ka'ba which I see has no power over me; what joy does the beauty of the Ka'ba bring to me?"[31]

In connection with this legend, which indicates how highly favoured by God Rábi'a was, in the eyes of her biographers, it is related that Ibráhím b. Adham[32] spent fourteen years making his way to the Ka'ba, because in every place of prayer he performed two *raka's*, and at last when he arrived at the Ka'ba, he did not see it.

He said, "Alas, what has happened? It may be that some injury has overtaken my eyes." An unseen voice said, "No harm has befallen your eyes, but the Ka'ba has gone to meet a woman, who is approaching this place". Ibráhím was seized with jealousy, and said, "O indeed, who is this?" He ran and saw Rábi'a arriving and the Ka'ba was back in its own place. When Ibráhím saw that, he said, "O Rábi'a, what is this disturbance and trouble and burden which thou hast brought into the world?" She said, "I have not brought disturbance into the world, it is you who have disturbed the world, because you delayed fourteen years in arriving at the Ka'ba". He said, "Yes I have spent fourteen years in crossing the desert (because I was engaged) in prayer". Rábi'a said, "You traversed it in ritual prayer (*namáz*) but I with personal supplication (*niyáz*)".[33] Then, having performed the pilgrimage, she returned to Basra and occupied herself with works of devotion.

For these early years only legends are available, but they give us a clear idea of a woman renouncing this world and its attractions and giving up her life to the service of God, the first step on the mystic Way to be trodden by the Ṣúfí saint.

1 Cf. al-Hujwírí: "You must know that the principle and foundation of Ṣúfism and knowledge of God rests on Saintship" (*Kashf al-Maḥjúb*, p. 210).

2 Cf. Shabistarí: "In God there is no duality. In that Presence 'I' and 'we' and 'thou' do not exist, 'I' and 'we' and 'thou' and 'he' become one. . . . Since in Unity there is no distinction . . . the Quest and the Way and the Seeker become one" (*Gulshan-i Ráz*, p. 27, l. 448).

3 The Mother of Jesus.

4 *Tadhkirat al-Awliyá*, I, p. 59.

5 Goldziher, *Muhamm. Studien*, II, p. 300.

6 Munawwar, *Asrár al-Tawḥíd*, p. 129.

7 Jámí, *Nafaḥát al-Uns*, p. 716.

8 "Ḥilya al-Awliyá".

9 *Tadhkirat al-Awliyá.*
10 "Ṣafwa al-Ṣafwa".
11 *Nafaḥát al-Uns.*
12 *Wafayát al-A'yán.*
13 Cf. Goldziher, *op. cit.* II, p. 300.
14 Cf. Dozy, *Hist. de l'Islamisme,* tr. Chauvin, pp. 318, 319.
15 Ṣibt Ibn al-Jawzí, "Mir'át al-Zamán", fol. 256a. Taghribardí, *al-Nujúm al-Záhira,* I, p. 365.
16 L. Massignon, *Textes Inédits Relatifs à la Mystique Musulmane.* (Proof kindly communicated to me by the author.)
17 Cf. St John of the Cross, *Spiritual Canticle,* p. 69: "The soul on fire with the love of God longs for the perfection and consummation of its love, that it may be completely refreshed."
18 A large number of the Traditions concerning Muḥammad, on which Muslims rely, were derived from his favourite wife 'Á'isha.
19 'Aṭṭár, *Tadhkirat al-Awliyá,* p. 59.
20 "Al-Kawákib al-Durriya", fol. 50. Cf. Muḥammad Zihní: "Although she was a woman, in character she was so enlightened of heart that she was manifestly superior to many men in the matter of human perfection, and for this reason she was called 'The Crown of Men'. Her works of piety and asceticism were so renowned that her praise was on everyone's tongue, and her exalted name became a kind of proverb for ascetic men and women" (*Meshâhír al-Nisá,* p. 225).
21 Cf. Massignon, *Lexique Technique,* p. 193, note 5.
22 M. Zihní, *Meshâhír al-Nisá,* p. 225.
23 See Part Two, Chapter IX.
24 The Ṣúfís would not make use of money unless it had been earned by means accounted lawful according to the sacred law of Islám.
25 'Aṭṭár, *op. cit.* pp. 59 and 60.
26 *Op. cit.* I, pp. 60 and 61.

[27] Cf. Goldziher, "Le culte des saints chez les Musulmans", *Revue de l'histoire des Religions*, 1880, pp. 270, 271.

[28] 'Aṭṭár, *op. cit.* I, p. 61.

[29] 'Aṭṭár, *op. cit.* Uyghur version, II, p. 56.

[30] 'Aṭṭár, *op. cit.* I, p. 61.

[31] *Op. cit.* I, pp. 61, 62.

[32] Prince of Balkh, converted to Ṣúfism by a heavenly voice while out hunting, who lived in the second century of Islám. Cf. al-Sulamí, "Ṭabaqát al-Ṣúfiyya", fols. 3 b ff.

[33] 'Aṭṭár, *op. cit.* I, p. 62.

CHAPTER II

RÁBI'A'S CHOICE OF CELIBACY

Rábi'a al-'Adawiyya received many offers of marriage, but rejected them all, feeling that in the celibate life only could she pursue her quest unhindered. Among those who sought her hand in marriage was 'Abd al-Wáḥid b. Zayd, who was renowned for his asceticism and the sanctity of his life, a theologian and a preacher and an advocate of solitude for those who sought the way to God; the reputed writer of verses declaring that

> The Ways are various, the Way to the Truth is one,
> Those who travel on the Way of Truth must keep
> themselves apart.[1]

He was the founder of one of the first monastic communities near Baṣra, and died in AD 793. Rábi'a did not welcome his offer but shunned him with the greatest loathing, and said to him, "O sensual one, seek another sensual like thyself. Hast thou seen any sign of desire in me?"[2]

Another who sought her hand was Muḥammad b. Sulaymán al-Háshimí, the 'Abbásid Amír of Baṣra from AH 145, who died in AH 172.[3] He offered a dowry of a hundred thousand *dínárs* and wrote to Rábi'a that he had an income of ten thousand *dínárs* a month and that he would bestow it all on her, but she wrote back, "It does not please me that you should be my slave and that all you possess should be mine, or that you should distract me from God for a single moment".

Another account of this offer says that the governor wrote to the people of Baṣra asking them to find him a wife, and they agreed upon Rábi'a, and when he wrote to her expressing his wishes, her reply was as follows:

> Renunciation of this world means peace, while desire for it brings sorrow. Curb your desires and control yourself and do not let others control you, but let them share your inheritance and the anxiety of the age. As for yourself, give your mind to the day of death; but as for me, God can give me all you offer and even double it. It does not please me to be distracted from Him for a single moment. So farewell.[4]

Another story tells how Ḥasan of Baṣra,[5] with whom the legends persistently associate her (though he died more than seventy years before her death), and others are also said to have come to Rábi'a, urging her to take a husband, and to choose from among the Ṣúfís of Baṣra whom she would. She replied, "Yes, willingly. Who is the most learned of you, that I may marry him?" They said, "Ḥasan of Baṣra", so she said to him, "If you can give me the answer to four questions, I will be your wife". He said, "Ask, and if God permit, I will answer you".

She said then, "What will the Judge of the world say when I die? That I have come out of the world a Muslim or an unbeliever?"

Ḥasan answered, "This is among the hidden things, which are known only to God Most High".

Then she said, "When I am put in the grave and Munkar and Nakír[6] question me, shall I be able to answer them (satisfactorily) or not?" He replied, "This also is hidden".

She said next, "When the people are assembled at the Resurrection and the books[7] are distributed, and some are given their book in the right hand and some in the left, shall I be given mine in my right hand or my left?" He could only say, "This also is among the hidden things".

Finally she asked, "When mankind is summoned (on the Day of Judgement), some to Paradise and some to Hell, in which of the two groups shall I be?" He answered as before, "This, too, is hidden, and none knows what is hidden save God, His is the glory and majesty".

Then she said to him, "Since this is so, and I have these four questions with which to concern myself, how should I need a husband, with whom to be occupied?"

She is said to have emphasised her refusal with the following beautiful lines, but they cannot be attributed to her with any certainty:

My peace, O my brothers, is in solitude,
And my Beloved is with me alway,
For His love I can find no substitute,
And His love is the test for me among mortal beings,
When-e'er His Beauty I may contemplate,
He is my "miḥráb", towards Him is my "qibla"
If I die of love, before completing satisfaction,
Alas, for my anxiety in the world, alas for my distress,
O Healer (of souls) the heart feeds upon its desire,
The striving after union with Thee has healed my soul,
O my Joy and my Life abidingly,
Thou wast the source of my life and from Thee also
came my ecstasy.
I have separated myself from all created beings,
My hope is for union with Thee, for that is the goal of
my desire.[8]

This story is given in more than one account, and though chronologically it is almost impossible that Ḥasan of Baṣra should be the suitor in the case, it is possible that it refers to some other offer of marriage.

Another legend also gives an account of an offer said to have been made by Ḥasan of Baṣra, in which the same feeling is evident in Rábi'a's answer. Ḥasan is reputed to have said, "I desire that we should marry and be betrothed". Her reply was:

> The contract of marriage is for those who have a phenomenal existence (*i.e.* who are concerned with the affairs of this material world). Here (*i.e.* in my case) existence has ceased, since I have ceased to exist and have passed out of Self. My existence is in Him, and I am altogether His. I am in the shadow of His command. The marriage contract must be asked for from Him, not from me.[9]

So, like her Christian sisters in the life of sanctity, Rábi'a espoused a heavenly bridegroom and turned her back on earthly marriage even with one of her own intimates and companions on the Way.

Rábi'a had many disciples and associates, who resorted to her house day and night to seek her counsel or her prayers or to listen to her teaching. As already stated, her biographers constantly associate her with Ḥasan of Baṣra, whom they portray as her disciple and follower, though he must have been so much her senior. Either her name has been introduced into anecdotes relating to Ḥasan, or else Ḥasan's name has been substituted for that of one of her own contemporaries in anecdotes which relate to her. Ḥasan of Baṣra was one of the earliest Ṣúfís, a saint who took the gloomiest view of life, both in this world and the next, and whose faith was overshadowed by the fear of Hell to such an extent that he even envied the man who would be saved after a thousand years in Hell, and said, "Would that I were like this man".[10] Ḥasan was a learned man, eloquent and a great preacher of sermons.[11] He was strict in ritual observances and constantly under the influence of godly sorrow.[12] He was the author of a number of works of a theological nature, and his opinions on Ṣúfí doctrine carried great weight with those who came after him. He died in AD 728.[13]

'Aṭṭár states that if Rábi'a were not present in Ḥasan's assembly, he left the assembly at once.[14]

The same writer relates that Ḥasan of Baṣra said about his relationship with Rábi'a, "I passed one whole night and day with

Rábi'a speaking of the Way and the Truth, and it never passed through my mind that I was a man nor did it occur to her that she was a woman, and at the end when I looked at her, I saw myself a bankrupt [*i.e.* spiritually worth nothing], and Rábi'a as truly sincere".[15]

Again, he tells a story of how once Rábi'a was passing Ḥasan's house and Ḥasan had his head out of the window and was weeping; and his tears fell on to Rábi'a's garment. She looked up, thinking it was not rain, and when she was certain that it was Ḥasan's tears, she at once came to him, and said, "O teacher, this weeping is from pride of self; rather weep tears (as a result) of looking into your heart, that within thee they may become a river such that within that river you will not by searching find your heart again unless you find it in the Lord of Might". Ḥasan, who had a sufficient opinion of himself, found that a hard saying and was silent.[16]

Another ascetic with whom she is associated, and in this case with great probability, since he was both her contemporary and also of the same school of thought, is Rabaḥ al-Qays of Baṣra, who died in AD 810. A modern writer, associating him with Rábi'a, says, "With these two ascetics, both of the school of Baṣra, the quest of the ascetic life leads to mystic states already differentiated and brings up delicate problems of casuistry and dogma".[17] He introduced ideas of the glorious light of God (*tajallí*), of the Divine friendship (*Khulla*) and of the superiority of the saint over the prophet. In the moral life, he advocated chastity, repentance and acts of piety.[18]

Abú Nu'aym gives an anecdote which shows how her associates depended upon Rábi'a's help when faced with a difficult problem. He says that Rabaḥ relates it thus:

> I came to Abrad b. Dirár of the Baní Sa'd and he said to me, "Are the days and nights long to you?" and I said, "Why?" He said, "Because of your desire to meet God". Rabaḥ said, "I was silent and said nothing until I

> came to Rábi'a and said 'Veil yourself with your garment, for al-Abrad has asked me a question and I could say nothing in answer to it'". She said, "What did he ask you?" I said to her, "He said to me 'Are the days and nights long to you from your desire to meet God?'" Rábi'a said to me, "And what did you say?" I said, "I did not say 'Yes', lest I should tell a lie, and I did not say 'No', lest I should debase his soul".
>
> I heard the rending of her chemise under her cloak as she said, "My answer is 'Yes'".[19]

Abú Nu'aym is also the source of a story related by Abú Bakr al-Sarráj about Rabaḥ and Rábi'a:

> Abú Ma'mur 'Abdallah b. 'Amr said: "I saw Rábi'a with Rabaḥ al-Qays and he was kissing a boy belonging to his family and embracing him and she said, 'Do you love him, O Rabaḥ?' He said, 'Yes', and she said, 'I did not suppose there was room in your heart for loving any but God'. Rabah cried out and fell in a swoon; when he recovered, he wiped the sweat from his brow and said, 'Compassion is from God Most High and He has put it into the hearts of his servants towards little children'."[20]

Sufyán al-Thawrí appears in all the biographies of Rábi'a as a very intimate friend and a constant visitor at her house, and much of the teaching attributed to her was the result of his questions or of conversation with him. He was born at Kúfa in AH 95 (AD 713–14) and died in AD 778; he was therefore contemporary with Rábi'a and it is reasonable to suppose that he would come into contact with her. He was a great authority on the Traditions, and Rábi'a appears to have taken him to task more than once for his devotion to them. Abú Ṭálib relates in this connection that Rábi'a al-'Adawiyya used to say of al-Thawrí, "Yes, Sufyán would be a (good) man, if he did not love the Traditions", and she used to say, "The seductive power of the Traditions is stronger than the enticement of property and children" (*i.e.* the study of the Traditions distracted him from the life with God even more than worldly possessions would have done), and she said once, "If only Sufyán did not love this world, that is to say the gathering of people round him for (discourse on) the Traditions, what a good thing it would be".[21]

The same writer relates how one day Sufyán al-Thawrí said in Rábi'a's presence, "O God, mayst Thou be satisfied with us!" and she said, "Are you not ashamed before God to ask Him to be satisfied when you are not satisfied with Him?"[22] and he said, "I ask forgiveness from God".[23]

Again Sufyán, who seems to have been somewhat of a *poseur*, or at least anxious to provoke Rábi'a to retaliation, said to her, "Alas, for my sorrow! (for my sins)", but she rejoined, "Do not lie, but say rather, 'Alas, for my lack of sorrow', and if you were truly sorrowful, life would have no delight for you".[24]

That her intercession was valued even in her lifetime by her disciples, is proved by an account of a man who said to Rábi'a, "Pray for me", and she said, "Who am I? Obey your Lord and pray to Him, for He will answer the suppliant when he prays."[25]

More than one episode, of doubtful authenticity, connects Rábi'a with the great Egyptian Ṣúfí Dhú al-Nún al-Miṣrí,[26] one of the chief exponents of the Ṣúfí doctrine and especially the doctrine of the heavenly gnosis (*ma'rifa*) derived from spiritual experience, not from acquired learning. He elaborates the Ṣúfí conception of unification (*tawḥíd*) and employs for the love of God to the saint and the saint's love to Him, the term which Rábi'a also used (*ḥubb*). He died in AD 856 and therefore survived Rábi'a for nearly half a century. It is quite possible, however, that he may have met her in his early years.

There is a story connecting the two which has a good deal of interest, related by Sa'd b. 'Uthmán, who says,

> I was with Dhú al-Nún the Egyptian . . . and behold, someone arrived and I said, "O teacher, someone has come", and he said to me, "See who it is, for no one sets foot in this place, except my friends", and I looked and lo, it was a woman, and I said, "It is a woman", and he said, "She is a friend, by the Lord of the Ka'ba", then he ran up to her and greeted her . . . and said, "I am your brother Dhú al-Nún and there is no one present (*i.e.* no strangers)", and she said, "May God welcome your soul in peace". Then he said, "What led you to enter this place?" and she said, "A verse from the book of God. . . . His most exalted Word says, 'Is not God's earth wide? Therefore wander about in it.'" Then he said to her: "Expound Love to me", and she said, "Praise be to God, for you speak with the tongue of knowledge and (yet) you ask me about it". He said to her, "The asker has a right to an answer".

Then she is said to have recited her famous verses on the two types of love to God.[27]

Another of her contemporaries and acquaintances was 'Abd al-'Azíz b. Sulaymán Abú al-Rasíbí of Baṣra, who died in AH 150 (AD 767), an ascetic and devotee whom Rábi'a called "The Chief of the Devotees" (Sayyid al-'Ábadín).[28]

Others mentioned as visitors to her house who came to discuss problems with her, were Ṣáliḥ b. 'Abd al-'Azíz and Kiláb b. Ḥarí, the latter a Ṣúfí Shi'ite.[29] More than one story associates Rábi'a with Málik b. Dínár, a very well known ascetic, who was one of the disciples of Ḥasan al-Baṣrí. As he died in AH 128 (AD 745) Rábi'a can have known him only in her youth.[30]

It was chiefly among men that Rábi'a found her disciples and friends; we hear less of her association with women. Among her companions who were evidently of her own kinsfolk we hear of Mu'adha al-'Adawiyya, a famous woman ascetic, and Layla al-

Qaysiyya.[31] Rábi'a's name is often connected with that of Umm al-Darda,[32] but the latter must have been considerably older than Rábi'a. We are given the names of two of her servants, who were themselves pious and devout women. One of these was Mariam of Baṣra, a devotee and ascetic who loved Rábi'a greatly and became her servant, and survived her for some time. She used to listen to and take part in discussions on love and was so deeply moved thereby that she would at times lose consciousness. On one occasion she was in the assembly (of the Ṣúfís) when they were speaking of love, and the effect on her was so great that she yielded up her soul, there in the assembly. Among her sayings was this, "I have not concerned myself with my daily bread, nor wearied myself in seeking it since I heard this verse from the Word of God, 'In Heaven is your provision and what has been promised to you'".[33] The other was 'Abda bint Shuwál, who is described as herself one of the virtuous handmaids of God Most High, of whom several stories are told in connection with her service to Rábi'a and who was with Rábi'a at the time of the latter's death.

The anecdotes related in this chapter show that Rábi'a al-'Adawiyya associated on equal terms with the Ṣúfí leaders of her day, and her biographers, despite the Oriental preference for the male sex and belief in its essential superiority, are prepared to grant to Rábi'a a position of equality with, even of pre-eminence above her contemporaries, including those who were accepted as leaders of thought and revered teachers of the Ṣúfí doctrine.

1 Abú Ṭálib, *Qút al-Qulúb*, I, p. 153.

2 *Op. cit.* II, p. 57. Hamadhání "Shakwa" MS. Berlin, fol. 37 b. See L. Massignon, *Textes Inédits*. (Proof kindly communicated by the author.)

3 Cf. L. Massignon, *Lexique Technique*, p. 193, note 5.

4 Munáwí, "Al-Kawákib al-Durríya", fol. 510. Ṣibt Ibn al-Jawzí "Mir'át al-Zamán", fol. 265 b.

5 Ob. AD 728.

6 The two angels of Death, who visit the dead Muslim in the grave and ask questions to test the faith of the deceased.
7 The record of each one's deeds, given into the right hand of those who have done good and the left hand of those who have done evil.
8 Al-Ḥurayfísh, *Al-Rawḍ al-Fá'iq*, p. 214.
9 'Aṭṭár, *op. cit.* I, p. 66.
10 Abú Ṭálib, *Qút al-Qulúb*, I, p. 101.
11 Cf. al-Jáḥiẓ, *al-Bayán*, III, p. 68.
12 *Op. cit.* III, p. 86.
13 For an account of his life and influence see L. Massignon, *Lexique Technique*, pp. 152–79.
14 'Aṭṭár, *op. cit.* I, p. 59.
15 *Op. cit.* I, p. 65.
16 *Op. cit.* I, pp. 64 and 65.
17 L. Massignon, *Textes Inédits*. (Proof kindly communicated by the author.)
18 Cf. L. Massignon, *Lexique Technique*, pp. 195–7.
19 "Ḥilya al-Abrár", Leyden MS. I, fol. 26 b. al-Sarráj, *Maṣári'*, p. 181.
20 Al-Sarráj, *Maṣári'*, p. 186. "Ḥilya", Leyden MS. I, fol. 27 a.
21 *Qút al-Qulúb*, I, pp. 156, 157.
22 See Part Two, Chapter X, pp. 113 ff.
23 *Op. cit.* II, p. 40.
24 Al-Qushayrí, *Risála*, p. 86. Ibn al-Jawzí, "Ta'ríkh al-Muntaẓam", fol. 132.
25 Ṣibt Ibn al-Jawzí, *op. cit.* fol. 265 b.
26 Cf. 'Abd al-Rahmán al-Sulamí, *op. cit.* fol. 6 b.
27 Al-Ḥurayfísh, *op. cit.* p. 213.
28 Taghribardí, *Al-Nujúm al-Záhira*, p. 406.
29 Al-Dhahabí says that Abú Dáwúd said about Málik b. Dínár: "He and Abú Ḥabíb al-Ḥaríri and Rábi'a are all four zindiqs" (heretics). *Mizán al-I'tidál*, p. 306.
30 Ṣibt Ibn al-Jawzí, *op. cit.* fol. 265 b.

[31] M. b. Hasan Imád al-Dín, *Ḥayát al-Qulúb* (on margin of *Qút al-Qulúb*, II, p. 196.

[32] Al-Jáḥiẓ, *Kitáb al-Ḥayawán*, I, p. 78.

[33] Jámí, *op. cit.* p. 717. Munáwí, *op. cit.* fol. 83 a.

CHAPTER III

RÁBI'A'S ASCETICISM AND PRAYER-LIFE

To the Ṣúfí, as to the Christian saint, the life of purgation was the first stage towards the attainment of the mystic's goal, and asceticism was enjoined on all who entered the novitiate. Only when the novice had purged himself of the carnal self and its desires, could he hope to enter on the way which would lead to union with the Divine. Ascetic (*záhid*) was the most common appellation of the Ṣúfí, and even those who had attained to sainthood, with few exceptions, practised asceticism to the end of their lives. As a Ṣúfí writer expresses it: "If you ask, Who is the traveller on the road (the mystic Way)? It is one who is aware of his own origin. . . . He is the traveller who passes on speedily; he has become pure from Self as flame from smoke".[1]

Rábi'a al-'Adawiyya was an ascetic who followed the path of poverty and self-denial with unwavering steps to the end. Again and again her friends would have given her of their substance to alleviate her poverty and discomfort, but she would have none of their proffered gifts and looked only to the Lord she served, to provide for the needs of His servant.

For some time after her release from slavery, according to 'Aṭṭár, she retired to the desert and there lived the life of a recluse in a cell, and even after her return to Baṣra she lived apart from the world, so far as the constant visits of her disciples and other visitors made it possible.

Al-Jaḥiẓ, our oldest authority, says that some of her friends said to Rábi'a al-Qaysiyya, "If we were to speak to the men of your kinsfolk, they would purchase a servant for you, who would look after the needs of your house", but she said, "Verily, I should be ashamed to ask for worldly things from Him to Whom the world belongs, and how should I ask for them from those to whom it does not belong?"[2]

A similar story is told of a man who brought her forty *dínárs* and said to her, "Spend them on something that you need", and she wept and lifted up her head and said, "God knows that I am ashamed to ask Him for this world, though He rules it, and how shall I take it from one who does not rule it?"[3]

'Aṭṭár relates that some people came to see her and she was tearing a piece of meat with her teeth, and they said to her, "Have you no knife with which to cut it?" She said, "From fear of cutting off (separation from God) I have never had a knife in my house, so I have none".[4]

He also tells a story of how Rábi'a learnt the lesson of giving up all worldly desires in order that she might serve God without distraction.

Once for seven days and nights she had been fasting and had eaten nothing, and during the night she had not slept at all, but had spent every night in prayer. When she was in extremity from hunger, someone came into the house and brought her a cup of food. Rábi'a took it and went to fetch a lamp. When she returned, a cat had upset the cup. She said, "I will go and fetch a jug and break my fast (on water)". When she brought the jug, the lamp had gone out. She intended to drink the water in the darkness, but the jug fell from her hands and was smashed to pieces. Rábi'a broke into lamentations and heaved such a sigh that it almost seemed as if the house would catch fire.

She said, "O my Lord, what is this which Thou art doing to wretched me?" She heard a voice saying,

> Have a care, if you desire it, I will endow you with all the pleasures of this world, but I shall take concern for Me out of your heart, for such concern and the pleasures of this world cannot dwell together in one heart. O Rábi'a, you have a desire and I have a desire, I cannot combine my desire and your desire in one heart.

She said,

> When I heard this warning, then I separated my heart from worldly things and so cut off my worldly hopes that for thirty years every prayer which I have performed, I have prayed as if it were my last, and I have cut myself off from the creatures so that when day broke, from fear lest anyone should distract me from Him, I have said, "O Lord, make me occupied with myself, lest they should distract me from Thee".[5]

The austerity of her views is further shown by a little anecdote which tells how Rábi'a once went out on a feast-day, and when she returned she was asked, "What did you think of the feast?" Rábi'a replied, "I saw how you went out (nominally) to make the Sunna a living force and to put a stop to heresy, but you displayed a love of luxury and soft living and thereby you brought humiliation upon the Muslims".[6]

Illness and suffering Rábi'a accepted as her Lord's will for her, enduring them with fortitude, and she even showed herself oblivious to pain; more than one story tells how she was unaware of injury until others reminded her of it.

It is related that one day her head was struck by some boughs and began to bleed, but she paid no attention to it, and when someone said to her, "Do you not feel the pain?" her reply was as follows: "My concern is to accommodate myself to His will; He has made me occupied with something other than the tangible things which you see."[7]

Another story to the same effect tells how one night she was making supplication and the result was that she fell asleep from the extremity of her absorption and a blood-vessel in her eye broke, but when she awoke, she was quite unaware of it.[8] The capacity of these ascetics for enduring physical pain and rising above it is exemplified by the story of another woman, of Rábi'a's time, named Batja, who followed the sect of Qádiriyya al-Ḥururiyya. Zayd, Amír of Baṣra, when he heard of this, took her and cut off her hands and feet. The people came to visit her in her illness and they said to her, "How do you feel, O Batja?" She answered, "Awe of the future has distracted me from the cold of your iron".[9]

On one occasion Rábi'a fell ill, and her sickness was serious. Her friends came and asked her what was the cause of her illness, and she said, "I looked towards Paradise and my Lord has chastened me. At daybreak my heart looked in the direction of Paradise (*i.e.* I longed for its joys) and my Friend has reproached me. This illness is a reproach from Him".[10]

Her unwillingness to depend on any save God is shown in another account by the same writer, who tells how Ḥasan of Baṣra once came to visit her when she was ill and said that on his way he saw one of the merchants of Baṣra at the door of Rábi'a's cell, with a purse of gold, weeping. Said Ḥasan, "O merchant, why are you weeping?" He said, "On account of this ascetic of our time [Rábi'a], for if her blessings upon mankind were to cease, mankind would perish", and he added, "I have brought somewhat as a recommendation to her, but I fear that she may refuse it. Do thou intercede for me, that she may accept it."

Ḥasan went in and spoke about it to Rábi'a, who looked at him out of the corner of her eye and said:

> Shall not He who provides for those who revile Him, provide for those who love Him? He does not refuse sustenance to one who speaks unworthily of Him, how then should He refuse sustenance to one whose soul is overflowing with love to Him? Ever since I have known Him, I have turned my back upon mankind. How should I take the wealth of someone of whom I do not know whether he acquired it lawfully or not? . . . Make my excuses to that merchant, that my heart may not be in bondage (to a creature).[10]

Rábi'a made clear her attitude on the subject of resignation and the renunciation of desire to certain visitors who came to see her during one of her illnesses. These were 'Abd al-Wáḥid 'Amr, and her constant visitor Sufyán. The former relates:

> I and Sufyán Thawrí visited Rábi'a when she was sick, and from awe I was not able to begin to speak, and I said to Sufyán, "Say something". He said (to Rábi'a), "If you would utter a prayer, (God) would relieve your suffering". She turned her face to him and said, "O Sufyán, do you not know Who it is that wills this suffering for me, is it not God Who wills it?" He said,"Yes". She said, "When you know this, why do you bid me ask for what is contrary to His will? It is not well to oppose one's Beloved".
>
> Sufyán said then, "O Rábi'a, what is your desire?" She replied, "O Sufyán, you are a learned man, how can you ask me such a question as 'What do I desire'? I swear by the glory of God that for twelve years I have desired fresh dates, and you know that in Baṣra dates are plentiful, and I have not yet tasted them.[11] I am a servant and what has a servant to do with desire? If I will (a thing) and my Lord does not will it, this would be unbelief. That should be willed which He wills, that you may be His true servant. If He Himself gives anything, that would be a different matter." Sufyán was silenced and offered no more on the subject.[12]

One of her acquaintances, Muḥammad b. 'Amr, says:

> I went in to Rábi'a, and she was a very old woman of eighty years, as if she were a worn-out skin almost falling down, and I saw in her house a reed-mat and a clothes-stand of Persian reed, of the height of two

> cubits from the ground and upon it were her shrouds and the curtain of the house was made of palm-leaves, and perhaps there was a mat and an earthen jug and a bed of felt, which was also her prayer-carpet.[13]

Another friend of hers, Málik Dínár,[14] once found her lying on an old rush mat, with a brick to serve as a pillow and drinking and making her ablutions from a cracked jar. His heart was pained and he said, "I have rich friends and if you wish, I will take something from them for you". She said, "O Málik, you have made a great mistake. Is it not the same One Who gives daily bread to me and to them?" Málik said, "It is". She said, "Will He forget the poor because of their poverty or remember the rich because of their riches?" He said, "No". Then she said, "Since He knows my state, what have I to remind Him of? What He wills, we should also will."[15]

Rábi'a's devotion to the life of prayer is evident in all the accounts given of her life, and her biographers speak frequently of her custom of spending her nights in prayer. As a modern authority on Ṣúfism has written, "In Moḥammedan mysticism it is Prayer that supplies the best evidence of personality – not the ritual prayer (*ṣalat*) but the free prayer (*du'á'*) and in particular the loving converse with God (*munáját*) when the mystic speaks out of the depths of his heart",[16] and Rábi'a's prayers reveal her personality more clearly perhaps than anything else.

It is told of her that at one time she was laid aside by sickness and, in the weakness which followed it, she gave up her night-prayers and slept instead and for some days she recited her portion when the day had risen, although it was the portion appointed for the night-prayer. Then God restored her to health, but for a time, through the languor produced by sickness, she went on reciting the portion by day and neglected rising at night. Then she says:

> One night, while I was sleeping, it seemed to me in my sleep as if I were lifted up to a green park containing

palaces and beautiful plants. While I was wandering about in it, astonished at its beauty, I saw a green bird and a maiden pursuing it as if she wished to take it, and her beauty distracted me from its beauty, and I said, "What do you want with it? Leave it alone, for truly I have never seen a bird more beautiful than that". Then she said, "Shall I show you something more beautiful than that?" I said, "Yes, surely". Then she took my hand and led me round that garden until she brought me to the gate of a palace and she sought to open it and it opened to her and from the door were cast rays from a candlestick the light of which shone before me and behind me, and she said to me, "Enter", and I entered the house, in which the sight was dazzled by the beauty of it, I know nothing in the world like it and while we were going round it, there appeared to us a door opening from it on to a garden and she hastened towards it and I with her and there met us a band of servants, with faces like pearls, and in their hands aloeswood, and she said to them, "What do you seek?" and they said, "We seek such a one, who was drowned in the sea, as a martyr". She said, "Will you not perfume this woman?" They said, "She had her portion in that, and she left it". Then (Rábi'a said) she withdrew her hand from mine, and approached me and said :

"Your prayers were light and your worship rest,
Your sleep was ever a foe to prayer,
Your life was an opportunity which you neglected, and a preparation
It passes on and vanishes slowly and perishes".

Then she vanished from before my eyes and I awoke as

> the dawn appeared and verily I remembered it, and thought of it only as confusion of my mind and a phantom of my soul.

When Rábi'a had related her dream she fell unconscious and her servant said that after this vision she never slept at night, until her death.[17]

It is related of her that at night she used to go up on to her roof and pray thus:

> O my Lord, the stars are shining and the eyes of men are closed, and kings have shut their doors and every lover is alone with his beloved, and here am I alone with Thee,

and then she began her prayers. When she saw the dawn appearing, she would pray:

> O God, the night has passed and the day has dawned. How I long to know if Thou hast accepted (my prayers) or if Thou hast rejected them. Therefore console me for it is Thine to console this state of mine. Thou hast given me life and cared for me and Thine is the glory. If Thou wert to drive me from Thy door, yet would I not forsake it, for the love that I bear in my heart towards Thee.[18]

Then she is said to have recited these verses:

> O my Joy and my Desire and my Refuge,
> My Friend and my Sustainer and my Goal,
> Thou art my Intimate, and longing for Thee sustains me,
> Were it not for Thee, O my Life and my Friend,
> How I should have been distraught over the spaces of

the earth,
How many favours have been bestowed, and how
much hast Thou given me.
Of gifts and grace and assistance,
Thy love is now my desire and my bliss,
And has been revealed to the eye of my heart that was
athirst,
I have none beside Thee, Who dost make the desert
blossom,
Thou art my joy, firmly established within me,
If Thou art satisfied with me, then
O Desire of my heart, my happiness has appeared.[19]

'Abda bint Shúwál, already mentioned in the last chapter, says of her:

> Rábi'a used to pray all night, and when the day dawned she allowed herself a light sleep in her place of prayer, until the dawn tinged the sky with gold, and I used to hear her say, when she sprang up in fear from that sleep, "O soul how long wilt thou sleep and how often wilt thou wake? Soon wilt thou sleep a sleep from which thou shalt not wake again until the trumpet call of the Day of Resurrection."[20]

A story is related of how Rábi'a visited Hayyúna, an ascetic who practised the greatest austerity and who used to pray, "O God, I would that the day were night that I might enjoy Thy proximity". In the middle of the night sleep overcame Rábi'a, and Hayyúna rose and came to her and kicked her with her foot, and said, "Rise up, the Bridegroom of the truly guided ones has come. The adornments of the brides of night are revealed by the light of the night-prayers."[21] This anecdote is remarkable in that it is the only passage I have met with which makes a reference to the spiritual marriage of lover and Beloved, in these terms, applied to Ṣúfís, and it appears also as if there might be a reference to the parable of the Ten Virgins.

One of the biographers tells how she used to pray a thousand *raka's* in the day and night, and someone said to her, "What are you seeking (to gain) by this?" and she replied, "I do not desire God's forgiveness (by this), I do it only that the Apostle of God on the Day of Resurrection may be able to say to the rest of the Prophets, 'Behold this woman of my community, this is her work'".[22]

Her friend, Sufyán al-Thawrí, relates:

> I approached Rábi'a, and she was in the miḥráb, where she was praying till day, while I, in another corner, was praying until the time of dawn and I said, " How shall we give thanks for His grace given to us, whereby we spent the whole night in prayer?" She said, "By fasting tomorrow".[23]

Rábi'a for the most part was filled with a radiant faith and joy in the service of God, which left little room for the gloomy fears by which Ḥasan of Baṣra was so constantly obsessed, but an old writer tells us how once, overcome by a dread of judgement, she prayed, "O my God, wilt Thou burn in Hell a heart that loves Thee?" and she heard an unseen voice speaking to her inner consciousness, "O Rábi'a, We shall not do this. Do not think of Us an Evil thought."[24]

Among the prayers recorded by her biographer 'Aṭṭár are several beautiful examples, showing how prayer to her in truth was "loving converse" with her Lord, not supplication on her own behalf or on behalf of others but simply communion with the Divine Friend, and perfect satisfaction in His presence. Among those quoted are the following:

> O my Lord, whatever share of this world Thou dost bestow on me, bestow it on Thine enemies, and

> whatever share of the next world Thou dost give me, give it to Thy friends. Thou art enough for me.[25]

One night Rábi'a said, "My God, when I make my prayer, take from my heart all Satanic suggestions, or through Thy generosity, accept my prayer with these suggestions".[26]

Again she used to pray,

> O my Lord, if I worship Thee from fear of Hell, burn me in Hell, and if I worship Thee from hope of Paradise, exclude me thence, but if I worship Thee for Thine own sake then withhold not from me Thine Eternal Beauty.[27]

Yet another prayer was this:

> O my God, my concern and my desire in this world, is that I should remember Thee above all the things of this world, and in the next, that out of all who are in that world, I should meet with Thee alone. This is what I would say, "Thy will be done".[27]

In the last sentence is fittingly summed up Rábi'a's attitude to this life and to the Lord of life.

We are given yet another prayer with which this chapter may close:

> O my God, the best of Thy gifts within my heart is the hope of Thee and the sweetest word upon my tongue is Thy praise, and the hours which I love best are those in which I meet with Thee. O my God, I cannot endure without the remembrance of Thee in this world and how shall I be able to endure without the vision of Thee in the next world? O my Lord, my

plaint to Thee is that I am but a stranger in Thy country, and lonely among Thy worshippers.[28]

1 Shabistarí, *Gulshan-i Ráz*, p. 19, ll, 313, 315.
2 *Al-Bayán wa al-Tabyín*, III, p. 66.
3 Munáwí, *op. cit.* fol. 51 a.
4 'Aṭṭár, *op. cit.* I, p. 68.
5 *Op. cit.* I, pp. 68 and 69.
6 Ṣibt Ibn al-Jawzí, *op. cit.* fol. 257 a.
7 Munáwí, *op. cit.* fol. 51 b.
8 'Aṭṭár, *op. cit.* I, p. 63.
9 M. b. Ḥasan Imád al-Dín, *op. cit.* II, p. 196. Cf. also the account of 'Amra, wife of Ḥabíb, the devotee, whose eyes were diseased, and when someone said, "Why do you not put medicine on them?" she replied, "The pain of my heart has distracted me from them". Munáwí, *op. cit.* fol. 70 a.
10 'Aṭṭár, *op. cit.* I, p. 70.
11 Cf. D. S. Margoliouth, *Early Development of Mohammedanism*, p. 154.
12 'Aṭṭár, *op cit.* I, pp. 70 and 71. Cf. Ramón Lull, *The Lover and the Beloved*, p. 70: "The Beloved bought a slave that He might show him His graces, and made him to suffer griefs and heavy thoughts, sighs and tears. And He asked him: 'What wilt thou eat and drink?' The slave replied: 'What Thou wilt'. 'But what wilt thou?' 'My will is as Thine'. 'Hast thou then no will?' asked the Beloved. He answered: 'A subject and a slave has no other will than to obey his Lord and his Beloved'".
13 Ibn al-Jawzí, "Ta'ríkh al-Muntaẓam", fol. 132.
14 Málik b. Dínár died in AH 127 (AD 744) and therefore cannot have known her in her old age, to which stage of her life this anecdote seems to belong.
15 'Aṭṭár, *op. cit.* I, p. 71.
16 R. A. Nicholson, *The Idea of Personality in Ṣúfism*, p. 36.
17 Al-Sarráj, *Al-Maṣári'*, p. 136. Ṣibt Ibn al-Jawzí, *op. cit.* fols. 256 b,

257 a.

18 This part of the story is attributed by al-Ghazálí to Ḥabíba 'Adawiyya, *Iḥyá*, IV, p. 353. Cf. al-Rúdhabárí, "Ṣúfism is abiding at the door of the Beloved, even when driven away from it". Al-Qushayrí, *op. cit.* p. 149.

19 Al-Ḥurayfísh *op. cit.* p. 213.

20 Ibn Khallikán, *Wafayát*, I, p. 34, No. 230.

21 Abú al-Qásim al-Nisábúrí, *'Uqalá' al-Majánín*, p. 128.

22 Munáwí, *op. cit.* fol. 50 b.

23 'Aṭṭár, *op. cit.* I, p. 72.

24 Al-Qushayrí, *op. cit.* p. 173.

25 'Aṭṭár, *op. cit.* I, p. 73.

26 'Aṭṭár, *op. cit.* Uyghur version, p. 68.

27 'Aṭṭár, *op. cit.* I, p. 73.

28 Abú al-Qásim al-'Árif, "Qaṣd ila Allah". Extract kindly communicated by Prof. Nicholson.

CHAPTER IV

Miracles

The saints of Islám, like the saints of Catholic Christendom, were expected to work miracles, as part of their claim to canonisation, and their biographers were not slow to attribute to them the power of performing these *karámát* (lit. favours from God). It is hardly necessary to say that most of these miracles rest on no historic foundation and yet, like other legends of the saints, they have their value in throwing light upon the personality of the one to whom these wonderful powers are ascribed and still more perhaps, in showing the high estimation in which such a saint was held.

The Ṣúfís themselves set little value upon the exercise of such miraculous powers. We are told that Abú Yazíd al-Bisṭámí[1] said:

> The saints do not rejoice at the answers to prayers which are the essence of miracles, such as walking on water, and moving in the air and traversing the earth and riding on the heavens, since the prayers of unbelievers receive an answer and the earth contains both Satans and men, and the air is the abode of the birds, and the water of the fish. Let not anyone who is perplexed by such things, put any faith in this trickery.[2]

Of Abú Yazíd it is also related that a man came to him and said, "I heard that you could pass through the air (fly)". He said, "And what is there wonderful in this? A bird which eats the dead passes through the air, and the believer is more honourable than a bird."[3]

There is no lack of stories of miracles ascribed to Rábi'a of Baṣra, and in any account of her life these must find a place. Most of them tend to show God's care for His servant and her needs and to justify her complete dependence upon Him. 'Aṭṭár has collected a number of these legendary stories, some of which are also to be found in other writers.

He tells how one night a thief came into Rábi'a's cell when she was asleep and took possession of her veil (in another account[4] it is said that he tried to steal all her clothes). Then he attempted to get away with his booty, but could not find the way to the door. He put down the veil, and found the way again, so he seized the veil once more, but again failed to find the way out. He repeated this seven times, then from a corner of the cell came an unseen voice, saying, "O man, do not trouble thyself since for all these years she has entrusted herself to Us and Satan has not had the courage to go round about her[5] and shall a thief have courage to go round about her veil? Concern not thyself with her, O pickpocket, if one friend is asleep, another friend is awake and keeping watch."[6] And al-Munáwí in his version of the story adds, "This is true and certain, as God Most High has said: 'There shall be angels in front of him (*i.e.* God's servant), and behind him.'"[7]

There is an anecdote given of provision for her bodily needs, to indicate her faith in God's promises, which is much more entertaining to the reader than her biographer can have intended it to be.

He tells how two religious leaders came to visit Rábi'a. Both of them were hungry and said to one another, "Perhaps she will give us something to eat, because her food is always obtained from a lawful source". When they sat down, a cloth containing two loaves was set before them and they were pleased. Before they had time to begin eating, a beggar came in and Rábi'a gave him both loaves. The two shaykhs felt annoyed but said nothing. After a time a slave-girl came in bearing a quantity of hot bread and said, "My mistress has sent this". Rábi'a counted the loaves and found that there were eighteen and said, "I think she has not sent me these", and whatever the slave-girl said was of no use. The slave-girl had brought all except two loaves, which she had taken out for herself; going away, she put the two loaves back in their place and then returned. Rábi'a counted the loaves again and found there were twenty. She said, "This is what you were ordered to bring", and she set the loaves before her guests and they ate. They were astonished at the number of them and said, "What is the secret of this? We were wishing for your bread, before you took it up and gave it to the beggar. Then of that bread (which was sent you) you said that there were eighteen loaves and that they did not belong to you. When they became twenty, you took them." She said:

> When you came in I knew you were hungry and I said, "How can I set two loaves before two honourable persons?" When the beggar came in, I gave them to him and I prayed to God Almighty, "O my Lord, Thou hast said that Thou wilt give ten for one, and I am sure of this. Now I have given two loaves for the sake of pleasing Thee in order that Thou mayest give me back ten for each of them." When the eighteen loaves came, I knew that either there was a deficiency due to misappropriation or that they were not meant for me.[8]

Another story, told quite naïvely by 'Aṭṭár, is equally entertaining to the modern reader.

He relates how on one occasion Rábi'a's servant was going to prepare wild onions, because for some days they had not prepared any food, and she needed an onion, so the servant said, "I will go and ask for one from a neighbour", but Rábi'a said, "Forty years ago I made an oath with God that I would not ask for anything except from Him. I can do without the onion." Immediately after she had spoken a bird flying in the air dropped an onion – ready skinned – into Rábi'a's frying-pan. But she was still doubtful and said, "I am not safe from a trick" (*i.e.* perhaps Satan had sent the onion), so she left the fried onion alone and ate bread without any seasoning.[9]

A much simpler and more probable account of this event is given by an earlier writer, who tells us that 'Abd Allah b. 'Ísá said,

"Rábi'a was boiling some food in a cooking pot and she needed an onion but had none, and there appeared a bird with a wild onion in its beak and threw it down to her".[10]

There is an attractive story told of Rábi'a, containing an element of the miraculous, which seems as if it might be drawn from Buddhist sources, and reminds us of stories told of Prince Gautama. 'Aṭṭár tells how one day Rábi'a had gone to the mountains and there a band of wild creatures gathered round her, deer and gazelle and mountain goats and wild asses, who came and looked at her and drew close to her. Suddenly Ḥasan al-Baṣrí appeared, and when he saw Rábi'a he approached her, and those wild creatures, when they saw Ḥasan, all fled away forthwith and Rábi'a was left alone. Ḥasan was vexed when he saw that, he looked at Rábi'a and said, "Why did they flee in terror from me, while they were friendly with you?" Rábi'a said, "What have you eaten today?" He said, "Some onions (fried) in fat". She said, "You eat of their fat, how should they not flee from you?"[11]

Al-Munáwí says that among Rábi'a's *karámát* it was related that she had sown corn and the locusts fell upon it, and she prayed, "O my Lord, this is my provision, upon which I have spent money, and if Thou willest, I will give it as food to Thine enemies or Thy friends". Then the locusts flew away as if they had never existed.[12]

The same writer relates a miracle which is perhaps a variant of a story told previously[13] of how Rábi'a went on pilgrimage, on a camel, and it died before she reached her destination, and she asked God to restore it to life. It recovered and she rode it until she reached the door of her own house.[14]

An amusing legend is told of how Ḥasan of Baṣra tried to exploit Rábi'a's power of working miracles for his own glory but only succeeded in reaping a rebuke for his vanity.

One day he saw Rábi'a near the river-side. Ḥasan cast his prayer-mat onto the surface of the water and said, "O Rábi'a, come and let us pray two *raka's* together", evidently counting on her powers to keep the carpet from sinking.[15] Rábi'a said, "O Ḥasan, was it necessary to offer yourself in the bazaar of this world to the people of the next? (*i.e.* was it needful to seek to win worldly reputation by a spiritual gift?) This is necessary for people of your kind, because of your weakness." Then Rábi'a threw her prayer-mat into the air and flew up onto it and said, "O Ḥasan, come up here that people may see us". But that station was not for Ḥasan and he was silent. Rábi'a, wishing to comfort him, said, "O Ḥasan, that which you did, a fish can do just the same, and that which I did, a fly can do. The real work (for the saints of God) lies beyond both of these and it is necessary to occupy ourselves with the real work."[16]

Another story tells of a miracle which has perhaps a mystical significance. One night Ḥasan and two or three friends are said to have come to Rábi'a and she had no lamp and she desired for them an illuminated heart. Rábi'a blew upon the tips of her fingers, and throughout that night, until daylight came, her fingers gave forth light like a lamp, and they sat until morning in that illumination. Her biographer adds by way of comment:

> If anyone were to say, "How was this?" I should say it was like the hand of Moses, and if it should be observed that he was a prophet, I should say, "Whoever obeys a prophet may obtain as his reward a share in the gift of prophecy". So the Prophet has said, "He who restores a small part of what was obtained unlawfully, has obtained one degree of prophecy".[16]

Yet another legend, proving that God provided for Rábi'a's needs when she herself was occupied in His service, tells how Ḥasan went one day to Rábi'a at the time of the second prayer of the day, when she was preparing to cook some meat in a pan and was putting water into it. He goes on to say:

> When she came to speak to me she said, "This discourse is better than anything cooked in a pan", so she

> went on talking till we performed the evening prayer. She brought a piece of dry bread and a jug of water that we might break our fast. Rábi'a then went to take off the pan and burnt her hand; we looked and there was the pan boiling and bubbling over, by the power of God Most High. She brought it and we ate of that meat and the food composed of that meat was the pleasantest we had ever tasted. Rábi'a said, "The food from that pan would have been suitable for an invalid just convalescent".[17]

Rábi'a herself disclaimed these miraculous powers and was anxious to avoid a reputation for working miracles. We are told of an interesting conversation between her and Zulfa bint 'Abd al-Wáḥid, who addresses Rábi'a as her aunt, while Rábi'a calls her her brother's daughter. If this represents a genuine relationship and not merely a term of affection, it is of great interest, as Zulfa is the only one of Rábi'a's own family who is mentioned by name by any of her biographers, nor have we any mention elsewhere of a brother of Rábi'a. But the terms "aunt" and "niece" are still used in the East as terms of endearment without any real relationship between the parties concerned.

Zulfa is reported to have said:

> I said to Rábi'a, "O my aunt, why do you not allow people to visit you?"[18] Rábi'a replied, "I fear lest when I am dead, people will relate of me what I did not say or do, what if I had seen, I should have feared or mistrusted. I am told that they say that I find money under my place of prayer, and that I cook (food) in the pot without a fire". I said to her, "They relate of you that you find food and drink in your house", and she said, "O daughter of my brother, if I had found such things in my house I would not have touched them, or laid

> hands upon them, but I tell you that I buy my things and am blessed in them".[19]

These anecdotes of Rábi'a are trivial in themselves, but they show that her biographers believed that she had the power to work miracles, attributed to all true saints of Islám, and moreover, that miracles were wrought on her behalf, that God might justify His servant in the eyes both of friends and enemies, and as 'Aṭṭár's own comment shows,[20] these miracles, wrought by, or for her, indicated to all who heard of them that the grace of God was with her.

1 Ob. AD 875 a native of Khurasán. For an account of his life and teaching cf. L. Massignon, *Lexique Technique*, pp. 243–56.
2 Munáwí, *op. cit.* fol. 123 a. For a full discussion of the miracles of Muslim saints cf. Goldziher, "Le culte des saints chez les Musulmans", *Revue de l'histoire des Religions*, 1880, pp. 335 ff.
3 Abú Nu'aym, "Ḥilya", Leyden MS. fol. 219 a.
4 Munáwí, *op. cit.* fol. 51 a.
5 Cf. Job i. 7: "The Lord said unto Satan, Whence comest thou? Then Satan answered the Lord and said, From going to and fro in the earth, and from walking up and down in it."
6 'Aṭṭár, *op. cit.* I, p. 63.
7 Munáwí, *op. cit.* fol. 51 a. This is surely a re-echo of Psalm xci. II: "He shall give His angels charge over thee, to keep thee in all thy ways."
8 'Aṭṭár, *op. cit.* I, pp. 63, 64.
9 *Op. cit.* I, p. 64.
10 Ṣibt Ibn al-Jawzí, *op. cit.* fol. 256 b.
11 'Aṭṭár, *op. cit.* I, p. 64.
12 Munáwí, *op. cit.* fol. 51 b.
13 See p. 25.
14 Munáwí, *op. cit.*, *loc. cit.*
15 This appears to be a favourite type of miracle among the Muslim claimants to sanctity.

[16] 'Aṭṭár, *op. cit.* I, p. 65.

[17] *Op. cit.* I, p. 72.

[18] Probably she refers here to people who wished to visit the saint simply out of curiosity, not to the Ṣúfís who sought counsel and instruction.

[19] Ṣibt Ibn al-Jawzí, *op. cit.* fol. 257 a.

[20] Quoted above, p. 57.

CHAPTER V

Rábi'a's Declining Years

Rábi'a, like so many of the saints, lived to a ripe old age, and must have been nearly ninety when she died. Some of the authorities quoted by her biographers apparently knew her only in her old age, when she was feeble in body and yet so clear in mind that she was still the guide and spiritual director of the many souls who came to seek counsel of her.

The author of the "Siyar al-Ṣáliḥát" says that when she heard others speak of death she shivered and her fingers trembled,[1] and others say that if she heard the mention of fire, or even the crackling of it, she became unconscious.[2]

An overwhelming dread of judgement after death and the constant fear of Hell was characteristic of the early Ṣúfís, as we have already noted, and especially of the school of Ḥasan al-Baṣrí. The most that he felt could be hoped for was an alleviation of the punishment for the believer, in that the period of torment in Hell would be shortened, and here seems to be in embryo the doctrine of purgatory for those who were true Muslims, and yet had fallen short and sinned.[3] It is plain that the early Ṣúfís had a strong sense of the moral turpitude of sin and the idea that it might mean separation from God – for the Ṣúfí the greatest of all deprivations – in the next world. The Christian doctrine that sincere repentance cannot fail to win forgiveness, together with the Christian doctrines of Atonement and Redemption, had not entered into the Ṣúfí conception of the relation between God and His servant. We are told of Sha'wána the ascetic that she said at the time of her death, "I cannot bear to meet with God", and when asked why, she said, "Because of the multitude of my sins".[4] The same feeling led to a different result with 'Ubayda bint Abí Kiláb,[5] who is said to have spent forty years in weeping, until her sight was lost. She was asked, "What do you desire?" She said, "Death", and when those with her asked "Why?"

she replied, "Because every new day that dawns I fear lest I should commit some sin which would mean my loss on the Day of Resurrection".[6]

Yet to some of the Ṣúfís the longing to be with their Lord was stronger than their fear of judgement. Al-Junayd was told that the Ṣúfí Abú Sa'íd al-Kharráz was in great ecstasy at the time of his death. "Is it to be wondered at?" said al-Junayd, "his soul has taken flight full of longing (to see God)".[7] Fáṭima, sister of the Ṣúfí Abú 'Alí al-Rúdhabárí, said that when her brother was at the point of death he opened his eyes and said, "Here are the gates of heaven opened and here is Paradise adorned and here is one saying, 'O Abú 'Alí, thou hast reached the highest rank'".[7]

As we shall see from the account of her teaching, it is hardly conceivable that Rábi'a was amongst those who were afraid of death, which to her represented union with her Beloved, above and beyond the temporary experience of union which was all that could be attained in this life. Her faith soared to heights above those to which Ḥasan attained or al-Fuḍayl,[8] of whom it was said that "sadness left the world when al-Fuḍayl left it"; hers was a confident and radiant faith founded on her intimate knowledge of – and communion with – her Lord. She would have said with 'Abd al-'Azíz, "Death is a bridge whereby the lover is joined to the Beloved".[9]

As regards the effect upon her of the mention of fire,[10] this element seems to have been chiefly associated with Hell and with evil in the minds of the early Ṣúfís, and a later Ṣúfí, Rúmí, contrasts fire with light, as evil with good, the defiled with the pure, that which perishes with that which is immortal.[11] Al-Hujwírí also contrasts the "fire of wrath" and the "light of mercy".[12] On the other hand the Persian writers constantly speak of the "fire" of love and its consuming power. 'Aṭṭár speaks of Rábi'a as "that woman on fire with love", and in this sense fire is regarded as a pure and holy element, causing suffering yet purging of dross. Al-Kalábádhí, using the term in such a sense, says, "He is burnt who feels the fire, but he who is fire, how shall he be burnt?"[13] *i.e.* he who is still under bondage to self and his sins, must feel the wrath of God, but he who is on fire with love to God, what fear has he of judgement? Again al-Ghazálí says of the longing of the mystic that it is "the fire of God which He has kindled in the hearts of His saints, that thereby may be burned away what exists in them of vain fancies and desires and purposes and needs".[14] This is the sense in which the Spanish mystic, St John of the Cross, says, "Love has set the soul on fire and transmuted it into love, has annihilated it and destroyed it as to all that is not love".[15]

Rábi'a, consumed by love and desire for God, might be compared with St Catherine of Genoa, who felt the consuming fire of her love to God so hot within her that she was dried up by it and her body was burning to the touch,[16] and fire for her had a significance equal to that felt by Rábi'a, who swooned from her strong emotion at its mention. Yet this emotion was more probably ecstasy than fear; to Rábi'a her Lord was "the One God Who is the Fire of Pain and the Light of Joy to souls, according as they resist Him or will Him, either here or hereafter".[17] In Rábi'a "the fire of her all-conquering love" demanded "eternal union with an eternal flame",[18] and the mention of death made her tremble, not with apprehension, but with infinite joy.

In one respect, certainly, Rábi'a was like her great successor, in that her health was frail, perhaps as the result of her ceaseless asceticisms, perhaps because of the hardships of her youth. We hear constantly of her illnesses and her sufferings from weakness. As with St Catherine, too, her illness sometimes had its source in spiritual rather than physical disturbance. We are told how one day she was suffering and lamenting and her friends said to her, "O venerable one of this world, we see no visible cause of illness and yet you are in pain and crying out". She said:

> My sickness is from within my breast, so that all the physicians in the world are powerless to cure it, and the plaster for my wound is union with my Friend;

> (only so) shall I be soothed. Not tomorrow (*i.e.* not yet) shall I attain my purpose. But since pain is not affecting me, I appear to be in pain, I cannot do less than this.

(*I.e.* the outward signs of my spiritual sickness should not be less than the outward signs of physical illness.)[19] So also the Christian mystic:

> The soul that loves God lives more in the next life than in this, because it lives rather where it loves than where it dwells, and therefore esteeming but lightly its present bodily life cries out: "Behold, the malady of love is incurable, except in Thy presence and before Thy face." The reason why the malady of love admits of no other remedy than the presence and countenance of the Beloved is that the malady of love differs from every other sickness, and therefore requires a different remedy . . . love is not cured but by that which is in harmony with itself. . . . There is no remedy for this pain except in the presence and vision of the Beloved.[20]

In what appears to have been her last illness, Rábi'a was said to have been visited by three of her friends, Ḥasan of Basṛa,[21] Málik Dínár and Shaqíq Balkhí, and they, like the friends of Job, endeavoured to teach her the duty of resignation.

Ḥasan said, "He is not sincere in his claim (to be a true servant of God), who is not patient under the chastisement of his Lord". Rábi'a said, "I smell egotism in this speech". So Shaqíq took up the thread and said, "He is not sincere in his claim who is not thankful for the chastisement of his Lord". Rábi'a said, "Something better than this is needed". Then Málik Dínár tried, "He is not sincere in his claim who does not delight in the chastisement of his Lord". Rábi'a said, "Even this is not good enough". They said, "Do thou speak", and she showed her idea of the true resignation in her reply, "He is not sincere in his claim who does not forget the chastisement in the contemplation of his Lord".

And 'Aṭṭár commends her answer, saying, "It would not be surprising, since the women of Egypt in their contemplation of a creature were oblivious to the pain of their wounds;[22] and therefore if anyone in the contemplation of the Creator were in this state, it would not be strange".[23]

One writer says that her shroud was always before her, in her place of worship.[24] When the time of her departure from this world drew near, she called her servant, 'Abda bint Abí Shuwál, and said to her, "O 'Abda, do not inform anyone of my (approaching) death, but shroud me in this gown of mine, of hair". So when she died, she was shrouded in that gown and in a woollen scarf which she used to wear. 'Abda relates further how she saw Rábi'a in a dream, a year or so after her death, and she was wearing a robe of green silk embroidered with gold and a scarf of fine green silk brocade and never had 'Abda seen anything in this world more beautiful, and she cried out, "O Rábi'a, what have you done with the shroud in which you were buried and the woollen scarf?" and Rábi'a answered her, "They were taken from me and I was clothed with what you see upon me and what I wore as a shroud was folded up and sealed and carried up to the angels, so that my garments might be complete on the Day of Resurrection". 'Abda said to her, "Were you working for this, in your earthly days?" She said, "What is this in comparison with the grace of God to His saints?"[25]

Her Persian biographer gives the following account of her death. He says:

> At her last moments many pious folk were sitting around her and she bade them, "Rise and go out; for a moment leave the way free for the messengers of God Most High". All rose and went out and when they had closed the door, they heard the voice of Rábi'a making

> her profession of faith and they heard a voice saying, "O soul at rest, return to thy Lord, satisfied with Him, giving satisfaction to Him. So enter among My servants and enter into My paradise."[26]
>
> There was no further sound heard, they returned and found that her soul had departed. As soon as she had rendered up her last breath, the doctors who were assembled had her body washed, recited over it the prayers for the dead and placed it in its last abode.[27]

The religious leaders said of her that Rábi'a came into this world and departed into the next and never was she wanting in reverence to her Lord, and never did she desire anything or say "Give me this or do this for me", much less did she desire anything from any of His creatures.

After her death, she was seen in a dream and the dreamer said to her, "Tell us of your state and how you escaped from Munkar and Nakír". She said, "Those beings came and said, 'Who is your Lord?' I said, 'Return and tell your Lord, Notwithstanding the thousands and thousands of Thy creatures, Thou hast not forgotten a weak old woman. I, who have only Thee in all the world, have never forgotten Thee, that Thou shouldest ask, Who is thy Lord?'"[28]

Rábi'a al-'Adawiyya died in AH 185 (AD 801) and was buried at Baṣra.

It is said that Muḥammad b. Aslam al-Ṭúsí and Na'mí Tarṭúsí both visited Rábi'a's grave, and said, "O thou who didst boast that thou wouldst not bow thy head for the two worlds, hast thou reached that exalted state?" and they heard a voice in reply, "I have reached that which I saw".[29]

She had attained the goal of her quest, she was united at last and for ever, with her Friend, she beheld the Everlasting Beauty, and so we leave her, with the closing words of her faithful biographer, "May God have mercy upon her".

1 "Siyar al-Ṣáliḥát", fol. 26 a.
2 Sha'rání, *Ṭabaqát*, p. 86. Munáwí, *op. cit.* fol. 51 a.
3 Cf. Shahrastání, *Kitáb al-Milal*, pp. 31, 33.
4 Munáwí, *op. cit.* fol. 58 b.
5 See p. 207.
6 Munáwí, *op. cit.* fol. 69 b.
7 Al-Ghazálí, *Ihyá*, IV, p. 411.
8 Died two years after Rábi'a.
9 Abú Nu'aym, "Ḥilya", Leyden MS. fol. 210 b.
10 Cf. also the account of Baríra, *Iḥyá*, IV, p. 354.
11 *Mathnawí*, II, l. 83.
12 *Kashf al-Maḥjúb*, p. 177.
13 Al-Kalábádhí, "Ma'ání al-Akhbár ", fol. 70 b.
14 Al-Ghazálí, *op. cit.* IV, p. 309.
15 *Spiritual Canticle*, p. 209.
16 Von Hügel, *Mystical Element in Religion*, I, p. 179; II, pp. 215–18.
17 *Op. cit.* II, p. 218.
18 John Cordelier, *The Spiral Way*, p. 158. For other examples of the mystical use of fire-imagery cf. E. Underhill, *Mysticism*, pp. 503, 504.
19 'Aṭṭár, *op. cit.* p. 69.
20 St John of the Cross, *Spiritual Canticle*, pp. 54, 84, 85.
21 On chronological grounds, it was impossible that Ḥasan could have visited Rábi'a when she had reached this age.
22 Referring to the story of "Yusef and Zulaykha", when the women of Egypt, sitting at a repast, beheld Joseph and cut their hands with their knives in amazement at his beauty. Qur'án, XII, 31.
23 'Aṭṭár, *op. cit.* p. 71.
24 Sha'rání, *op. cit.* p. 86. Cf. also Ibn al-Jawzí, *op. cit.* fol. 132.
25 Ṣibt Ibn al-Jawzí, *op. cit.* fol. 257 a. Ibn Khallikán, *op. cit.* No. 230.
26 Qur'án, LXXXIX, 27–30. Cf. the Catholic commendation of the departing soul, "Go forth Christian soul, from this world . . . let thine habitation today be in peace. . . . I commit thee to Him whose creature thou art that thou mayst return unto thy Maker."

27 'Aṭṭár, *op. cit.* Uyghur version, II, p. 68.

28 *Op. cit.* p. 73.

29 *Op. cit., loc. cit.* In the Uyghur version, II, p. 68, her reply is given as "Ah, what I did was what needed to be done, and it was the right Way that I discovered".

Part Two

RÁBI'A'S TEACHING AND WRITINGS

CHAPTER VI

The Ṣúfí Doctrine

Rábi'a's teaching on mysticism and her contribution to the development of Ṣúfism are of considerable importance, and in dealing with her teaching we stand on surer ground than was possible in collecting material for her biography. As a teacher and guide along the mystic Way, Rábi'a was greatly revered by the Ṣúfís and practically all the great Ṣúfí writers speak of her teaching, and quote her sayings, as being of the highest authority. Abú Ṭálib al-Makkí, one of the first to write a systematic treatise on Ṣúfí doctrine; al-Qushayrí, in his *Risála* on the subject; the great Muslim theologian al-Ghazálí, of whose works frequent editions have been brought out during the past century, and whose teaching is widely accepted by Muslims up to the present day; and al-Suhrawardí, also a well-known writer on Ṣúfism, all refer to Rábi'a's teaching on the main doctrines of Ṣúfism. These writers are chiefly concerned with expositions, doctrinal and theological, but Rábi'a's biographers also make it plain that teaching to others, what she herself had learned of the Way, played an important part in her life. It is to be noted that we do not hear of Rábi'a herself learning from any great shaykh or teacher.

'Aṭṭár says of her, "Rábi'a was unique, because in her relations (with God) and her knowledge (of things Divine) she had no equal; she was highly respected by all the great (mystics) of her time and she was a decisive proof, *i.e.* an unquestioned authority, to her contemporaries".[1] A later writer, 'Abd al-Rá'úf al-Munáwí, gives her equally high commendation when he says that Rábi'a was in the rank referred to by 'Abd al-Qádir al-Jílání, when he said that there were two classes of true believers. First, those who seek a master in the Way that leads to the majesty of God, who may act as an intermediary between them and God, people who persuade themselves that there is no way for them to God except by the Prophet, who was the "chamberlain" (*i.e.* the one who admitted them into the presence of God), so they do not accept as evidence of the right way, anything in which they do not see the footsteps of the Prophet before them. The second class are those who, when they seek to follow the right Path, do not see before them the footprint of any of God's creatures, for they have removed all thought (of what He has created) from their hearts and concern themselves solely with God. It is in this latter class that Rábi'a is placed. As al-Munáwí writes: "This state is the state of 'Abd al-Qádir and Abú Sa'úd b. Shiblí and Rábi'a al-'Adawiyya and whoso follows where they lead, will attain his desire".[2]

Before continuing further, it is necessary to give here a very brief outline of the Ṣúfí doctrine, in order to understand the extent and value of Rábi'a's contribution to its development. The Ṣúfí view was that

> man's business is to eliminate, so far as may be, the element of Not-Being, and to attain to that union with God, that absorption into the Divine, which though to be fully achieved only after the death of the body, is possible in a certain measure even in this present life.
>
> But how is one to overcome the element of Not-Being?
>
> By conquering self. . . . And how is self to be conquered? By Love. By Love and Love alone can the dark shadow of Not-Being be done away; by Love and by Love alone, can the soul of man win back to its Divine source and find its ultimate goal in re-union with the Truth.[3]

The preparation, then, for those who sought to follow the mystic Way of the Ṣúfís, was the life of purgation, that is, a life of asceticism, through which the carnal soul, the *nafs*, might be purified from its sins, which ultimately had their source in the desires of self, the *shahawát*. When cleansed from these lusts of the flesh, the soul could enter on the Path which was destined to lead it to union with the Divine. The Ṣúfís often held that such asceticism was necessary only at the beginning of the quest, as a preparatory stage, and some, such as the famous Ṣúfí Shaykh Abú Sa'íd b. Abí al-Khayr,[4] felt no need of continuing their ascetic practices when they had attained to a higher degree of the spiritual life. Others, like Rábi'a, as we have seen in the foregoing pages, practised asceticism to the end of their lives, and so came nearer to the fulfilment of the Christian idea of sainthood.[5]

The Way, upon which the soul, cleansed from its sins, now entered, was made up of a number of stages, in its passage through which the soul acquired certain qualities, which enabled it to rise higher and higher, and to attain to more exalted stations, until at last, partly through its own striving, partly through the grace of God, it reached the heavenly gnosis (*ma'rifa*). Through this knowledge, based upon intuitions of the truth (*Khawáṭir al-yaqín*) the mystic proceeded to the final goal, the contemplation of God Himself, and the abiding in union with Him for ever.[6]

As Abú Ṭálib writes in the *Qút al-Qulúb*, to the mystic who has attained, it is said, "Thou shalt worship God as if thou sawest Him", and the same writer, dealing with the derivation of this intuitive knowledge of God, says:

> The Gnostic is not one who commits to memory passages from the Qur'án, who if he forgets what he has learned, becomes ignorant. He only is the Gnostic who takes his knowledge from his Lord at all times, without having to learn it, and without studying, and this (knowledge) lasts throughout his lifetime, he does not forget his knowledge, but he remembers it for ever. He has no need of a book, and he is the (true) spiritual Gnostic.[7]

Abú Ṭálib states that there are indeed myriad ways to God and quotes a gnostic who said, "The ways to God are as many as the believers", and another who held that "the ways to God are as many as created things, that is, that to the contemplative there is a way to be found through every creature",[8] and this is in accordance with the later Ṣúfí view that the whole world is the book of God Most High[9] and that beneath the veil of each atom is hidden the soul-ravishing beauty of the face of the Beloved.[10]

But in spite of these more pantheistic views, the serious exponents of Ṣúfism held that the mystic must expect to pass through certain stages, as stated above, and in Abú Ṭálib's *Qút al-Qulúb*, al-Qushayrí's *Risála* and al-Ghazálí's *Iḥyá 'Ulúm al-Dín*, whole chapters are devoted to these stages on the Way and the qualities to be acquired by the mystic as he traverses them. These degrees to be attained are given by the Ṣúfí writers, in varying order, as penitence (*tawba*), patience (*ṣabr*), gratitude (*shukr*), hope (*rajá'*), holy fear (*khawf*), voluntary poverty (*faqr*), asceticism (*zuhd*) – here considered as applied to the adept, involving renunciation of all save God, not the mere purification from sensual desires needed for the novice – abnegation of the personal will in the Will of God (*tawḥíd*), complete dependence upon God (*tawakkul*), and finally love (*maḥabba*), including in this last, passionate longing for God (*shawq*), intimacy with Him (*uns*) and satisfaction (*riḍá'*) considered both objectively and subjectively, *i.e.* God's satisfaction in His servant's obedience and the servant's satisfaction in God's service when he casts aside all that belongs to this world and its desires and is content to "glorify God and to enjoy Him for ever".[11] Other stages mentioned by Ṣúfí writers are sincerity, contemplation, self-examination and meditation on death,[12] but the stage of love includes so much that in practice it is the final stage.[13]

These stages passed,[14] the Ṣúfí attains to the true Gnosis and the beatific vision, through which, becoming one with the Divine, he abides with and in Him for ever.

1 'Aṭṭár, *op. cit.* I, p. 59.
2 Munáwí, *op. cit.* fol. 51 b.
3 E. J. W. Gibb, *History of Ottoman Poetry*, I, p. 20.
4 Died at Mayhana, Khurásán, AD 1049. For a full account of his life and writings cf. R. A. Nicholson, *Studies in Islamic Mysticism*, Chapter I.
5 Cf. Francis Thompson: "Sanctity is genius in religion: the saint lives for and in religion, as the man of genius lives for and in his peculiar attainment. Nay, it might be said that sanctity is the supreme form of genius. Both are the outcome of a man's inner and individual love and are characterised by an eminent fervour, which is the note of love in action. . . . In like manner does the Saint receive into himself and become one with divine law, whereafter he no longer needs to follow where the flocks have trodden, to keep the beaten track of rule, his will has undergone the heavenly magnetization by which it points always and unalterably towards God" (*Health and Holiness, Works*, III, p. 260).
6 Abú Ṭálib, *Qút al-Qulúb*, I, p. 120.
7 *Op. cit.* I, p. 121.
8 *Op. cit.* I, p. 83.
9 Maḥmúd Shabistarí, *Gulshan-i Ráz*, p. 13, l. 201.
10 Shabistarí, *op. cit.* p. 11, l. 165. Cf. also Jalál al-Dín Rúmí, *Mathnawí*, II, l. 191.
11 Cf. Rábi'a's verses quoted above, p. 48 last two lines.
12 Cf. R. A. Nicholson, arts. on "Ṣúfís" and "Asceticism (Muslim)" in *Encyclopaedia of Religion and Ethics*.
13 See p. 72.
14 Compare the Christian mystic: "The Soul that would be perfect begins to mortify its passions; and when 'tis advanced in that exercise, it denies itself; then with the Divine Aid, it passes to the state of Nothing . . . from hence springs the dying in itself and in its senses . . . insomuch that when the Soul is once dead to its will and understanding, 'tis properly said to be arrived at the perfect and happy state of Annihilation, which is the last disposition for

Transformation and Union . . . this Annihilation, to make it perfect in the Soul, must be in a man's Judgment, in his Will, in his Works, Inclinations, Desires, Thoughts and in itself; so that the Soul must find itself dead to its Will, Desire, Endeavour, Understanding and Thought; willing, as if it did not will; desiring, as if it did not desire; understanding, as if it did not understand; thinking, as if it did not think. . . . O what a happy Soul is this, which is thus dead and annihilated! It lives no longer in itself, because God lives in it and now it may most truly be said of it, that . . . 'tis changed, spiritualised, transformed and deified" (Molinos, *The Spiritual Guide*, pp. 179 ff.).

CHAPTER VII

Repentance, Patience, Gratitude

Repentance (*tawba*) was the first stage on the Way to God. It found a place also in orthodox Muslim doctrine. In the Qur'án punishment is laid down for the sinner, "Except those who repent (after apostasy) and amend, then surely Allah is forgiving, Merciful". Yet there may be repentance which is unacceptable, "Surely those who disbelieve after their believing, then increase in unbelief, their repentance shall not be accepted and these are they that go astray".[1] "Repent" (lit. to come back to) is used of the sinner, meaning to return to God, to a state of obedience to Him, and also of God Himself to express the Divine act of the acceptance of repentance.

The same idea is expressed in the following Súra: "Repentance with Allah is only for those who do evil in ignorance, then turn soon, so these it is to whom Allah turns, and Allah is ever-Knowing, Wise". "And repentance is not for those who go on doing evil deeds until when Death comes to one of them he says, 'Surely now I repent', nor (for) those who die while they are unbelievers."[2]

The Ṣúfís made repentance a much more essential part of the life lived with God. Al-Hujwírí says, "There is no right service without repentance. Repentance is the first of the 'stations' in this Path."[3] He considers that there are three things involved in repentance: (*a*) Remorse for disobedience, (*b*) Determination not to sin again, (*c*) Immediate abandonment of sin.[4] This corresponds to a later exposition of the Ṣúfí doctrine of repentance, as involving first conviction of sin, then contrition, which in its turn must lead to a purpose to amend.[5]

> "Some Ṣúfís", says al-Hujwírí, "take the view that Repentance consists in not forgetting sins, but always regretting them. Junayd and others take the view that

repentance consists in forgetting the sin, for the penitent is a lover of God, and the lover of God is in contemplation of God, and in contemplation it is wrong to remember sin, since remembrance is a veil between God and those who contemplate Him."

This is the repentance of the adept in the mystic life.[6] Al-Hujwírí regards repentance as a Divine strengthening: "God hath said, And he turned towards him (Adam), for He is the Disposer towards repentance, the Merciful" (Al-Qur'án, II, 35 (37)). Repentance may be from what is wrong to what is right – the common kind, from what is right to what is more right – that of the elect, and from selfhood to God, which belongs to the degree of Divine love.[7] Again, he quotes Dhú al-Nún as saying that there is the repentance of return (*tawba al-inába*), through fear of the Divine punishment, and repentance (*tawba al-istiḥya*) through shame of Divine clemency. "The repentance of fear is caused by revelation of God's majesty, the repentance of shame by the vision of God's Beauty."[8]

This is the repentance spoken of by Abú al-Ḥusayn al-Núrí when he said, "Repentance is repenting (turning away) from all save God Most High",[9] and the same idea that the highest type of repentance is entirely different from the type normally practised is found in the statement that "The sins of those who are near (to God) are the good deeds of the righteous".[9]

Rábi'a, like all the great saints of God, had a deep sense of the exceeding sinfulness of sin and the need for repentance and forgiveness, and the Ṣúfí writers, in their chapters on the stage of *tawba*, more than once mention her teaching on this subject. In a fragment quoted by Ḥurayfísh, which he appends to her verses on the two loves, she prays thus:

O Beloved of hearts, I have none like unto Thee,
Therefore have pity this day on the sinner who
comes to Thee.

> O my Hope and my Rest and my Delight
> The heart can love none other but Thee.[10]

In one of her prayers quoted by the same writer she speaks of God as a comforter in sorrow, the One who can cleanse her from sin.[11]

In verses already quoted,[12] she addresses her Lord as "Healer of Souls", and says that her soul has been healed through Him.

That Rábi'a sorrowed constantly for her sins is plain from the frequent mention of her grief. 'Aṭṭár says, "It is related that Rábi'a was always weeping and it was said to her, 'Why do you weep like this?' She said, 'I fear that I may be cut off from Him to Whom I am accustomed, and that at the hour of death a voice may say that I am not worthy'." Someone asked her, "If a person commits many sins and repents, will (God) accept him?" She replied, "How can anyone repent unless his Lord gives him repentance and accepts him?" and she emphasised her conception of repentance as a "gift from God" in another saying of hers, to the effect that "Seeking forgiveness with the tongue is the sin of lying. If I seek repentance of myself, I shall have need of repentance again."[13]

Al-Qushayrí, in dealing with the subject of "tawba", gives a similar account of Rábi'a's view when he says, "A man said to Rábi'a, 'I have sinned much and rebelled (against God). If I repent, will He accept my repentance?' and she answered, 'No, but if He turns towards you, you will turn towards Him'."[14]

In the "Siyar al-Ṣáliḥát", her biographer gives a vivid picture of the impression made by her deep grief for her sins, saying:

> 'Abd Allah b. 'Ísá said, "I entered Rábi'a's presence and I saw the light on her face, and she used to weep much, and a man related of her that at every mention of fire (representing the punishment of the unrepentant sinner), she swooned, and I heard the falling of her tears on the ground like the sound of (water) filling a vessel",

and he reports that Ibn Manṣúr said:

> I came into Rábi'a's presence and she was worshipping, and when I reached my place, she raised her head, and lo, the place of her worship was like a marsh from her tears and I saluted her. Then she received me and said, "O my son, do you need anything?" and I said, "I came to you to greet you", and she wept and said, "May God censure thee!" Then she rose up for (the ritual) prayer and said, "I ask forgiveness of God for my lack of sincerity when I say (those words) 'I ask forgiveness of God'",

and the writer adds in comment, "How God has blessed her! God has illuminated her heart among those who are dearest to Him."[15]

Jámí relates that Sufyán al-Thawrí exclaimed once in her hearing, "Alas for my sorrow", and Rábi'a rebuked him, saying, "Do not lie. If you were really sorrowful, life would not be so pleasant to you." Again she said, "My sorrow is not for the things which make me grieve, but my sorrow is for the things for which I do not grieve".[16]

Sha'rání also tells how Rábi'a wept and sorrowed much, and of her emotion at the mention of fire (so often synonymous with the torments of Hell to the Muslim), and how she used to say, "Our asking forgiveness of God, itself needs forgiveness", and he also adds that her oratory was like a swamp of water from her tears.[17]

Rábi'a, then, felt and taught that sin was hurtful in the highest degree to the soul, since it was a cause of separation between the soul and its Beloved. This conviction of sin as a barrier between the servant and his Lord[18] must lead to godly sorrow, contrition. This sorrow evinced itself in her case by the outward signs of grief, the constant weeping, which is recorded of her and of other saints as a mark of godliness, and also in remorse for sins of commission and omission, and this burning grief left no place for taking pleasure in the transient delights of this world. Sin to Rábi'a was hateful because it separated her from God, not because it involved punishment hereafter.

Rábi'a's teaching on repentance, as we have seen, includes the doctrine that "tawba" is the gift of God, not something due to the effort of the sinner – "If God turns towards thee, thou wilt turn to Him" – and this is quite in accordance with her general view that "every good gift and every perfect gift is from above", and that only God has the power so to touch the sinner's heart that he will turn away from his wickedness and repent. This is, of course, also the Christian view, set forth by St Paul, "Despisest thou the riches of His goodness and forbearance and longsuffering; not knowing that the goodness of God leadeth thee to repentance?"[19]

But for the sincere penitent forgiveness is sure, since repentance is a sign of grace, and sin and grace are incompatible in the same soul. As al-Ghazálí expresses it, "Darkness cannot dwell with light, nor filthiness abide with the whiteness of the fuller's soap".[20]

So if the Lord grants repentance, He will not withhold forgiveness, and since faith is the beginning, justification will be the end.[21]

Patience (*ṣabr*) is dealt with at length by the Ṣúfí writers as an essential stage in the progress of the spiritual life, or perhaps rather as an essential quality to be acquired by the saint. Hujwírí quotes a saying of Ḥasan al-Baṣrí to the effect that patience is of two sorts, firstly, patience in misfortune and affliction, and secondly, patience to refrain from the things which God has commanded us to renounce and has forbidden us to pursue.[22]

Abú Ṭálib gives us the view of the Ṣúfís that patience has three stages, first, to leave off complaining, and this is the stage of the repentant; second, to be satisfied with what is decreed, and this is the rank of the ascetics; third, to love whatever his Lord does with him, and this is the stage of the true friends of God.[23] Al-Qushayrí speaks of patience as being as necessary to faith as the head to the body.[24] Al-Ghazálí, in dealing with *ṣabr*, regards it as a necessity for the saint, whose spiritual life must be a militant one, making war upon the passions and seeking after victory. In this world trials and misfortunes must come, losses, pain, injury to feelings, and the saint may expect that these will come with greater force to him, since "whom the Lord loveth, He chasteneth and scourgeth every son whom He receiveth", that through the fire of affliction, the faith of the saint may shine more brightly. By patient endurance the saint may cease to feel the effects of adversity, and in the end, for his patience, he will win the greater reward.[25]

Rábi'a's life is her plainest teaching on this subject, and many of the anecdotes related in her biography witness to her practice of this virtue. In her early years we note her patience under the heavy affliction of slavery,[26] and she met the trials and adversities of life in the same spirit. The loss of her goods, the poverty and discomfort of her life, the sufferings of mind and body she was called upon to endure, were all accepted as part of the will of God for her and as a training of her character.[27] We have already seen how Rábi'a, when in pain, reminded those who called her attention to her injury, that her concern was to accommodate herself to her Lord's will and to occupy herself with something better than physical affliction.[28] The secret of her patience is to be found in her answer to Sufyán, when he tempted her to seek what she desired from God, and she said, "If I will a thing, and my Lord does not will it, I shall guilty of unbelief",[29] thereby confirming the view of both al-Qushayrí and al-Ghazálí that patience is an essential part of faith.[30] The faithful servant must accept in patience what is sent to him, since if he doubts either his Lord's wisdom or His loving care for those who depend on Him, he commits *kufr*, and Rábi'a did not fail to teach this lesson both by precept and example, as we have already seen.

Gratitude (*shukr*) is the complementary quality to patience, representing the same attitude towards God's benefits that patience represents towards His chastisements. Like the other qualities to be acquired at the different stages on the mystic Way, gratitude contains the elements of faith, feeling and action.[31] Faith must accept the fact that all benefits come from God and are His free gift, which

He might have withheld, and that He has not withheld them is due to His unfailing goodness towards His elect. This faith that all good gifts come from God must produce the feeling of joy for the gift but humility before the Giver. Joy comes from the sense of the graciousness which is the sign of God's love for us, but also because the act of giving establishes a relation between us, the beneficiaries, and the Lord who bestows the benefit and to the Ṣúfí, this relationship will mean ultimately union with the Giver.[32]

These feelings of joy and humility and aspiration will lead to action – acts of gratitude, taking the form of praise and thanksgiving to God for His beneficence[33] – and the recipient of His bounty will seek to do all things in accordance with His Will and to avoid all that is contrary to it.[34]

Gratitude must extend to misfortunes as well as blessings and here it joins forces with patience, but whereas the latter is but a passive form of the virtue, the former is an activity arising from it. "Real resignation consists not in bowing down under the Will of God, but in rising up into it."

Even in adversity we can be thankful because our misfortunes might always be greater than they actually are, our spiritual state might be worse than it is; in any case all temporal adversity is less than we deserve for our unworthiness, and finally, all comes from God Himself and is the outcome of the Divine Volition.[35]

Al-Qushayrí goes to the heart of the matter when he says that "Gratitude is the vision of the Giver, not of the Gift",[36] and he goes on to say that "Gratitude is a gift from God Himself".[37]

Rábi'a both taught and practised this quality of *shukr*. Much of her time was spent in praise to her Lord for His goodness to her, and her prayers, already quoted, are full of thanksgiving. She says in one, "Thou hast given me life and hast provided for me, and Thine is the glory", and again she says, "How many favours hast Thou bestowed on me, gifts and grace and help".[38]

There is one story told of her, in which she made her teaching on gratitude very plain. Her biographer says:

> It is related that at one time she saw someone who had a bandage bound about his head. She said, "Why is this bandage bound (round your head)?" He said, "My head is paining me". Rábi'a asked him how old he was. "Thirty years old", he replied. She asked him, "Were you in pain and trouble for the greater part of your life?" "No", he answered. Then she said, "For thirty years (God) has kept your body fit and you have never bound upon it the bandage of gratitude, but for one night of pain in your head you bind it with the bandage of complaint".[39]

Another story shows how to her, too, gratitude meant the vision of the Giver rather than the gift, and how she turned aside from the gifts in order to look up and beyond to Him who gave them.

Once in the spring, she was in the house, giving praise to God, and her servant-maid came to her and said, "O mistress, come out to behold the works (of God)", but Rábi'a replied, "Come you inside that you may behold their Maker. Contemplation of the Maker has turned me aside from contemplating what He has made."[39] In her disregard of the beautiful creations of God, for the sake of their Creator, Rábi'a's attitude is in contrast to that of the more pantheistic later Ṣúfís, who felt that God was to be seen (and could be worshipped) in all His creation. The view of Maḥmúd Shabistarí that "Beneath the veil of each atom is hidden the soul-ravishing beauty of the face of the Beloved",[40] would have met with little response from Rábi'a, and likewise the view of Jámí, expressed in *Yusef u Zulaykha*:

> Each speck of matter did He constitute
> A mirror, causing each one to reflect
> The beauty of His visage. From the rose
> Flashed forth His beauty and the nightingale
> Beholding it, loved madly. From that fire

The candle drew the lustre which beguiles
The moth to immolation. On the sun
His beauty shone, and straightway from the wave
The lotus reared its head. Each shining lock
Of Layla's hair attracted Majnún's heart
Because some ray Divine reflected shone
In her fair face. 'Twas He to Shírín's lips
Who lent that sweetness, which had power to steal
The heart from Parríz and from Farhád life.
His Beauty everywhere doth show itself,
And through the forms of earthly beauties shines
Obscured as through a veil. . . .
    Where'er thou seest a veil,
Beneath that veil He hides.[41]

Rábi'a, however, desired to look upon her Lord unveiled, the beauties of His gifts were as nothing in her eyes compared with the beauty of the Giver, and gratitude to Him outweighed the thought of the things for which she was grateful.[42]

In that degree of gratitude which can feel thankfulness for adversity as well as prosperity, Rábi'a went beyond the limits to which her friends among the Ṣúfís managed to attain. She attributed her sufferings to the Will of God and said that she would not oppose her Beloved in seeking to be rid of them.[43] She speaks with gratitude of "warnings" given to her by her Lord, through suffering and affliction, that she might turn wholly to Him and so win the great reward at last.[44] We are told by an old writer that Rábi'a or another of the Ṣúfís said, "If Thou hadst not set me apart by affliction, I had not increased Thy lovers",[45] *i.e.* my afflictions have led me to do Thy work and lead others to love Thee.

Rábi'a, then, had the faith which accepts all gifts as from God the Giver and regards misfortune and adversity in the same light as favour and happiness. Her faith led her to joy in the chastening of the Lord as being His goodness to her, and to a humble acceptance of all that He might send, and thence to acts of praise and thanks-giving, and an eager looking forward to the great Gift, of which these gifts were but an earnest, of union, for ever, with the Giver. She might well have identified herself with the words of a later Ṣúfí, Bábá Kúhí of Shíráz,[46] who wrote:

In the market, in the cloister – only God I saw
In the valley and on the mountain, – only God I saw.
Him I have seen beside me oft in tribulation;
In favour and in fortune – only God I saw.
In prayer and fasting, in praise and contemplation,
In the religion of the Prophet – only God I saw.
Neither soul nor body, accident nor substance,
Qualities nor causes – only God I saw.
Like a candle I was melting in His fire
Amidst the flames outflashing – only God I saw.
Myself with mine own eyes I saw most clearly,
But when I looked with God's eyes – only God I saw.
I passed away into nothingness, I vanished,
And lo, I was the All-living, – only God I saw.[47]

1 Al-Qur'án, III, 88, 89 (Woking Press Edition).
2 Al-Qur'án, IV, 17, 18.
3 *Kashf al-Maḥjúb*, p. 79.
4 *Op. cit.* p. 294.
5 Al-Ghazálí, *Iḥyá*, IV, p. 11. See also p. 14 for his definition of sin as all that is contrary to the law of God, whether by omission or commission.
6 Al-Hujwírí, *op. cit.* p. 296. Cf. also al-Sarráj, *Kitáb al-Luma'*, p. 43.
7 Al-Hujwírí, *op. cit.* p. 297.
8 *Op. cit.* p. 299.
9 Al-Sarráj, *op. cit.* p. 44.
10 *Al-Rawḍ al-Fá'iq*, p. 213.
11 Al-Ḥurayfísh, *op. cit.* p. 212.

12 See p. 31.
13 'Aṭṭár, *Tadhkirat al-Awliyá*, I, p. 67.
14 *Risála*, p. 62.
15 "Siyar al-Ṣáliḥát", fol. 26 a.
16 Jámí, *Nafaḥát al-Uns*, p. 716. Cf. Romans vii. 15–23.
17 Sha'rání, *Al-Ṭabaqát al-Kubrá*, p. 86.
18 Cf. Romans vi. 16: "Know ye not, that to whom ye yield yourselves servants to obey, his servants ye are to whom ye obey; whether of sin unto death, or of obedience unto righteousness?"
19 Romans ii. 4.
20 Al-Ghazálí, *Iḥyá*, IV, 12. Cf. also Mal. iii. 2: "He is like a refiner's fire and like fullers' soap".
21 "Now being made free from sin, and become servants to God, ye have put your fruit unto holiness, and the end everlasting life", Romans vi. 22.
22 Al-Hujwírí, *Kashf al-Maḥjúb*, p. 86.
23 *Qút al-Qulúb*, I, p. 199.
24 *Risála*, p. 111.
25 *Iḥyá*, IV, pp. 55 ff. Cf. al-Kalábádhí, "Ma'ání al-Akhbár", fol. 169 b.
26 See pp. 23–4.
27 See above, Part One, Chapter III.
28 See p. 43.
29 See p. 44.
30 Cf. Heb. vi. 12: "them who through faith and patience inherit the promises".
31 Al-Qushayrí, *op. cit.* p. 105. Al-Ghazálí, *op. cit.* IV, p. 71.
32 Cf. al-Qushayrí, *op. cit.* p. 106. Al-Kalábádhí, "Ma'ání al-Akhbár", fol. 50 b.
33 Cf. 2 Cor. ix. II: "Being enriched in every thing to all bountifulness, which causeth through us thanksgiving to God".
34 Al-Qushayrí, *op. cit.* p. 106. Al-Ghazálí, *op. cit.* pp. 72, 73.
35 Al-Qushayrí, *op. cit.* pp. 107, 108. Al-Ghazálí, *op. cit.* IV, p. 74.
36 Cf. Bishr-i-Yásín: "Certainly the Giver is better for you than the

gift. How should you want the gift, when you possess the very Philosopher's Stone?" (R. A. Nicholson. *Studies in Islamic Mysticism*, p. 5). Cf. also Mme Guyon:
"'Tis the Giver, not the Gift
Whence the joys I feel proceed"
(*Poems*, tr. W. Cowper, p. 90).

37 *Risála*, p. 106.

38 See pp. 47–8.

39 'Aṭṭár, *op. cit.* p. 68.

40 *Gulshan-i Ráz*, p. 11, l. 165.

41 Tr. E. G. Browne, *Religious Systems of the World*, p. 329. Cf. also Plato's *Symposium*, ed. Jowett, pp. 581 ff.

42 Cf. the similar view taken by Mme Guyon, *op. cit.* pp. 3, 4:
"Far from enjoying what these scenes disclose,
* * * * * * * * * * * * *
Their form and beauty but augment my woe
I seek the Giver of those charms they show".

43 See p. 44. Cf. Mme Guyon, *op. cit.* p. 52.

44 See p. 42. Cf. St Paul's view: "I reckon that the sufferings of this present time are not worthy to be compared with the glory which shall be revealed in us" (Rom. viii. 18).

45 Al-Kalábádhí, "Ma'ání al-Akhbár", fol. 2 b.

46 Ob. AD 1050.

47 Tr. R. A. Nicholson, *Eastern Poetry and Prose*, p. 101.

CHAPTER VIII

Hope and Fear

The Ṣúfí writers have much to say on the stages of hope and fear and are agreed that both have their place in the progress of the saint towards the Goal.

Al-Hujwírí considers that right hope and right fear are both necessary to man in this world,[1] and regards fear and hope as the two pillars of faith. Those who fear, serve God through dread of separation from Him, and those who hope, serve in the expectation of union with Him.[2] It is interesting to note that this writer, who maintains that every prophet has his special "station", says that to Jesus belonged the station of Hope and to John the Baptist that of Fear.[3]

Al-Sarráj states that hope and fear are as two wings without which the work of the saint cannot make progress[4] and al-Qushayrí, developing this simile, which he attributes to Abú 'Alí al-Rúdhabárí, says that hope and fear are like the two wings of a bird when it is flying straight (to its destination); if one wing fails, its flight fails, and if both fail, it dies.[5] Both are concerned with the future, hope looks forward to what is desired and fear dreads what is hated.

Al-Kalábádhí, writing on fear, says that when the Ṣúfí, Abú 'Abd Allah b. al-Jilí, was asked about the man who fears, he said, "He is the man who is made to trust (in God) by those things which are rightly feared, because he does not let fearful things disturb his mind, being removed from them by his fear of God, so that such things will be removed from him".[6]

Another Ṣúfí, being asked about such a God-fearing man, said, "He is the man who fears what is worthy of fear, and being dominated by the fear of God, he becomes all fear, and all things make him fear". Yet this fear does not make him wretched, "He is burnt who feels the fire, but he who is fire, how shall he be burnt?"[6] Abú 'Amr al-Dimashqí is reported to have said, "The man who fears rightly is he who fears his carnal self more than his enemy".[7]

Among the sayings of al-Fuḍayl, one of the earliest of the Ṣúfís, contemporary with Rábi'a, is that

> He who knows God by way of love without Fear perishes through pleasure and ease. He who knows Him by way of Fear (only) is separated from Him by the spirit of servitude and avoidance, but he who loves Him, and is near to Him, and is a matter of concern to Him, and has knowledge of Him, and he who knows God in reality, is far from error, and he who gives to death (*i.e.* the chief object of Fear) its true significance, will not be unmindful of it.[8]

That is, he will always bear in mind that death must bring him to the judgement of God and he will so live that he need not fear it.

Like the other qualities to be attained by the Ṣúfí on the path of enlightenment, these two can be analysed into the elements of faith, emotion and action. In hope there is faith in the thing desired, based upon knowledge of God's mercy, upon the warm recollection of His favours received – through grace, not merit – and upon the proofs of His love and forgiveness towards His elect, and upon His promise of rewards to His servants.[9]

This faith leads to joy in the prospect of God's future favour, and the practical results are that the soul strives to fight against all that may hinder it from gaining these delights in the future and to develop those virtues which may help towards their attainment.

But hope of such a kind is too much tinged with self-interest to be a help along the mystic Way and it is of such hope that al-Hujwírí says, "No one who has imbibed the doctrine of hope can tread the way of purgation, because it leads to indolence"[10] and the Ṣúfí sets before himself a higher ideal of hope. Al-Qushayrí, with his gift for going to the heart of the matter, defines hope as "the vision of God in His perfect Beauty" and al-Sarráj says that the true servant's hope is in God alone, and he hopes for nothing from God except God Himself.[11] Such hope will lead the saint onward and upward.

Fear, like hope, is conditioned by faith and leads through emotion to action calculated to ward off that which is dreaded and hence it is salutary for the Ṣúfí if of the right type.

Al-Sarráj speaks of three kinds of fear, the commonest being fear of punishment. Others fear being cut off from God, or anything that might hinder their attainment of gnosis. But there is a higher type of fear even than this and the holy fear of the elect is the fear of God alone.[12]

Al-Qushayrí calls fear "the scourge of God" wherewith He corrects those who would flee from His door. Terror of the common sort (*rahba*) makes a man run away, but holy dread (*khashya*) brings him near to God. Fear is as a lamp to the heart, making it see what is good and what is evil; and godly fear leads a man to turn his back on what is feared, because it is evil. "He who truly fears a thing flees from it, but he who truly fears God, flees unto Him."[13]

Al-Ghazálí also speaks of the fear of Hell as "a whip to drive to Paradise".[14]

All the early Ṣúfí writers are agreed that fear is superior to hope in its influence on the will and its effect on the life of devotion, and in freeing the soul from deceptive confidence in itself or the future. It may be interesting here to compare the Christian view on this subject as set forth in the Franciscan doctrine of the place of holy fear:

> He that fears not, shows that he hath nought to lose. The holy fear of God orders, governs and rules the soul and maketh it come to grace. If a man possesseth any grace or divine virtue, it is holy fear that keepeth it safe. And whoso hath not yet obtained virtue or grace, holy fear maketh him obtain it. . . . But this holy gift of fear is not given save unto the perfect, for the more

> perfect a man is, the more doth he fear and humble himself. . . . A man should have greater fear of his own wickedness lest it overcome him and lead him astray, than of any other of his enemies. . . . Whoso hath not the fear of God, is in danger of perishing and of being altogether lost.[15]

To the Ṣúfí also, fear is a gift from God, who has decreed that His servants should fear, and holy fear, that dread which is salutary for the soul, is produced by meditation on the Divine justice as evidenced in the punishment of Iblís and of Adam, and on death and judgement and Hell. Fear is a fire which burns away the desires which hinder the soul. "The fear of the Lord", says a tradition, "is the chief part of wisdom."[16]

Yet the conclusion of the matter, for the Ṣúfí, as we have said above, is that the most sublime form of fear is that which has for its object not chastisement, nor even sin, but God Himself, fearing lest at the last the soul should be deprived for ever of the vision of His Everlasting Beauty.[17]

Al-Sarráj, summing up the Ṣúfí doctrine of these two stages, says that hope and fear are two fetters of the soul, hindering it from wandering from the straight path and safety and from turning aside to despair and separation (from God). Fear is like a state of darkness, in which the soul wanders, bewildered, seeking always to escape from it, and when hope comes to lighten it, the soul goes out to a place of refreshment and grace prevails. The fairness of the day would not appear to advantage except in contrast with the darkness of the night. The best state (for the mystic) includes both, and the heart is sometimes a slave in the darkness of fear and sometimes a prince in the brightness of hope. Love and hope and fear are bound up together. Love is not perfect without fear, nor fear without hope, nor hope without fear.[18]

With this question of hope and fear is bound up the eschatological teaching of the Ṣúfís and their conception of Paradise and Hell.

For them Hell was not so much a place of punishment as a means of separation from the presence of God, and Paradise to them was not a place of sensual or even spiritual joys, but simply the vision of the Beloved and the state of abiding union with Him.

Of Rábi'a's teaching on these stages, we are told that she was much subject to fear and the effect upon her of the mention of Hell fire, already referred to, was due to her belief in the judgement that must be passed upon the sinner, a judgement which, in her weaker moments, she feared might be ordained for her, and once she prayed that she might not be condemned to Hell and was rebuked for thinking an evil thought.[19]

One of her biographers says that she remained for forty years without raising her head to heaven, out of her reverence towards God, and she used to say, "Whenever I have heard the call to prayer, I have remembered the trumpet call of the Day of Resurrection, and whenever I have seen the snow I have seen also the pages of the records[20] fluttering."[21] She was once asked, "In what do you hope most of all?" and she replied, "In my sorrow for most of my deeds".[22]

But it is plain from teaching of hers already quoted that she held the motive of fear of punishment or hope of reward to be altogether unworthy of the saint of God. In the incident related by Aflákí[23] she sought to remove both these motives as being hindrances to the attainment of the mystic goal. Again she thought that it was but a poor servant who worshipped his Lord either to escape punishment or to win reward.[24] To her only God Himself was to be feared with the reverence due to His awful holiness, and equally to her, hope was only in God Himself, in the vision of His beauty.

Al-Munáwí relates that she heard a reader read that "the inhabitants of Paradise are occupied in enjoying themselves" and she said, "The inhabitants of Paradise are unfortunate in their occupation and their companions". Ibn 'Arabí blamed her for this and said that she did not know (what she was speaking of) and that it was she who was unfortunate and that they were occupied only with God and this was His will for them.[25] She probably wished to make it clear that in her view Paradise was not a place for sensual delights, but rather a state of contemplation of the Face of God.

When Rábi'a was asked what she had to say about Paradise she said, "First the Neighbour, then the house", and al-Ghazálí, after quoting her statement, goes on to say that she meant that in her heart was no leaning towards Paradise, but to the Lord of Paradise, and

> no-one who does not know God in this world will see Him in the next, and he who does not find the joy of gnosis in this world will not find the joy of vision in the next, since none may appeal (to God) in the next world who has not sought His friendship in this world and none may reap who has not sown.[26] A man is raised up only in the state in which he has died, and he dies only in the state in which he has lived and the only gnosis he takes with him is that wherewith he was blessed in himself, unless it is changed into the Vision (of God) by the removal of the veil, when his joy in it is greatly increased just as the joy of the lover is doubled if the imaginary picture of the loved is exchanged for the vision (*i.e.* the reality) of the picture, that is the highest joy.
>
> For the delights of Paradise are to each one there, only what he desires, and to him who desires only to meet with God Himself there is no delight save in Him, indeed he may suffer thereby, for since the delights of Paradise are only in proportion to (his) love of God and his love of God is in proportion to his gnosis, then the origin of (that spiritual) happiness is the gnosis which has been revealed by God through faith, and if you say, "Then the joy of the Vision, if it is in proportion to the joy of gnosis, in this world is but

> weak", verily it shall be increased to an almost infinite degree of power, so that all the other joys of Paradise shall be despised beside it.[27]

All this al-Ghazálí reads into Rábi'a's teaching on the true significance of Paradise, for the Ṣúfí. Another writer, later than al-Ghazálí, also comments on this saying of Rábi'a's. He relates that Rábi'a al-'Adawiyya, when the state of love was dominating her, was asked, "Why do you not ask God for Paradise?" and she replied, "The Neighbour before the house". He compares this with a story of Ásiya,[28] a daughter of Mazáham, who said, "O Lord build for me a house with Thee in Paradise"; thus she chose the neighbour before the house. He also compares the saying of the Prophet, "I ask Thee for Thine approval and for Paradise", as containing an indication of what Rábi'a said about the neighbour before the house.[29]

It is plain that Rábi'a's teaching on hope and fear, seen in an eschatological setting, is closely linked with her teaching on the doctrine of disinterested love to God,[30] and since she appears to have been among the first to bring this doctrine into prominence among the Ṣúfís and to lay particular stress upon it as the essential element in the saint's relation to God, it is possible that she was also one of the first to teach this exalted ideal of hope and fear and to conceive of Paradise as a spiritual state.

Ibráhím b. Adham, of Balkh, a contemporary of Rábi'a's, is reputed to have said, "O God, Thou knowest that in my eyes Paradise hath not the value of a gnat, if Thou hast blessed me with Thy love",[31] and Abú Yazíd al-Biṣṭámí, somewhat later than Rábi'a, said that "Paradise is of no worth to those who love",[32] but these fall somewhat short of Rábi'a's conception of life eternal as pure contemplation and adoration of the Beloved.

Al-Qushayrí, writing nearly three hundred years after Rábi'a's death, includes her views as an accepted element in the Ṣúfí doctrine of hope and fear, and it may well be, since al-Ghazálí, with so much material at his disposal, gives her authority for this high conception of the only worthy motive of Hope or Fear, that Rábi'a was largely responsible for this important development in Ṣúfí doctrine.

1 *Kashf al-Maḥjúb*, p. 112.
2 *Op. cit.* p. 122.
3 *Op. cit.* p. 371. Cf. St Matt. iii and Isaiah xl.
4 *Kitáb al-Luma'*, p. 62.
5 *Risála*, p. 82.
6 "Ma'ání al-Akhbár", fol. 70 b. "Kitáb al-Ta'arruf", fol. 26 b.
7 "Kitáb al-Ta'arruf", fol. 26 b .
8 Munáwí, *op. cit.* fol. 17 a.
9 Al-Sarráj, *op. cit.* p. 62. Al-Ghazálí, *op. cit.* IV, pp. 124–9.
10 *Kashf al-Maḥjúb*, p. 133.
11 *Kitáb al-Luma'*, p. 62.
12 *Op. cit.* p. 60.
13 *Risála*, pp. 78–80.
14 *Iḥyá*, IV, p. 130.
15 *Little Flowers of St Francis*, p. 266.
16 Cf. St Luke xii. 4, 5.
17 *Iḥyá*, IV, p. 135.
18 Al-Sarráj, *op. cit.* p. 63. Cf. the higher conception of St John: "There is no fear in love; but perfect love casteth out fear: because fear hath torment. He that feareth is not made perfect in love" (I John iv. 18).
19 See p. 49.
20 A reference to the records of their deeds which all were required to take in their hands on the Day of Judgement, the righteous being given their record in the right hand and the wicked in the left. See p. 30.
21 Munáwí, *op. cit.* fol. 51 a.
22 M. b. Ḥusayn, *Al-Kashkúl*, p. 273.
23 See p. 123.
24 See p. 124.
25 Munáwí, *op. cit.* fol. 51 b.

26 Cf. with this his teaching on hope (*Iḥyá*, IV, p. 124).

27 *Iḥyá*, IV, p. 269.

28 Cf. Qur'án, LXVI, 11. See also J. Walker, "Ásiya, the wife of Pharaoh", *The Moslem World*, Jan. 1928.

29 M. b. H. Imád al-Dín, "*Ḥayát al-Qulúb*" on margin of *Qút al-Qulúb*, II, p. 193.

30 See Part Two, Chapter X.

31 Abú Nu'aym, "Ḥilya al-Awliyá", Leyden MS. fol. 200 a.

32 *Op. cit.* fol. 219 a.

CHAPTER IX

Poverty, Renunciation, Unification, Dependence

The stages of poverty, of asceticism or renunciation, of the merging of the individual will in the Will of God, and of complete trust in and dependence upon Him, can be considered together.

Poverty (*faqr*) is held in high estimation by the Ṣúfí writers, but it is only poverty for the sake of God, which is meritorious. Those who are poor for His sake are promised entrance into Paradise five hundred years before the rich, even the virtuous rich.[1] Such teaching of course is similar to that of the New Testament, "How hardly shall they that have riches enter into the kingdom of God".[2]

Again, al-Sarráj says that the poor are the richest of God's creation[3] – they dispense with the gift for the sake of the Giver. Poverty he describes as a sea of tribulation, but all its tribulations mean glory.[4] There are different grades of those who possess nothing and do not desire outwardly or inwardly anything from anyone (*i.e.* not only do they refrain from expressing desire, but they do not even feel it) and they do not expect anything from anyone, and if given anything, they refuse to receive it; this station belongs to those who are in proximity (to God).[5] It is, indeed, the first of the stages (*manázil*) of unification (*tawḥíd*).[6] In a like spirit, St Francis embraced the Lady Poverty as his bride, for the love of God. Brother Giles gives an account of the Franciscan doctrine of holy poverty as

> the immeasurable treasure of the most holy poverty, for it is a treasure so high excelling and so divine that we be not worthy to lay it up in our vile vessels; since this is that celestial virtue whereby all earthly things and fleeting are trodden under foot, and whereby all hindrances are lifted from the soul, so that freely she

> may join herself to God Eternal. And this is the virtue that makes the soul, still tied to earth, hold converse with the angels in heaven . . . which also in this life grants to the souls that love it an easier flight to heaven; in that it guards the arms of true humility and love;[7]

and again St Francis speaks of the bread of poverty as "this it is that I account vast treasure, wherein is nothing at all prepared by human hands, but whatsoever we have is given by God's own providence".[8]

This was the spiritual poverty of the adept in Ṣúfism, for which Rábi'a craved, while she was yet a novice, and incapable of understanding the depths of its meaning.

'Aṭṭár tells the story of how on one occasion, when she was making the pilgrimage and had reached 'Arafát, she heard the voice of God saying to her, "O you who invoke Me, what request have you to make of Me? If it is Myself that you desire, then I will show you one flash of my glory (but in that) you will be absorbed and melt away." She said then, "O Lord of Glory, Rábi'a has no means of attaining to that degree, but I desire one particle of (spiritual) Poverty". The voice said:

> O Rábi'a, Poverty is the scourge (lit. the drought or famine, *i.e.* that which withers up and destroys life) of Our wrath, which we have placed in the way of men. When but a hair's breadth remains between them and Union with Us, everything is changed and Union becomes separation. As for you, you are still within seventy veils of self-existence; until you have come forth from beneath those veils, and set forth on the way towards Us, and passed the seventy stations, you will not be fit even to speak of that Poverty.[9]

Here poverty (*faqr*) signifies the state of complete self-loss, exceedingly hard to attain, and not leading to union, unless it is perfect, and even then the mystic may, in the good pleasure of God, be subject to a dark night of the soul before attaining to union. Such poverty could be attained only by the adept, divested of every attribute of "self".

Renunciation, or asceticism (*zuhd*), is to be considered side by side with this high conception of poverty. The first stage of *zuhd*, to the Ṣúfí, is initiatory and represents the purgative life, through which the novice must pass before setting foot on the mystic Way.[10] But where the soul has been purified from all sensual desires, and the mystic "pure from Self as flame from smoke" sets forth upon his journey towards God,[11] then he passes beyond this early degree of *zuhd* and aims at the last stage, renunciation of all but God, attained only by the adept.

This question of *zuhd* is of the greatest importance in the study of early Ṣúfism, because at that stage Ṣúfism consisted of asceticism carried to the point of quietism, rather than the acceptance of a theosophy or a mystical doctrine as the term is generally understood. The Way was the subject of study rather than the Goal. So the Ṣúfí writers have much to say concerning *zuhd*. Al-Sarráj states that love of the world is the root of all sin, and that renunciation of the world is the root of all good and obedience (to God).[12]

Abú Ṭálib says that the beginning of *zuhd* is concern for the next world, in the soul, and then the coming into existence of the sweetness of hope in God, and concern for the next world does not enter in until anxiety for this world goes out,[13] nor does the sweetness of hope enter in until the sweetness of desire has departed. True *zuhd* means the thrusting out from the heart of all thought of worldly things and the counting of them as vanity and only so will *zuhd* become perfect.[14]

Zuhd leads ultimately to intimacy with God. Piety in the servants leads on to *zuhd* and *zuhd* to love of God, and these two states are the aim of those who seek to love God and to be intimate with

Him and he is not truly a *záhid* who does not attain to the station of love or the mystic state of intimacy (*uns*).[15]

Al-Qushayrí, in dealing with this subject, defines *zuhd* as leaving all that distracts the soul from God, freeing the hand from wealth and the heart from desire; and he quotes the misanthropic Ḥasan of Baṣra as saying that "*zuhd* in this world is to hate its people and all that is in it and to leave what is in this world to those who dwell in it".[16]

Aḥmad b. Hanbal[17] distinguishes three kinds of *zuhd*, the renunciation of what is unlawful, which is common enough; the renunciation of what is lawful, which is a more special type; and, finally, the renunciation of all, whatever it may be, that distracts the servant from God Most High, and this is the *zuhd* of the gnostics.[18] The gnostic seeks to cut himself off from all else in order that, undistracted, he may obtain the beatific vision, and therefore he counts even the delights of Paradise as contemptible in comparison with the beauty of God.[19]

Renunciation involves unification (*tawḥíd*). The doctrine of the unity of God was from the first the central doctrine of Islám, and to Muslims the unpardonable sin was *shirk*, the admission by word or act that anything or anyone was worthy to share that which was due to God alone. Further, this doctrine meant that within the Godhead itself no duality could be admitted. God must be one in His essence and one in His activity, and therefore must be the sole Cause of all that exists and all that comes to pass.

To the Ṣúfí, the doctrine of *tawḥíd* meant far more than the confession of God's unity; it was to him the sinking of the self and the abnegation of the personal will, in the will of God. So the doctrine of the unity for the Ṣúfí was developed into the doctrine of unification. This was expressed in the plainest terms by the Persian mystic Abú Sa'íd b. Abí al-Khayr, who lays it down that

> it is the vision of the heart that is of value, not the tongue's speech . . . the (true servant) is he who fears

the majesty of God and frees himself from carnal desires. Until you empty yourself of Self, you will not be able to escape from it. It is not enough for me to repeat, "There is no god but God", to become a Muslim. (It is written) "Most of them have not believed in God, but are polytheists", that is, they have made profession of faith with the tongue, but most of them in their hearts are polytheists. God has said, "I do not pardon the polytheist", that is, God will not forgive one who gives Him a partner, but apart from that He will forgive whom He will. All the members of thy body are filled with doubt and polytheism. Thou must cast out this polytheism from thy heart that thou mayst have peace . . . thou canst not believe in God until thou dost deny thyself, that self which keeps thee far from God Most High and which says, "So and So has done thee an injury and such a one has treated thee well". All this leads to dependence on creatures and all this is polytheism. The creatures are nothing, the Friend is everything. After this manner it must be known and declared and having been declared, it is necessary to abide by it and in it. And to abide by it means that when thou hast said, "One", thou must not again say "Two" and the creature and the Creator are two. The right faith is to say God and therein to stand fast. And to stand fast means that when thou hast said, "God", thou shouldst no more speak of the creatures nor think upon them in thine heart, so that it is as if the creatures were not. Whatever thou dost see or say, see and say from what is existent, which will never cease to be. Love that One, Who, when thou shalt cease to be, will not Himself cease to be, that thou, too, mayst become one who will never cease to be.[20]

The older Ṣúfí writers had expressed the same idea. Al-Sarráj quotes a saying of Ruwaym b. Aḥmad b. Yezíd al-Baghdadí that *tawḥíd* is the effacement of human nature, and keeping separate that which is Divine, and explains the latter phrase as meaning the separation of what is eternal from that which has been brought into phenomenal existence and is therefore evanescent.[21]

Al-Hujwírí also states that sharing in the unity involves cessation of human volition and affirmation of the Divine Will so as to exclude all personal initiative.[22]

Al-Qushayrí speaks of the servant being like a body in the hands of God, plunged in the depths of the ocean of His unity, having passed away from his self and from the claims of created things, so that at the last the servant returns to what he was at first, before he had begun to be.[23]

So also writes the Christian mystic:

> We ought to offer ourselves entirely to Him, studying only His good pleasure, not our own . . . O complete submission of a disinterested soul; most sweet and tender in that the soul's whole feeling is divine! To attain to this, is for the soul to be deified; as a small drop of water appears lost if mixed with wine, taking its taste and colour; and as, when plunged into a furnace, a bar of iron seems to lose its nature and assume that of fire; or as the air filled with the sun's beams seems rather to become light than to be illuminated. So it is with the natural life of the Saints; they seem to melt and pass away into the Will of God.[24]

Here is the doctrine of *tawḥíd* stated quite plainly, but it is to be noted that it is only unification, not yet union. The drop of water may appear to be absorbed into the wine, yet the two are of different natures, the iron may take on the heat and colour of the fire and yet the two remain distinct substances, there is still duality, still

"Thou" and "I". Not yet has the mystic attained to complete union, when "Thou" and "I" cease to exist, the union symbolised rather by the drop of water merged in the ocean, the spark absorbed in the flame, when the part becomes one with the whole, not losing its identity, but returning to its source, the spirit of man made one with the Eternal Spirit.

This stage involves also that of complete dependence upon God and trust in Him (*tawakkul*) which is the natural consequence of renunciation of this world and the abnegation of the individual will.

Abú Ṭálib says of the people of *tawakkul* that they are the elect of God, whom He has chosen, and these put their trust in Him, and are contented with Him, and so they rest from the troubles of this world and the next.[25] The true dependent is the one who knows that his Lord's provision for him is better than his own for himself, and that his Lord can see him (and know his needs) better than he can himself.[26] Then he ceases to think of what is, or to be concerned with what shall be, and he takes no thought (for himself) for to God belong the results of our affairs, and in all cases He is worthy of praise and thanks.[27]

Al-Sarráj gives a definition of the *tawakkul* of the chosen of God, which he attributes to al-Shiblí, to the effect that "you should be to God as if you were not and God should be to you as One Who was and is and shall be to eternity",[28] and elsewhere he says the *mutawakkil* should put his trust in God as the birds do.[29]

Abú Nu'aym relates of Dhú al-Nún that he was asked concerning *tawakkul* and he said that it meant getting rid of earthly masters and the removal of motives, *i.e.* true dependence on God means that we should no longer let earthly things or earthly influences weigh with us, nor let our actions be the result of interested motives, and he added that dependence meant bringing the self into obedience to God and withdrawing it from the power of controlling its own destiny.[30]

The same writer tells of a woman among the devotees who said,

"Verily God has bestowed on those who long to meet Him a state, which if they lost they would have lost eternal bliss". They said to her, "What is that state?" She said, "Complete independence from their carnal selves" (and consequent dependence upon God), and those who heard were amazed at her, wondering how she had attained to such enlightenment.[31]

Al-Ghazálí holds that *tawakkul* is a question of faith in the unity of God. Since God is the sole cause of all that exists or can exist, and all His acts are the result of His perfect goodness and wisdom, and all things depend on His power, then the servant can in perfect trust give up his will to the Divine Will and abandon himself to God, trusting in Him to provide for all needs.[32] To him *tawakkul* is practically identical with the Ṣúfí conception of *tawḥíd*.[33] As the child knows only his mother's breast, so the one who trusts in God knows only his Lord's care and in His hands is as the dead body in the hands of those who prepare it for burial.[34] So we reach the doctrine of quietism, very characteristic of the early Ṣúfís, and very possibly founded on the teaching of the Christian Gospel.[35]

Rábi'a, who belonged to this early school, was an ascetic of extreme other-worldliness, as we have already noted in the account of her life and her relations with others.

'Aṭṭár relates of her that she was asked, "Whence have you come?" She said, "From that world". They asked her, "Whither are you going?" She replied, " To that world". She was asked, "What are you doing in this world?" and she answered, "I am sorrowing". "In what way?" they asked, and she said, "I am eating the bread of this world and doing the work of that world". Then someone said, "One so persuasive in speech is worthy to keep a rest-house", and she responded, "I myself am keeping a rest-house, whatever is within, I do not allow it to go out and whatever is without, I do not allow it to come in. If anyone comes in or goes out, he does not concern me, for I am contemplating my own heart, not mere clay",[36] *i.e.* she was concerned only with what belonged to God and was oblivious to all other thoughts and interests. Others might come and go, but she was occupied with the things of the spirit and was not to be distracted by what belonged to the things of sense.

In this connection there is an interesting little anecdote related, so far as I know, only by Abú Ṭálib, since none of Rábi'a's biographers include it. He says:

> They told us that Rábi'a al-'Adawiyya, may God Almighty have mercy upon her, once said, "I praised God one night with the praises of dawn, then I slept and I saw a bright green tree, indescribable in its size and beauty, and lo, upon it were three kinds of fruit, unknown to me among the fruits of this world, like virgins' breasts, white, red and yellow, and they shone like spheres and suns in the green spaces of the tree, and I admired them and said, 'Whose is this?' and one said to me, 'This is yours, for your praises aforetime'. Then I began to walk round it, and lo, under it were eighteen fruits on the ground, of the colour of gold, and I said, 'If only these fruits were with the fruits on the tree, it would surely be better'. That personage said to me: 'They would have been there, but that you, when you offered your praises, were thinking, "Is the dough leavened or not?" and this fruit fell off'." This is a warning to those of insight and an exhortation to those who are pious and worship God.[37]

This feeling that even the most homely and necessary things in life might be a cause of separation from God was shown in a story related of her by 'Aṭṭár and already quoted.[38] Abú Ja'far b. Sulaymán relates how Sufyán al-Thawrí once took him by the hand and said, "Come with us to that teacher, for I can find no refreshment in any but her". And when they came in Sufyán lifted up his hands and said, "O God, I ask Thee for freedom from this world (earthly things)", and Rábi'a wept, and he said to her, "Why do you weep?" and she said, "You are the cause of my weeping". He said, "How is that?" She said, "Do you not know that freedom from this world comes only from renouncing what is in it and how can that be when you are defiled by it?"[39] and she went on to say, "You have abundance of days, and when a day has passed part of you has passed away, and it must come to pass, when part has gone, that the whole will go. You are a teacher, therefore learn."[40]

Among Rábi'a's sayings it is reported that she said to some devotees, "Despise the world, for it is the pleasantest thing for you, when you look down upon it".[41]

Jámí tells how Sufyán once asked her, "What is the best thing for the servant to do, who desires proximity to his Lord?" She said, "That the servant should possess nothing in this world or the next, save Him".[42]

In the same strain she once said, "If a man possessed the whole world, he would not be wealthy thereby". They said to her "Why?" She said, "Because it perishes and passes away".[43]

Here the Ṣúfí view is in accordance with the Franciscan contempt of the world:

> Many sorrows and many woes will that wretched man have, who setteth his desire and his heart and his hope on earthly things, for which he abandons and loses the things of heaven, and at the last will also lose those things of earth. The eagle flieth high; but if she had a weight tied to her wings, she could no more fly high; so man for the weight of earthly things cannot fly high, to wit cannot attain to perfection.[44]

Al-Jáḥiẓ notes that Rábi'a feared even the possession of the reputation of a saint, lest it should give her satisfaction in something other than her Lord's service. He says, "Rábi'a al-Qaysiyya was asked, 'Have you done any work at all that you can show (*i.e.* any miracle) so that you may be accepted thereby (as a saint)?' and she replied,

'If there were anything, I should fear that it might be a source of profit to me'."[45]

Among the sayings recorded of her is this to the same effect, "What appears of my (good) works, I count as nothing at all",[46] and among her counsels to those who asked her advice was this, "Conceal your good deeds as you conceal your evil deeds",[47] again with the desire to receive nothing, not even commendation, at the hands of mankind.

The desire of these early Ṣúfís to be free from all that concerned the phenomenal world, in order to be free for the world of spiritual things, is illustrated by a quaint story which finds a place in 'Aṭṭár's biography of Rábi'a. He relates that one day she gave three silver *dirhams* to a man to buy a garment (for her) because she was in need of it, and after he had started out, he turned back and said, "O lady, what colour shall I buy?" Rábi'a said, "Since it is a question of colour (*i.e.* something which belongs to this world of the senses) give me the money back", and she threw it into the Tigris. That is to say, adds 'Aṭṭár, that even a garment should not be a cause of separation (from God).[48]

She gave a shrewd rebuke to certain visitors for their worldliness, according to a story which relates that some eminent men of Baṣra came and sat by her pillow (when she was ill) and reviled the things of this world – no doubt with a desire to please the saint. But Rábi'a, with her usual ability to perceive insincerity, said to them, "You must be very fond of this world: if you were not fond of it, you would not say so much about it. Who breaks the goods must have bought them. If you were detached from this world you would not speak of it, either good or ill – remember that 'whoso loves a thing speaks much of it'."[49]

A story is told of how one day a rich merchant, having come to see Rábi'a, saw that her house was falling into ruin. He gave her a thousand pieces of gold, and made her a present of a house in good repair. Rábi'a came, and was no sooner installed than, seeing the paintings on this house, she became absorbed in contemplating them. At once, returning to the merchant the thousand pieces and the house, she said to him: "I fear lest my heart should become attached to this house, and it would be no longer possible to occupy myself with the works of the other world. My only desire is to consecrate myself to the service of the Most High Lord."[50]

It was probably in this connection that, when asked why she had parted with her house, Rábi'a answered, "In order to leave what did not concern me and find fellowship with One who is Eternal",[51] that is, she turned her back on the transient that her face might be towards that which endures for ever. She might have said, with St Paul, "We look not at the things which are seen, but at the things which are not seen: for the things which are seen are temporal, but the things which are not seen are eternal".[52]

Many of the stories already quoted show plainly that Rábi'a lived the life of the true ascetic, embracing poverty for the love of God, choosing to live in a hut, provided only with the barest necessities of life, though she had rich and solicitous friends who would have surrounded her with comfort.[53] She attained as much by her practice as her precepts to the Ṣúfí ideal of the sincere *záhid* in turning aside from all things, lawful or unlawful, that might distract her from the service due to God alone: she indeed counted all things loss for the sake of her Lord. In verses already quoted in full, she says, "I have fled from the world and all that is within it. My hope is for union with Thyself: for that is the Goal of my desire."[54]

As one of the "elect of the elect" among the *mutawakkilín*, she merges her will in the Divine Will and leaves all her needs in the hands of God. For thirty years, she says of herself, she had sought nothing save from Him and He had never failed her.

From this stage, in which she casts behind all that is of this world, she passes on to the last stage of the mystic Way, that of love with all that it includes, which leads on to the final state which is the goal of the mystic's quest, contemplation of the vision of God, unveiled in all His beauty, and the abiding union of the lover with the Beloved.

1 Abú Ṭálib, *Qút al-Qulúb*, I, p. 242.
2 St Mark x. 23–5.
3 *Kitáb al-Luma'*, p. 48.
4 Cf. again St Mark x. 29, 31.
5 *Kitáb al-Luma'* , p. 221.
6 *Op. cit*. p. 48.
7 *Little Flowers of St Francis*, p. 38.
8 *Op. cit*. p. 37.
9 'Aṭṭár, *op. cit*. pp. 62, 63.
10 See p. 72.
11 Maḥmúd al-Shabistarí, *Gulshan-i Ráz*, p. 19, l. 315.
12 *Kitáb al-Luma'*, p. 46.
13 Cf. St Matt. vi. 24.
14 *Qút al-Qulúb*, I, pp. 248, 250.
15 *Op. cit*. I, pp. 270, 271.
16 *Risála*, p. 74.
17 See al-Hujwírí, *Kashf*, pp. 117, 118.
18 Al-Qushayrí, *Risála*, pp. 74, 75. Cf. also al-Sarráj, *op. cit*. p. 46.
19 Al-Ghazálí, *op. cit*. IV, p. 195.
20 Munawwar, *Asrár al-Tawḥíd*, p. 371.
21 *Kitáb al-Luma'*, p. 31.
22 *Kashf al-Maḥjúb*, p. 252. Cf. E. Underhill's description of "the transformation of the individual outlook into the universal out look, the complete surrender of man's personal striving to the overruling Will of God, and thus the linking up of all the successive acts of daily life with the Abiding" (*Man and the Supernatural*, p. 246).
23 *Risála*, p. 177.
24 St Bernard on *The Love of God*, pp. 44 and 45. Cf. also Grou, "The soul has reached the highest degree of sanctity when having become perfectly simple, she sees God only in all things, and has no interests but His interests" (cited by E. Underhill, *Man and the Supernatural*, p. 245).
25 *Qút al-Qulúb*, II, p. 3.

26 Cf. Ps. xxxiii. 18, 19: "Behold, the eye of the Lord is upon them that fear Him, upon them that hope in His mercy; To deliver their soul from death, and to keep them alive in famine".

27 Abú Ṭálib, *op. cit.* II, p. 38.

28 *Kitáb al-Luma'*, p. 52.

29 *Op. cit.* p. 117.

30 "Ḥilya", Leyden MS. fol. 203 b.

31 *Op. cit.* fol. 232 a.

32 *Iḥyá*, IV, p. 211.

33 See p. 101 ff.

34 Al-Qushayrí, *op. cit.* p. 102 and p. 99.

35 Cf. St Matt. vi. 24–34.

36 'Aṭṭár, *op. cit.* p. 67. Cf. Ramón Lull: "'Say, O Fool, what is this world?' He answered, 'It is the prison-house of those that love and serve my Beloved'. 'And who is he that imprisons them?' He answered: 'Conscience, love, fear, renunciation and contrition and the companionship of wilful men'. 'And who is he that frees them?' 'Mercy, pity and justice'. 'And where are they then sent?' 'To eternal bliss and the joyful company of true lovers, where they shall laud, bless and glorify the Beloved everlastingly, to whom be ever given praise, honour and glory throughout all the world'" (*The Lover and the Beloved*, p. 106).

37 *Qút al-Qulúb*, I, p. 103.

38 See p. 41.

39 Ṣibt Ibn al-Jawzí, "Ta'ríkh Mir'át al-Zamán", fol. 256 b.

40 Munáwí, *op. cit.* fol. 51 b.

41 M. b. Ḥ. Baha al-Dín, *Al-Kashkúl*, p. 134.

42 *Nafaḥát al-Uns*, p. 716.

43 Munáwí, *op. cit.* fol. 51 a.

44 *Little Flowers of St Francis*, p. 276.

45 *Al-Bayán*, III, p. 85. Cf. also Ṣibt Ibn al-Jawzí, "Mir'át al-Zamán", fol. 257 a.

46 *Al-Kashkúl*, p. 134.

47 Ibn Khallikán, I, p. 34, No. 230.

[48] 'Aṭṭár, *op. cit.* p. 68; also Ṣibt Ibn al-Jawzí, *op. cit.* fol. 265 b.

[49] 'Aṭṭár, *op. cit.* p. 72.

[50] 'Aṭṭár, *op. cit.* Uyghur version, Part II, p. 66.

[51] Abú Nu'aym, "Ḥilya", Leyden MS. fol. 241 a. Al-Ghazálí, *Ihyá*, IV, p. 291.

[52] 2 Cor. iv. 18.

[53] See Part One, Chapter III above.

[54] Al-Ḥurayfísh, *op. cit.* p. 214.

CHAPTER X

LOVE, GNOSIS, THE VISION, UNION

Though, as we have already mentioned, some Ṣúfí writers give a place to the stages of sincerity, contemplation, self-examination and meditation on death, yet love as conceived by the Ṣúfís was so all-embracing that we shall here consider it as the last and highest stage to be attained by the adept, including satisfaction (*riḍá'*), longing (*shawq*) and fellowship (*uns*); *riḍá'* representing, on one side, the acquiescence of the lover in the will of the Beloved, *shawq* the longing of the lover to meet with the Beloved, and *uns* the intimate relation which exists between the lover and the Beloved. From love the adept passes directly to the true knowledge of the Divine mysteries (*ma'rifa*), is enabled to see God unveiled in His beauty and becomes one with Him in mystic union – a union obtained for brief moments only in this life, but for ever in the life to come.

Satisfaction (*riḍá'*) has two sides to it; it is both subjective and objective; there is human satisfaction with God and Divine satisfaction with man.[1] Al-Hujwírí makes the distinction plain when he says:

> Divine satisfaction really consists in God's willing that man should be recompensed and in His bestowing grace upon him. Human satisfaction really consists in Man's performing the command of God and submitting to His decree. Accordingly the satisfaction of God precedes that of Man . . . because Man's satisfaction is connected with God's satisfaction and subsists thereby. In short, human satisfaction is equanimity towards Fate, whether it withholds or bestows, and spiritual steadfastness in regarding events, whether they be the manifestation of Divine Beauty or of Divine Majesty,

> so that it is all one to a man whether he is consumed in the fire of wrath or illuminated by the light of mercy, because both wrath and mercy are evidences of God and whatever proceeds from God is good in His eyes.[2]

Al-Qushayrí quotes the sayings of a Ṣúfí: "If my heart is satisfied with God Most High (*i.e.* acquiesces in His Will) I know that He is satisfied with me".[3] Ruwaym gives a striking illustration of his conception of *riḍá'*. "Satisfaction means that if God were to put Hell on His right side, (the servant) should not ask Him to change it to His left",[4] and Ibn Khafíf defines satisfaction as "the acquiescence of the heart in God's decisions and the agreement of the heart with what He wills and chooses", and again "Satisfaction is the acceptance of God's decisions with joy".[4] Al-Qushayrí gives as another example of the satisfaction of the true Ṣúfí that 'Atba al-Ghulám spent the night until dawn saying, "If Thou dost chastise me I will love Thee (for it) and if Thou dost have compassion on me, I will love Thee (for it)".[5] Al-Hujwírí speaks of four classes of those who are satisfied: (1) those who are satisfied with God's gift, which is gnosis; (2) those who are satisfied with happiness, which is this world; (3) those who are satisfied with affliction, which consists of diverse probations; and (4) those who are satisfied with being chosen, which is love. Of the last two classes he says:

> He who is satisfied with the affliction that God sends is satisfied because in the affliction he sees the Author thereof and can endure its pain by contemplating Him Who sent it; nay, he does not count it painful, such is his joy in contemplating his Beloved. Finally, those who are satisfied with being chosen by God are His lovers, whose existence is an illusion alike in His anger, and in His satisfaction: whose hearts dwell in the presence of Purity and in the garden of Intimacy; who have no thought of created things and have

> escaped from the bonds of "stations" and "states" and have devoted themselves to the love of God. Their satisfaction involves no loss, for satisfaction with God is a manifest kingdom.[6]

So he finally identifies satisfaction in its highest form, with love.

Another element in *maḥabba* is *shawq*, the passionate yearning of the soul for God. A dervish once asked Shaykh Abú Sa 'íd b. Abí al-Khayr, "What is this tumult within our breasts?" The Shaykh replied:

> This is the fire of supplication, and God Almighty has created two fires, one unto life and one unto death. The living fire is the fire of supplication which He has placed in the breasts of His servants in this world, so that their carnal Self may be consumed; that fire burns brightly and when the Self is consumed away, suddenly that fire of supplication becomes the fire of longing and that fire of longing will never die either in this world or the next, and this is that flame of which the apostle of God spoke when he said, "When God willed good to His servant He kindled a light in his heart". They asked the Apostle of God what was the sign of that light, and he said, "Separation from the abode of vanity and turning towards the abode of eternity, and preparing for death, before the descent of death".

The questioner asked the Shaykh, "When God grants that fearful vision, does that fire of longing become rest?" The Shaykh said:

> That vision increases thirst, it does not produce satiety . . . everyone who sees it, sees it according to the measure of his faith. That was the light of faith which came into the hearts through sight, so that that light of faith

> sees (God's) majesty and beauty according to (the capacity of) the eye of faith.[7]

Al-Sarráj also speaks of *shawq* as "the fire of God Most High which He has kindled in the hearts of His saints, so that it may burn up in their hearts all vain desires and wishes and hindrances and needs".[8]

Again he says that the highest degree of *shawq* is attained by the one who beholds his Lord near at hand, and sees that He is present and not absent, and so his heart rejoices in His worship and says to itself that longing is only for the absent, but He is present, not absent, and so he, in his desire is without consciousness of *shawq* and he is the true *mushtáq* without *shawq*.[8]

Bound up with *maḥabba* too, is *uns*; where the worshipper feels awe, the lover feels the sense of intimacy. Al-Sarráj describes it as the heart's joy in the Beloved and he defines the highest degree of *uns*, like that of *shawq*, as becoming unconscious of *uns*, in the sense of reverence (in the presence of God) and proximity to Him, and of His greatness, all combined with intimacy with Him.[9] Al-Hujwírí shows the difference between the relation of the ordinary worshipper, who fears God, and the mystic, who loves Him. He says:

> When God manifests His glory to a man's heart, so that His Majesty predominates, he feels awe, but when God's beauty predominates he feels intimacy, those who feel awe are distressed, while those who feel intimacy are rejoiced. . . . A servant of God seeing His favour, cannot fail to love Him, and when he has loved, he will become intimate, because awe of one's beloved is estrangement, whereas intimacy is oneness. . . . The power of awe is exerted upon the lower souls and its desires, and tends to annihilate human nature, while the power of *uns* is exerted upon the heart and tends to foster gnosis in the heart. Therefore God annihilates the souls of those who love Him by revealing

> His Majesty and endows their hearts with everlasting life by revealing His beauty.[10]

Abú Ṭálib, comparing *shawq* and *uns*, says that *shawq* is a longing to see what is invisible and hidden and this state causes sorrow, but *uns* is a state of proximity through the unveiling of God's presence, and in this station is joy. He quotes al-Junayd as saying with regard to *uns* that the sign of perfect love is the abiding remembrance of God in the heart, in joy and delight and great longing for Him and intimacy with Him.[11] Love includes all these elements and transcends them. To the Ṣúfí mystic the servant was the lover and God the Beloved. Since the origin of every action must be referred to God, He is also the Giver of Love, and Abú Ṭálib writes that God's love to His saints precedes their love to Him,[12] but the Ṣúfís have little to say of the love of God to man, in comparison with what they say of man's love to God. The latter was incumbent upon the servant, the former but an act of grace to which the servant had no claim. The Ṣúfís would not dream of attributing to God feelings akin to their own, He was to them the unique and incomparable object of adoration. Such a conception as that of the Christian mystic who thought of God's love as pursuing the soul,[13] a conception which had reached its highest development in the Christian doctrine of Redemption, was impossible to the Ṣúfís; hence they describe God as the Beloved and throw all the emphasis on the human side. Al-Hujwírí says that

> God's love to Man is in His goodwill towards him and His having mercy on him. Man's love to God is a quality which manifests itself in the heart of the believer . . . so that he seeks to satisfy his Beloved and becomes impatient and restless in his desire for vision of Him and cannot rest with anyone except Him and grows familiar with the remembrance of Him and abjures the remembrance of everything besides.

He goes on to say that

> Believers who love God are of two kinds: (1) those who regard the favour and beneficence of God towards them, and are led by that regard to love the Benefactor; (2) those who are so enraptured by love that they reckon all favours as a veil (between themselves and God) and by regarding the Benefactor are led to His favours.[14]

To this latter class al-Sarráj refers when he says that the love of the saints and the gnostics arises from their vision and their knowledge of the eternal and causeless love of God, therefore they also love Him without any cause.[15]

Al-Qushayrí defines love as the enduring inclination of the love-intoxicated heart, the preference of the Beloved over all companions, harmony with the Beloved, whether present or absent, the effacement of the lover's qualities and the establishment of the Beloved's essence, and finally the agreement of the heart with the Will of the Lord.[16]

Among the sayings of the Ṣúfís which he quotes is that of al-Junayd defining love as "the entering in of the qualities of the Beloved in place of the qualities of the lover" – being changed into the same image till the two become one; that of Abú 'Abd Allah al-Qurashí to the effect that love "means to give all that thou hast to (Him) whom thou lovest, so that nothing remains to thee of thine own"; and those of Shiblí when he says of love that "it is called love, because it obliterates from the heart all save the Beloved", and again, "Love is a fire in the heart consuming all save the Will of the Beloved".[17] Of the effect of this love upon the mystic it is related that Yaḥyá b. Mu'adh wrote to Abú Yazíd: "What do you say of one who drinks a single drop of the ocean of Love[18] and becomes intoxicated?" Báyazíd wrote in reply, "What do you say of one who, if all the oceans in the world were filled with the wine of Love, would drink them all and still cry for more to slake his thirst?" and Hujwírí explains that this intoxication with the cup of love arises from regarding the Benefactor.[19]

Abú Ṭálib also, speaking of the effect of love and that to which it brings the lover, says that love leads to knowledge of the Divine mysteries and those who love abide in God and look to Him only and He is nearer to them than all else, and to them is given the vision of Him unveiled, and they see Him with the eye of certainty.[20]

Thus, through the stage of love, the mystic attains to his goal, and having cast aside all the veils, which hindered him from seeing God, he at last beholds the Divine Beauty unveiled. So Plato also describes the reward of love:

> He who has been instructed thus far in the things of Love, and who has learned to see the beautiful in due order and succession, when he comes toward the end will suddenly perceive a nature of wondrous beauty – not growing and decaying, or waxing and waning . . . but Beauty only, absolute, separate, simple and everlasting. . . . He who under the influence of true love rising upward begins to see that Beauty, is not far from the end. . . . This . . . is that life above all others which a man should live, in the contemplation of Beauty absolute. . . . What if man had eyes to see the true beauty – the Divine Beauty, pure and clear and unalloyed, not clogged with the pollutions of mortality and all the colours and vanities of human life – thither looking, and holding converse with the true Beauty – Divine and Simple? Remember how in that communion only, beholding Beauty with the eye of the mind, he will be enabled to bring forth, not images of beauty, but realities and . . . to become the friend of God and be immortal, if mortal man may.[21]

So he makes Diotima of Mantineia set forth the doctrine of love leading to the beatific vision, and foreshadow the ideals of the mystics of all creeds who were to come after her, and who were to seek the way to God through love.

On the subject of the vision of God which is the reward of the mystic who, having passed through the stages of the Path, reaches the knowledge which comes to him directly from God, and from knowledge passes to sight and from sight to union, al-Junayd says that

> God gives to the adept the sharp desire to behold His Essence, then knowledge becomes vision, and vision revelation, and revelation contemplation, and contemplation existence (with and in God). Words are hushed to silence, life becomes death, explanations (necessary for finite minds in this world) come to an end, signs (a concession to those who are weak in faith) are effaced, disputes are cleared up. Perishability (*faná'*) is ended and subsistence (*baqá'*) is made perfect. Weariness and care cease, the elements perish and there remains what will not cease, as time that is timeless ceases not.[22]

So also writes the Christian mystic, John of Ruysbroeck, of the attainment of union through love:

> The spirit perceives that through love it has plunged itself into the depth . . . and through this intimate feeling of union, it feels itself to be melting into the Unity and, through dying to all things, into the life of God. And there it feels itself to be one life with God.[23]
>
> The Godseeing man who has forsaken self and all things and does not feel himself drawn away because he no longer possesses anything as his own, but stands empty of all, he can always enter, naked and unencum-

> bered with images, into the inmost part of his spirit. There he feels himself to be an eternal life of love, which craves above all else to be one with God.
>
> In the transformation within the Unity, all spirits fail in their own activity, and feel nothing else but a burning up of themselves in the simple Unity of God.
>
> Where the soul is burnt up . . . it feels nothing but unity . . . for the flame of the Love of God consumes all that it can enfold in itself. . . . And in this Love we shall burn and be burnt up without end, throughout eternity – for herein lies the blessedness of all spirits.[24]

The Ṣúfís, and chief among them Rábi'a, felt within themselves, or at least sought diligently that they might attain to "that eternal life of love, which craves above all else, to be one with God". Though Rábi'a was not the first among the Ṣúfís to realise that the way to God must be sought through love, she was perhaps the first to lay stress upon the doctrine and to combine with it the doctrine of *Kashf*,[25] the unveiling at the end of the Way, of the Beloved to His lovers.

'Aṭṭár speaks of her as "that woman on fire with love and ardent desire . . . consumed with her passion (for God)",[26] and a writer of the present day says of her, "With Rábi'a . . . Love, the unquenchable flame smouldering in the ashes of ceremonial religion and kindling the torch of Mysticism through the darkest ages began its conquest of Moḥammedan hearts".[27]

She was one of the first to teach the doctrine of disinterested love to God, a new conception to many of her fellow-Ṣúfís, who for the most part served God in hope of eternal reward or in fear of eternal punishment. With regard to the element of *riḍá'* in the stage of love Abú Ṭálib relates that Sufyán al-Thawrí said one day in Rábi'a's presence, "O God, mayst Thou be satisfied with us", and she said, "Are you not ashamed before God to ask Him to be satisfied, when you are not satisfied with Him?" (*i.e.* not acquiescent in

His Will for you) and Sufyán said, "I ask forgiveness from God".

Ja'far then said to her, "When is the servant satisfied with God Most High?" and she said, "When his pleasure in misfortune is equal to his pleasure in prosperity".[28]

> Some people were speaking in Rábi'a's presence of a devotee, who was known to be holy and in the favour of God, and who lived on what he collected from the refuse-heap of one of our kings, and a man said in her hearing, "What harm would there be in this, if he is in favour with God, that he should ask of Him to provide him with food by some other means?" and Rábi'a said to him, "Be silent, O worthless one, have you not realised that the saints of God are satisfied with Him, that they accept His Will even if He takes from them their means of livelihood, so long as it is He Who chooses this for them?"[29]

Of *shawq* Rábi'a said, "The groaning and the yearning of the lover of God will not be satisfied until it is satisfied in the Beloved".[30] In verses quoted by Al-Hujwírí, for which no author is assigned,[31] but attributed to Rábi'a by Suhrawardí, she says of the one who claims to be a lover of God but does not accept His Will unquestioningly, "You rebel against God, yet appear to love Him. I swear by my faith, that this is most strange. If your love were sincere, you would have obeyed Him, since the lover obeys that one whom he loves."[32] She said further in regard to *uns*, "Everyone who obeys (*i.e.* the true lover) seeks intimacy", and then recited these lines:

> I have made Thee the Companion of my heart,
> But my body is available for those who desire its
> company,
> And my body is friendly towards its guests,
> But the Beloved of my heart is the guest of my soul.[33]

There is an incident recorded by the Persian writer Aflákí which shows how Rábi'a sought to make her contemporaries understand how the true Ṣúfí must love God for Himself alone.

One day a number of saints saw that Rábi'a had taken fire in one hand and water in the other and was running with speed. They said to her, "O lady of the next world, where are you going and what is the meaning of this?" She said:

> I am going to light fire in Paradise and to pour water on to Hell so that both veils (*i.e.* hindrances to the true vision of God) may completely disappear from the pilgrims and their purpose may be sure, and the servants of God may see Him, without any object of hope or motive of fear. What if the hope of Paradise and the fear of Hell did not exist? Not one would worship his Lord or obey Him.[34]

Al-Ghazálí, in dealing with the love of the servant for his Lord, relates that Rábi'a al-'Adawiyya said one day when in the company of the Ṣúfís, "Who shall lead us to our Beloved?" and her servant (probably that 'Abda bint Shuwál, who had learnt much from her mistress)[35] answered, "Our Beloved is with us, but this world cuts us off from Him".[36] Then someone asked Rábi'a, "What is your love to the Apostle of God like?" and she replied, "Verily I love him greatly, but love of the Creator has turned me aside from love of His creatures".[37]

'Aṭṭár also mentions among her sayings on this great subject of all-absorbing love to God, that one day Rábi'a was asked, "Do you love the Lord of Glory?" Perhaps her questioner thought it was impossible or presumptuous for her to love One so far above her. But she said, "I do". Then she was asked, "Do you hold Satan as an enemy?" She replied, "No", and the other, astonished, asked, "How is that?" Rábi'a said, "My love for God leaves no room for hating Satan", and she went on to say, "I saw the Prophet in a dream, and he said to me, 'O Rábi'a, dost thou love me?' I said, 'O Prophet of God, who is there who does not love thee? But my love to God has so possessed me that no place remains for loving or hating any save Him.'"

Then someone said to her, "What is Love?" a question no less searching than Pilate's "What is Truth?" She said, "Love has come from Eternity and passes into Eternity and none has been found in seventy thousand worlds who drinks one drop of it until at last he is absorbed in God, and from that comes the saying 'He loves them (His saints) and they love Him'" (Qur'án, V, 59).[38]

'Aṭṭár gives another anecdote showing how she tried to emphasise her teaching of disinterested love to God, in which he relates how a number of elders came to Rábi'a, and she asked one of them, "Why do you worship God?" He said, "There are seven degrees in Hell, which are a source of dread to me, and everyone must pass by them, willy-nilly, in fear and terror".

Another said, "The different spheres of Paradise are places of rare delight, and much rest is promised".

Then Rábi'a rejoined, "He is a bad servant who worships God from fear and terror, or from the desire of reward – but there are many of these".[39] They asked her, "Why do you worship God, have you no desire for Paradise?" and she replied, "The Neighbour first, and then the House. Is it not enough for me that I am given leave to worship Him? Even if Heaven and Hell were not, does it not behove us to obey Him? He is worthy of worship without any intermediary (motive)."[40]

Al-Qushayrí, in the chapter on love in his *Risála*, mentions Rábi'a in connection with what is really the right conception by the servant of God's love to him. He says: "It is related that Rábi'a prayed once, 'O my God, wilt thou burn in Hell a heart which loves Thee?' and an unseen voice answered her, 'We shall not do thus. Do not think of Us an evil thought!'"[41] which may be considered as a rebuke to Rábi'a for lack of faith or for having too low a conception of God's love for His saints, but her view is in accordance with the view of the earlier Ṣúfís, that it was incumbent on the servant to love his Lord, but not incumbent on Him to return that love.[42] It is told how someone blamed worldliness in her presence, and Rábi'a said, "The Prophet of God said, 'If anyone loves anything more than the remembrance of God, then your remembrance of that thing leads your heart astray, since you are a vessel for something else that you are remembering besides Him'".[43]

Another story showing how Rábi'a felt that love to God must be all absorbing and exclude all else but Him is related by Abú Sa'íd b. Abí al-Khayr, who says that he heard it from Abú 'Alí the Jurist. Rábi'a was asked by what means she had attained to such pre-eminence in the spiritual life and she replied, "By constantly saying this, 'I take refuge in Thee, from everything which has distracted me from Thee, and from every hindrance which has hindered me from Thee'".[44]

Abú 'Abd al-Raḥmán al-Sulamí in his "Ṭabaqát", dealing with devout women,[45] says that a group of them were in his cell seeking a blessing, and they asked for a benediction to be pronounced for them and Rábi'a gave them what they desired in quoting the words, "God has separated from you every cause of separation which has separated you from Him".[46] Sufyán al-Thawrí asked her once what was the basis of her faith, and her answer revealed the secret of her whole life and the essence of all her teaching, when she said, "I have not served God from fear of Hell, for I should be like a wretched hireling, if I did it from fear; nor from love of Paradise, for I should be a bad servant if I served for the sake of what was given, but I have served Him only for the love of Him and desire for Him".[47]

It was on this occasion that she is said to have recited her famous verses on the two types of love, the type which seeks its own ends, and that love which seeks only the Beloved and His glory.[48] Abú Ṭálib says that these verses were attributed to Rábi'a by the people of Baṣra, and by others to either Ja'far b. Sulaymán al-Duba'í or Sufyán al-Thawrí or Ḥammád b. Zayd or 'Abd al-Wáḥid

b. Zayd, but Abú Ṭálib himself gives them as Rábi'a's own. They run thus:

> I have loved Thee with two loves, a selfish love and a love that is worthy (of Thee),
> As for the love which is selfish, I occupy myself therein with remembrance of Thee to the exclusion of all others,
> As for that which is worthy of Thee, therein Thou raisest the veil that I may see Thee.
> Yet is there no praise to me in this or that,
> But the praise is to Thee, whether in that or this.[49]

Abú Ṭálib comments on these verses in detail and says that in regard to her saying "The Selfish love" and her saying "the love of which Thou art worthy" and her distinction between the two loves, it is necessary to make this distinction and he will explain her meaning to those who do not understand these sayings or the nature of the two loves. In the selfish love, she has seen God and loved Him through contemplation, which is the essence of certainty, not through mere report and hearsay, but she has been given assurance through God's grace and kindness. Her love has come by way of personal intercourse, and she has drawn near to God and fled to Him (away from this world) and occupied herself with Him, to the exclusion of all but Him. Before this she had earthly desires, but when she saw her Lord, she cast these away and He became all-in-all to her heart and the sole object of her love. God had freed her from all (objects of desire) save Himself, and this although she was not worthy of that love and was not fit to look upon Him at the last, unveiled and manifest in the place of satisfaction. Her love for God need not have been reciprocated by Him, though it must needs be given by her to Him.[50] He had shown favour to her and He was worthy to bestow favour, and He had shown her His face in His presence at the last (*i.e.* when the vision was revealed to her), as He had shown it to her at this time in her presence first. To God was due the praise for the grace He had shown in this world (*i.e.* while she was still traversing the Way) and to Him was the praise for the grace He had shown in the next world (*i.e.* when the goal was attained and she saw Him unveiled and face to face), and there was no praise due to her in this here, or in that yonder, because it was God who had brought her to both stages. So Abú Ṭálib explains Rábi'a's words, believing that she had reached the highest truth in regard to love.[51]

Al-Ghazálí also, in dealing with the Ṣúfí doctrine of love, gives these verses of hers, and adds commentary upon them in which he explains how he believes they should be interpreted. His discussion is as follows:

> She meant by the selfish love, the love of God for His favour and grace bestowed and for temporary happiness, and by the love worthy of Him the love of His Beauty which was revealed to her, and this is the higher of the two loves and the finer of them. The delight arising from the Beauty of the Lord is that which the Prophet of God explained when he said, speaking of his Lord Most High, "I have prepared for my faithful servants what eye hath not seen nor ear heard and what has not entered into the heart of man",[52] and some of these delights are given beforehand in this world to the one who has wholly purified his heart. Someone said, "If a man reaches this high knowledge, he will be stoned,[53] because his words have passed beyond the limits of their minds (the minds of those who lack enlightenment) and they will consider his speech mad and unbelieving". The purpose of the gnostics is only to attain to this knowledge and possess it, for it is a consolation unknown to the souls from which it is hidden, and when it is attained it destroys

> all anxieties and sensual desires and the heart becomes filled with its grace. Even if the gnostic were cast into the fire he would not feel it because of his absorption and if the favours of Paradise were spread out before him, he would not turn towards them because of the perfection of the grace that is in him and his perfect attainment, which is above all else that can be attained. How can he who understands only the love of sensible things, believe in the joy of looking upon the Face of God Most High? For such a one there is no vision or form, and what meaning is there for him in the promise of God Most High to His worshippers and in His statement that He gives the greatest of all graces? But he who knows God, knows that all joys (save only sensual desires) are included in this joy.[54]

With the Ṣúfí doctrine of the beatific vision, and the joy of the mystic to whom it is granted at the end of the path, we may compare the conception of Plotinus, from whom indeed the Ṣúfís have plainly derived something of their own mystical doctrine.[55] Plotinus, dealing with the vision beautiful, says:

> Such vision is for those only who see with the Soul's sight – and at the vision, they will rejoice, and awe will fall upon them and a trouble deeper than all the rest could ever stir, for now they are moving in the realm of Truth.
>
> This is the spirit that Beauty must ever induce, wonderment and a delicious trouble, longing and love and a trembling that is all delight. For the unseen all this may be felt as for the seen: and this the souls feel for it, every soul in some degree, but those the more deeply that are the more truly apt to this higher love – just as all take delight in the beauty of the body, but all are

not stung as sharply, and those only that feel the keener wound are known as Lovers.[56]

Therefore we must ascend again towards the Good, desired of every Soul. To attain it is for those that will take the upward path, who will set all their forces towards it . . . until, passing, on the upward way, all that is other than God, each in the solitude of himself, shall behold that solitary dwelling Existence, the Apart, the Unmingled, the Pure, that from Which all things depend, for Which all look and live and act and know, the Source of Life and of Intellectuation and of Being.

And one that shall know this vision – with what passion of love shall he not be seized, with what pang of desire, what longing to be molten into one with This, what wondering delight! If he that has never seen this Being must hunger for It as for all his welfare, he that has known must love and reverence It as the very Beauty . . . he loves with a veritable love, with sharp desire; all other loves than this he must despise, and disdain all that once seemed fair.

What are we to think of one that contemplates Absolute Beauty in Its essential integrity – so perfect Its purity, far above all things?

Beholding this Being . . . resting, rapt, in the vision and possession of so lofty a loveliness, growing to Its likeness, what Beauty can the soul yet lack? For This, the Beauty supreme, the absolute and the primal, fashions Its lovers to Beauty and makes them also worthy of love.

And for This, the sternest and the uttermost combat is set before the Souls: all our labour is for This, lest we be left without part in this noblest vision, which to attain is to be blessed in the blissful sight, which to fail

> of is to fail utterly.
>
> Only he has failed, that has failed of only This, for Whose winning he should renounce kingdoms and command over earth and ocean and sky, it only, spurning the world of sense beneath his feet, and straining to This, he may see.[57]

Al-Ghazálí, turning aside from the distinction between the two loves in Rábi'a's verses, seems to concentrate on the vision which is the object of the higher love. He and Plotinus are at one in their conception of "the delight arising from the Beauty of the Lord"; in the course of his travels and of his studies of different schools of philosophical thought, it is not unlikely that al-Ghazálí had come across the ideas of Plotinus, who may also have affected the earlier Ṣúfís, if not directly by access to his writings, at least indirectly by his influence.

A later Ṣúfí, the greatest of all the Arabic mystic poets, wrote in a like strain on this same theme:

> With my Beloved I alone have been,
> When secrets tenderer than evening airs
> Passed, and the Vision blest
> Was granted to my prayers,
> That crowned me, else obscure, with endless fame,
> The while amazed between
> His Beauty and His Majesty
> I stood in silent ecstasy
> Revealing that which o'er my spirit went and came.
> Lo, in His face commingled
> Is every charm and grace;
> The whole of Beauty singled
> Into a perfect face
> Beholding Him would cry,
> "There is no God but He, and He is the most High".[58]

It is possible that Abú Ṭálib and al-Ghazálí read more into Rábi'a's verses than she meant to express. She seems to have been chiefly concerned to distinguish between the love towards God – which finds a satisfaction for itself and seeks to gain something, out of loving Him, even though it loves Him exclusively, and which is therefore only of the same type as the human love of the lover for the beloved, which includes its own satisfaction and enjoyment[59] – and the love which seeks nothing for itself, but only the glory of the beloved, a height to which the love of one human being for another rarely attains. The former has always some taint of selfishness, but in the second type the soul is content to seek only the glory of God and to carry out the will of the Beloved, even to its own hurt, and in beholding the vision of the Everlasting, is content.

So we read in *The Dream of Gerontius* of the eager soul, after death, inspired by pure love and adoration, escaping from the hold of its companion angel, darting to the very throne of God and there, scorched by the Divine fire of God's perfect purity, lying in acquiescent rapture, seeking only to carry out the will of God.[60] Only this type of love is worthy of God.

To sum up Rábi'a's teaching on love, that is the love of the servant to his Lord: she teaches, first, that this love must shut out all others than the Beloved, that is, the saint must turn his back on the world and all its attractions, he must cut himself off from the creatures of God, lest they should distract him from the Creator,[61] he must even rise above the claims of the senses and allow neither pleasure nor pain to disturb his contemplation of the Divine. To Rábi'a God seemed to be a jealous God, who will suffer none to share with Him that love which is due to Him alone.[62]

Then, secondly, she teaches that this love, directed to God to the exclusion of all else, must be disinterested, that it must look neither to hope of reward, nor to relief from punishment, but seek only to do the Will of God and to accomplish that which is pleasing to Him, that He may be glorified. So will the love of the servant be transmuted into that higher love, which is truly worthy of the Beloved.

Only to the servant who loves thus, can God reveal Himself in His perfect beauty and only by treading this Way of self-renouncing love, can the loving soul at last be united with its Beloved and in His Will find its peace.[63]

By means then of love and all the stages which have passed before, the Ṣúfí attains to the mystic gnosis and "the heart becomes filled with its grace". That knowledge comes directly as a gift from the Lord and from it the gnostic proceeds to contemplation of the unveiled essence of God.[64] With the enlightened eye of gnosis, the mystic gazes upon that vision, and thus beholding, is rapt up into union with the Divine, and the final goal of the quest, the end of the Path, is attained, not by annihilation, but by absorption and transmutation, so that the soul transmuted into the Divine image, and become itself part of God, in Him abides and lives for ever.[65] As Suso, the Christian mystic, describes it in his *Book of Truth*:

> This highest state of union is an indescribable experience, in which all idea of images and forms and differences has vanished. All consciousness of self and of all things has gone, and the soul is plunged into the abyss of the Godhead and the spirit has become one with God. . . . In this highest state God becomes the inner essence, the life and activity within, so that whatever the person does, it does as an instrument. . . . Like a being which loses itself in an indescribable intoxication, the spirit ceases to be itself, divests itself of itself, passes into God, and becomes wholly one with Him, as a drop of water mingled with a cask of wine. As the drop of water loses its identity and takes on the taste and colour of the wine, so it is with those who are in the full possession of bliss; human desires influence them no longer; divested of self they are absorbed in the Divine Will, mingled with the Divine Will and become one with it.[66]

So Rábi'a in one of her poems says, "My hope is for union with Thee, for that is the goal of my desire",[67] and again she says, to Ḥasan of Baṣra, "I have ceased to exist and have passed out of self. I am become one with Him and am altogether His."[68] Again she said in a time of spiritual distress that the cure for her sickness was union with her Friend and in the next life she would attain it.[69] Rábi'a, throughout her life, had her eyes fixed upon that goal, and when the end of life came she might have said, with Jalál al-Dín Rúmí:

> Up, O ye lovers, and away! 'Tis time to leave the
> world for aye. . . .
> O heart, toward thy heart's love wend; and O friend,
> fly toward the Friend.[70]

She had looked upon the vision and experienced union for brief moments in this life, and it was not without reason that her Ṣúfí friends, after her death, believed they heard her say, "I have attained to that which I beheld".

1 Cf. the saying attributed to Abú Sa'íd: "That man is a Ṣúfí who is satisfied with whatever God does so that God will be satisfied with whatever he does" (*Asrár al-Tawḥíd*, p. 381). Cf. also St John of the Cross: "This is therefore a test to discern the true lover of God. Is he satisfied with anything less than God? Do I say satisfied? Yea, if a man possess all things, he cannot be satisfied: the greater his possessions, the less will be his satisfaction, for the satisfaction of the heart is not found in possessions but in detachment from all things and in poverty. This being so, the perfection of love in which we possess God, by a grace most intimate and special, lives in the soul in this life when it has reached it, with a certain satisfaction" (*Spiritual Canticle*, p. 26).

2 *Kashf al-Maḥjúb*, p. 177.

3 *Risála*, p. 116.

4 Al-Qushayrí, *op. cit.* p. 117.
5 *Op. cit.* p. 118.
6 *Kashf al-Maḥjúb*, pp. 178, 179.
7 *Asrár al-Tawḥíd*, pp. 388, 389.
8 *Kitáb al-Luma'*, p. 64.
9 *Op. cit.* p. 66.
10 *Kashf al-Maḥjúb*, pp. 376, 377.
11 *Qút al-Qulúb*, II, p. 64.
12 *Op. cit.* II, p. 52. Cf. also *Asrár al-Tawḥíd*, p. 377.
13 Francis Thompson in *The Hound of Heaven*.
14 *Kashf al-Maḥjúb*, pp. 307, 308.
15 *Kitáb al-Luma'*, p. 59.
16 *Risála*, p. 188. Cf. also Ramón Lull: "'What meanest thou by love?' said the Beloved, and the lover answered, 'It is to bear on one's heart the sacred marks and the sweet words of the Beloved. . . . It is to long for Him with desire and with tears. It is boldness. It is fervour. It is fear. It is the desire for the Beloved above all things. It is that which causes the lover to grow faint when he hears the Beloved's praises. It is that in which I die daily and in which is all my will'" (*Book of the Lover and the Beloved*, p. 59).
17 *Risála*, pp. 189, 190.
18 See p. 124.
19 *Kashf al-Maḥjúb*, p. 187.
20 *Qút al-Qulúb*, II, p. 53.
21 *Symposium*, ed. Jowett, 1892, pp. 581 ff.
22 *Asrár al-Tawḥíd*, p. 378. Cf. John Cordelier: "Like some homing star which has burned its way swifter and ever swifter to the sphere that called it, purged and made shining by the ardour of its flight, it rushes through the shrouding darkness to its Origin. All its desire now is to be lost in Him . . . the choice, the effort, the self-stripping, the purging and transmuting fires . . . even the darkness, desolation and abandonment, the bitterness of the spiritual death . . . were they not needed, the soul had almost demanded them, that thus it might test for Him its courage and

its truth" (*The Spiral Way*, p. 113).

23 *The Book of the Sparkling Stone*, p. 184.

24 *Op. cit.* pp. 185, 186.

25 Not itself unknown to earlier Ṣúfís. Cf. al-Sulamí, "Ṭabaqát", fols. 6 b and 7 a on Dhú al-Nún's view.

26 *Tadhkirat al-Awliyá*, I, p. 59.

27 R. A. Nicholson, *Selected Poems*, Introd. p. xxvii.

28 *Qút al-Qulúb*, II, p. 40.

29 Abú Ṭálib, *op. cit.* p. 40.

30 Suhrawardí, "*'Awárif al-Ma'árif*", *Iḥyá*, IV, p. 343, margin. Cf. also "Kashf al-Asrár": "My cup and my wine and the Beloved are three, And I, filled with the yearning of Love, am the fourth" (Rábi'a), fol. 12.

31 *Kashf al-Maḥjúb*, p. 58.

32 *Op. cit. Iḥyá*, IV, p. 344, margin. Also "*Ḥayát al-Qulúb*", *Qút al-Qulúb*, II, p. 169, margin. Kalábádhí, "Ma'ání al-Akhbár", fol. 207 b.

33 *Op. cit. Iḥyá*, IV, p. 358, margin. Ibn Khallikán, *Wafayát*, vol. I, No. 230.

34 Afláki, "Manáqib al-'Árifín", fol. 114 a.

35 See p. 37.

36 Cf. St James iv. 4: "The friendship of the world is enmity with God".

37 *Iḥyá*, IV, p. 308.

38 'Aṭṭár, *op. cit.* p. 67.

39 So also St Basil (ob. AD 389): "We obey God . . . from fear of punishment and in that case we take on the resemblance of Slaves. Or we keep the precepts, because of the utility that we desire from the recompense, thus resembling Mercenaries. Or finally, from love of Him Who has given us the law, we obey with joy at having been judged worthy of serving so great and good a God and thus we imitate the affection of children towards their parents." (Von Hügel, *op. cit.* p. 165).

40 'Aṭṭár, *op. cit.* p. 69.

41 *Risála*, p. 192. Cf. above, p. 49.
42 See Abú Ṭálib's commentary on Rábi'a's verses, p. 142.
43 Munáwí, "Al-Kawákib al-Durríya", fol. 51 a.
44 *Asrár al-Tawḥíd*, p. 345.
45 Now, unfortunately, unavailable.
46 *Asrár al-Tawḥíd*, p. 410.
47 Abú Ṭálib, *Qút al-Qulúb*, II, p. 57. Cf. also Ghánim al-Maqdísí, "Kashf al-Asrár", fol. 12. Cf. also St Francis Xavier's *Hymn of Love*:
"O Deus, ego amo Te
Nec amo Te ut salves me,
Aut quia non amantes Te
Aeterno punis igne".
48 Cf., for the Christian doctrine of pure love, Von Hügel, *Mystical Element of Religion*, II, pp. 152 ff.
49 Ḥurayfísh adds another fragment to these verses:
"O beloved of hearts, I have none like unto Thee
Therefore have pity this day on the sinner who has come to Thee,
O my Hope and my Rest and my Delight,
The heart can love none other but Thee".
Rawḍ Al-Fá'iq, p. 213. For different readings, cf. al-Sarráj, *Maṣári'*, p. 180, and Kalábádhí, "Kitáb al-Ta'arruf", fol. 30 b. Cf. also al-Antákí, *Tazyín al-Aswáq*, p. 55.
50 See p. 117.
51 *Qút al-Qulúb*, II, pp. 57, 58.
52 I Cor. ii. 9: " Eye hath not seen, nor ear heard, neither have entered into the heart of man, the things which God hath prepared for them that love Him".
53 Perhaps a reference to the fate of al-Ḥalláj, who revealed his "high knowledge" and suffered martyrdom, AD 922.
54 Al-Ghazálí, *op. cit.* IV, p. 267.
55 Cf. E. G. Browne, *Literary History of Persia*, p. 420, and R. A. Nicholson, *Selected Poems*, p. xxx.
56 Plotinus, *1st Ennead*, VI, p. 82.

57 *Op. cit.* pp. 85, 86. Cf. the Franciscan concept of the vision: 'That grade of contemplation is a heavenly fire and a sweet devotion of the Holy Spirit, and a rapture and uplifting of the mind intoxicated in the contemplation of the unspeakable savour of the Divine sweetness, and a happy, peaceful and sweet delight of the soul, that is rapt and uplifted in great marvel at the glorious things of heaven above; and a burning sense within of that celestial glory unspeakable" (*Little Flowers of St Francis*, pp. 290, 291).

58 Ibn al-Fárid, *Eastern Poetry and Prose*, p. 142.

59 Cf. al-Hujwírí, *Kashf al-Maḥjúb*, p. 308.

60 Cf. also R. Browning, *Johannes Agricola*:
"I keep the broods of stars aloof
For I intend to get to God.
That's why I haste to God so fast,
For in God's Breast, my own abode,
Those shoals of dazzling glory past,
I lay my spirit down at last".

61 Cf. Browning's *Saul*:
"So shall crown thee the topmost, ineffablest, uttermost crown,
And thy love fill infinitude wholly, nor leave up nor down,
One spot for the creature to stand in!"

62 Cf. incident related on pp. 41–2.

63 Cf. E. Hamilton King, *The Hospital*:
"Measure thy life by loss instead of gain,
Not by the wine drunk, but by the wine poured forth,
For Love's strength standeth in Love's sacrifice,
And he who suffers most, has most to give".

64 *Qút al-Qulúb*, I, pp. 120, 121.

65 Cf. St John of the Cross: "Thus the soul, when it shall have driven away from itself all that is contrary to the Divine Will, becomes transformed in God in love . . . the soul then becomes immediately enlightened by and transformed in God because He communicates His own supernatural being in such a way that

the soul seems to be God Himself and to possess the things of God . . . the soul seems to be God rather than itself and indeed is God by participation" (*Ascent of Mount Carmel*, pp. 77 ff.).

66 Quoted by Rufus Jones, *Studies in Mystical Religion*, p. 290.

67 See p. 31.

68 'Aṭṭár, *op. cit.* I, p. 66.

69 *Op. cit.* I, p. 69.

70 *Selected Poems*, p. 140.

Part Three

WOMEN MYSTICS IN ISLÁM

CHAPTER XI

The Position of Woman in Muslim Lands

It has been commonly held that Islám has implied the degradation of women and, therefore, in order to ascertain to what extent the position of women was affected, unfavourably, by the adoption of the new faith, it is necessary to consider what was the position of women in Arabia and other countries which accepted Islám, before the time of the Prophet.

The lawlessness of the times in which the Arab tribes were constantly at war with each other, naturally involved hardship to the women and the fate of women captured in war was pitiable in the extreme. The great poverty of the wandering Arabs and the uncertainty and scarcity of their food supply, were probably the origin of the barbarous custom of female infanticide, which was prevalent in primitive Arabia and was rendered more cruel by the fact that such infants were buried alive in order to avoid the necessity of shedding the blood of kindred.

Yet with all this, there is little doubt that the free Arab woman in pre-Islamic and even early Islamic times held a more independent and more respected position than the Muslim woman of today and that her present degraded position is due to Islamic teaching which has prevailed since the second and third centuries of the Muslim era, to keep her in a position of almost complete subordination to the male sex.

It seems plain that before the time of Muḥammad there was a family system, matriarchal in type, in which kinship was reckoned through the female side. Under this system, the wife received her husband into her tent, the children belonged to her and were reckoned as members of her tribe, while she had the right to dismiss her husband at her pleasure.[1] This is not to say that the Arab woman was absolutely free, but control was vested, not in the husband, but in her own male relatives, and the head of the family was not the father, but the mother's brother,[2] and it is reasonable to suppose that such a system would give far more extensive rights to the woman – since, in case of dispute, she would be supported by her relations against her husband – than the Islamic type of marriage. This state of things was still in existence to some extent in Muḥammad's time and such customs did not die out altogether during the first two centuries after the rise of Islám. It would seem even to be possible that Muḥammad's first marriage was more of this type. His wife was older than himself, she was wealthy, and it is more than likely that she proposed marriage to one who, though of good family, was an orphan, poor, and actually in her service. That a man of such strong passions, and with such ideals of Paradise as he sets forth in the earlier Súras of the Meccan period,[3] should have remained content with one wife, no longer young, in a state of society in which polygamy was rife, would have been unlikely had he not been bound by economic limitations and the dominant personality of his wife. When her influence was removed, he was not slow to take advantage of his freedom.

Abú al-Faraj (*ob.* AD 967) in his *Kitáb al-Aghání*, throws much light on the position and character of the women of the period immediately preceding the rise of Islám, and of the earliest period of the Muslim era, and some of his stories show a very chivalrous attitude on the part of the pagan Arabs towards their womenkind, and also make clear the independent character of the women themselves.

There is the story of Durayd b. Ṣimma, living in the last century before Islám. Durayd b. Ṣimma went out with the horsemen of the Bení Jusham, and when they reached the valley of the Bení Kunayna, which is called al-Akhram, with the intention of raiding the Bení Kunayna, he saw a man on the side of the valley and a woman in a camel-litter with him, and when Durayd beheld him, he said to one of his horsemen, "Call out to him to leave the woman in the litter and save himself", for he did not know him. The man went up to the stranger and delivered his message and refused to leave him, whereupon the stranger threw down the reins of the camel and said to the woman:

Go on at thy gentle pace, in safety,
The pace of a laden camel, walking quietly,
For to turn aside from a foeman who sought me would
be base,
Test my gallantry and tell (others) of my achievement.

Then he attacked the horseman and flung him down and took his horse and gave it to the woman. Durayd sent another horseman to see what his companion was doing; he found him prostrate and cried out to the stranger, who appeared to be deaf; then, thinking that he had not heard him, he approached him. This latter threw down the reins once more and flung himself on the horseman and knocked him down, bidding him:

Stand aside from the way of the free-born lady,
she is well protected,
For you meet in front of her Rabi'a.
In his hand is that which defends from wrong,
Then take it, a swift thrust, for my thrust in war is
swift.

When Durayd thought that a long time had passed, he sent another horseman to see what the other two were doing; when he reached them, he found them both stretched on the ground, and the horseman said to Rabi'a, "Let go the woman in the litter". Then Rabi'a said to her, "Make your way to the encampment", and turning to the other, he said:

What do you seek from a grim-faced lion?
Do you not see horseman upon horseman?
The hand on the spear destroyed them both despairing.

Then he pierced him and slew him, breaking his own spear.

Now Durayd was puzzled and supposed that they had taken the woman and slain the man, and he went to meet them and found Rabi'a without a spear. Meanwhile the tribesmen had come down and found those who were slain. Durayd said to him:

> O rider, one such as you should not be slain, and my horsemen will be roused on account of their friends; I see no spear with you and I see you are young. Take this spear (of mine) and I will return to my friends and will keep them from you.

So Durayd came to his friends and said, "The rider with the woman has defended her and slain your horsemen and taken my spear. Do not hope for anything from him," and the people went away, and Durayd said:

> I have not seen or heard of one like him, as protector
> of his lady, a cavalier not to be slain.
> He slew horsemen, who were not an easy prey; then
> went his way as if nought had happened;
> Smiling in appearance, unlined was his face; like the
> sharp sword, as the hands of the burnisher
> polished it;
> He took his lady and trailed his spear; gazing to the
> right, towards their abode.
> Dost thou see the horsemen, from fear of his sword,
> like the prey under the fierce swoop of the hawk?
> Would that (I knew) who were his father and mother,
> O friend, one like him cannot be unknown.[4]

There is also a sequel to the story, in which the lady shows no less chivalry than Durayd and Rabi'a had done on this occasion.

Not long after, the Bení Málik b. Kunayna, the tribe of Rabi'a b.

Mukaddam, raided the Bení Jusham, the tribe of Durayd, and slew and captured and took booty, and they took prisoner Durayd b. al-Ṣimma and he concealed his identity. While he was with them, there came some women walking by him, and one of them cried out and said, "Ye have slain and brought destruction. What have our people brought upon us? Verily, this is he who gave Rabi'a his spear on the day of the camel-litter." Then she cast her robe over him and said, "O people of Firás, I will protect him from you, this is our friend of the day of the Valley". Then they asked him who he was, and he said, "I am Durayd b. al-Ṣimma. What has happened to Rabi'a b. Mukaddam?" They said, "The Bení Salím slew him". He said, "Who was the woman in the litter who was with him?" She said, "Rayṭa bint Judhal al-Ta'an, and I am she and I was his wife". The people kept Durayd in prison and discussed with one another and said, "We must not be ungrateful for Durayd's kindness towards us", but someone said, "Certainly he must not go out of our hands except with the consent of al-Mukháriq who took him captive".

But the woman that night made an impassioned appeal in verse for Durayd, and next morning the people arose and helped one another and set him free, and Rayṭa clothed him and gave him food and sent him to his own people. And never again, up to his death, did he make raids against the Bení Firás.[5]

There is yet another story told of Durayd in his old age, and the poetess al-Khansa,[6] which shows the independent spirit of the latter.

Durayd one day passed by when al-Khansa, the daughter of 'Amr b. al-Shurayd, had been smearing a camel with tar and was anxious to finish the task. When she was bathing herself afterwards, Durayd b. Ṣimma saw her, though she was unaware of him, and she struck him with astonishment and he composed an ode on her. Next morning he went to her father and sought her in marriage.

Her father said to him, "You are welcome, Abú Qurra, you are noble, one whose merit is not questioned, a chief not to be turned from his desire and a man of energy not to be rebutted – but this woman has qualities unlike any other, but I will mention you to her and she will decide".

Then he went in to her and said to her, "O Khansa, the cavalier of Hawázin has come to thee and the chief of the Bení Jusham, Durayd b. al-Ṣimma, seeking thee in marriage, and he is such as thou knowest", and Durayd was listening to their talk.

She said, "O my father, dost thou suppose that I will leave my cousins who are like sharp-pointed spears and marry an old man of the Bení Jusham, who will be a corpse today or tomorrow?"

Her father went out to him and said, "O Abú Qurra, she has refused thee, but maybe she will give (another) answer later", but he said, "I heard what you were saying", and so went away.[7]

A picture of the ideal woman of pagan Arabia is drawn by the poet al-Shanfará of Azd, whose description shows a much higher and more appreciative conception of womanhood than is commonly found in Islám:

Alas! Ummu 'Amr set firm her face and has flitted
and gone: she bade no farewell to her neighbours
what time she went away.
She gave us no warning of what she purposed, but
suddenly the necks of her camels towered above us
as forth they sped.
She dwelt in my eyes at even, at night and when
morning dawned; and now has she ended all
things, and flitted and passed and gone.
Alas my heart for Umaimah and all my longing for
her! yea, she was my life's delight, and now all its
joy is fled.
O thou sweet comrade! not one thou to start men's evil
tongues; not thou, when thy name is mentioned, to
draw a word of reproach.
She dwells in a tent pitched high above all the

slandering herd, when many a tent stands where
there gathers around it scorn.
She won me whereas, shamefaced, no maid to let fall
her veil, no wanton to glance behind, she walked
forth with steady tread.
Her eyes seek the ground, as though she looked for a
thing lost there, straight forward she goes: if thou
speak to her, few are her words and low.
At night after little sleep she rises to carry forth her
supper to wives who have need, when such gifts
are few enow.
Not one is Umaimah for gossip to bring to her
husband shame: when mention is made of women,
pure and unstained is she.
The day done, at eve glad comes he home to his eye's
Delight; he needs not to ask of her – "Say, where
didst thou pass the day?"
And slender is she where meet and full where it so
beseems, and tall, straight, a fairy shape, if such
upon earth there be.
And nightlong as we sat there, methought that the tent
was roofed above us with basil sprays, all fragrant
with evening's dew –
Sweet basil from Halyah dale, its branches abloom and
fresh, that fills all around with balm, no starveling
of droughty sands.[8]

To the pagan period, too, belongs the story of Buhaysa, daughter of Aws b. Ḥáritha.

Al-Ḥárith b. 'Awf, a famous Arab chieftain, was minded to seek a wife of the daughters of Aws b. Ḥáritha, though warned that he might be rejected. When he rode up to the dwelling of Aws, the latter first bade him welcome, but when he understood that he came as a suitor, he dismissed him curtly. The wife of Aws inquired whom her husband had sent away so summarily, and when she heard that it was the most renowned of the Arab chiefs who had come as a suitor, she rebuked him for rejecting such an alliance and bade him ride after al-Ḥárith and tell him that she had not been consulted and did not approve the reply. So Aws rode after the wooer and gave his wife's message and brought al-Ḥárith back to partake of his hospitality.

Aws then went to his eldest daughter and asked her if she would marry this chief of Arab chieftains, but she refused, saying that she was not fair to look upon, and that she had many faults, and that he was not related to her, nor one who belonged to a neighbouring tribe and that he might divorce her. Her father agreed with her view and sought his second daughter, who gave a like reply. So he went to his youngest daughter, Buhaysa, who said, "I am fair of face, skilled in handwork, tall of stature, of noble lineage. If he divorces me, God will requite it to him with evil." So the marriage was arranged and the bridegroom thought he had won his bride, but found himself mistaken: she would not receive him there among her own people. So they set off, and when they arrived at his abode the bride demanded that the customary feast of slain camels and sheep should be provided for the Arab guests. When all was done as she wished, the bridegroom came to his bride, but she said, "Is this a time for dallying with your wife, while the Arabs are at war with each other? Go, reconcile the tribes and then return to our own people."

So al-Ḥárith went at her behest and reconciled the warring tribes and paid the blood-money due, to the amount of three thousand camels. Then he returned, amid the plaudits of his people, and claimed the reward he had so hardly earned. His wife received him gladly, and they were blessed with a goodly family.[9]

These free Bedouin women not only exercised a good deal of freedom in the choice of a husband, but constantly refused to marry a man who already had a wife, and also freely exercised the right to leave their husbands as they saw fit. This freedom prevailed during the earliest period of Islám, before the legislation of the Islamic theologians had produced the deadening effects which we find later. Thus we are told of the wife of 'Abbas b. Mirdás, son of al-Khansa, the poetess already mentioned,[10] who, on hearing of the conversion of her husband to Islám, struck her tent and returned to her own people.[11] Again, there was Umm Ḥabtar, wife of Abú Duwád, who took her husband to task for dissipating his wealth by extravagance; he could not gainsay her, and she parted from him.[12]

Again we are told of Salmá bint 'Amr, Umm 'Abd al-Muṭṭalib, a noble woman, who would not marry a man except on condition that she retained her own freedom of action, and if she disliked anything in a man, she left him. When she was married to Uḥayḥa, the latter planned a raid against her people. She was with Uḥayḥa in his fortress and with her was her son 'Amr, then a baby. She tied the boy up so that he cried all night and kept Uḥayḥa awake, and then in the morning she loosed the child and he slept, and Uḥayḥa, tired out by his wakeful night, slept also. Salmá tied a rope to the top of the fortress, let herself down and went and warned her people. The raid took place, but there was little bloodshed, as it was expected, and her people named her the *Mutadalliyya* because she let herself down from the fortress.[13]

Of 'Á'isha bint Yaḥyá we hear that she refused to marry her betrothed unless he left the Hijáz, where he was living at the time, and came to live in Baṣra with her, and she also demanded that she should be the only wife. The fiancé was not willing, and her father said to him: "She is a woman of excellent intelligence, and I have not found her equal, but she is also a woman of strong character and jealous. I have heard that you have two wives and she will not endure being the third." As the man would not put away his wives and live with her in Baṣra, she refused to marry him.[14]

The poets, too, had reason to complain that their wives failed to treat them with the respect they expected. We are told that Miskín al-Dárimí was reciting a *qasída* and sang:

My fire and my neighbour's fire are one,
The pot falls to him, before it falls to me.

His wife said to him:

> I believe it; certainly your neighbour sits and cooks his pot, and enjoys himself by the fire, then he takes it down and eats and you take a share, like a dog, and when he is satisfied, you eat, no doubt. Truly the pot falls to him before you.[15]

This does not suggest the submissive wife who was the ideal of Islám, nor does the account given of a woman of the early generations of Islám, who displayed a like spirit in her relations with her husband. This was 'Á'isha, daughter of Ṭalha and Umm Kulthúm and granddaughter of Abú Bakr. She refused to veil her face from anyone, and when her husband, Muṣ'ab, reproached her with it, she said, "Since God Almighty has sealed me with the stamp of beauty, I desire that men should behold it and recognise His grace towards them, and I will not veil it. Verily, there is no defect in me, that anyone should speak of it."

Since her husband could not restrain his jealousy, she broke off all relations with him for a time, and was not reconciled with him until he returned victorious from battle.[16]

Other writers speak of heroic women of these early days, who even went into battle with their menfolk.[17] Such was the gallant Nuṣayba, daughter of Ka'b, Umm Ḥabíb, who lived in Muḥammad's time, who fought on the day of Yamáma and returned wounded, and also fought on the day of Uḥud AD 625. One writer says that in battle she lost a hand and sustained twelve wounds. She was one of the two women who offered allegiance on the day of 'Aqaba.[18] We are told, too, that on the day of the Yarmúk, AD 634, certain Muslim women fought zealously, among them Hind, daughter of 'Utba, Umm Mu'wíya.[19]

We hear of another warrior woman of this period who fought against Islám named Umm Qirfa Fáṭimá, daughter of Rabi'a, and widow of Málik, son of Hudhayfa. When Zayd, the adopted son of Muḥammad, was conducting a caravan on its way from Medína to Syria he was attacked by the tribe of the Fezára, acting under the orders of Umm Qirfa; the caravan was captured and Zayd was wounded. This woman lived not far from the Wadí al-Kora, in a fortress well-stocked with weapons of war, and had such a reputation that the people of her time used to say proverbially, "more unassailable than Umm Qirfa".

Zayd swore that he would be revenged on her, and when he recovered from his wounds he invested her fortress, surprised her troops, slew and scattered them and put her to a cruel death.[20]

Yet another woman of the same martial spirit was Saján, daughter of al-Ḥárith b. Suwayd b. 'Uqfán, who belonged to Mesopotamia, and was brought up among the Bení Taghlib. She had been brought up as a Christian, but after the death of Muḥammad she proclaimed herself a prophetess.[21] She advanced from Mesopotamia with a large number of tribesmen into the country of the Bení Tamím, announcing her intention of attacking Abú Bakr. The Bení Tamím were divided, some supporting the prophetess, while others fought against her claims. Finally, she agreed to an exchange of prisoners, to payment of blood-money for the slain, and to leaving the country with her troops.[22] She then led her followers on to Yamáma, where the false prophet Musaylima was established. He was in difficulties from other directions and thought it wise to treat with Saján, who granted him a private interview. The result was that they agreed to marry, and the marriage took place immediately. Saján agreed to withdraw her army to Mesopotamia and Musaylima to give her a year's revenue from Yamáma. She took half of the sum with her and left three of her generals behind to receive the rest. She herself continued to live in Mesopotamia as a nominal Christian, but in the end accepted Islám. Later she went to live in Baṣra, where she died.[23] Such a type of woman-warrior had little chance of survival in any country where Islamic legislation was strictly enforced.

Again, the picture drawn by Jalál al-Dín Rúmí in the *Mathnawí* of the Bedouin and his wife shows that the Bedouin woman had a great reputation for independence of spirit and freedom of speech:

> If he (the husband) be Rustam, son of Zál or greater than Hamza, he is yet as a captive under the authority of his old woman.
> Even though outwardly you dominate your wife, yet inwardly you are dominated (by her).[24]

Here the Ṣúfí poet is speaking allegorically of the domination of the carnal soul, but the choice of comparison which he makes suggests that the Bedouin woman of his own time (Rúmí died AD 1273) could at least hold her own with her husband.[25]

Such women as these were not the product of a community in which women were regarded as slaves, or one in which they regarded themselves as on anything but an equal footing with their menfolk. Not only was this the case, but the women of these early days inspired much of the most beautiful poetry of this period.[26]

The chivalrous devotion that could be felt by the Arabs of pre-Islamic times towards their women we have already illustrated by the story of Rabi'a and his wife Rayṭa, and even in the beginning of Islám itself we find traces of a tenderness and reverence which the attitude towards women adopted by the theologians after the second century or so was destined to destroy.

In the lament of Muwaylik al-Mazmúm, who wrote probably about the beginning of the third century AH, over his wife, we find a spirit of touching devotion to both her and her motherless babe, though of the sex later so despised:

> Let us pass along by the grave wherein she lieth;
> Umm al-'Alá, calling her, if haply she may hear!

Hast thou then come to dwell, thou who wast very
fearful,
In a land where even the brave go on their way in
fear?
May God bless and keep thee, O thou lamented one,
For that desolate, lonely place is not meet for thee.
Thou hast left behind for our pity thy little one;
She knows not why she should grieve for thee, and
yet she grieves,
She misses the sweetness of thy loving care for her.
She keeps us wakeful at night, our soothing is in
vain.
When I hear the sound of her wailing, throughout
the night,
My thoughts are turned to thee, and mine eyes are
filled with tears.[27]

This is a cry from the heart of a man who loved tenderly and deeply, and who mourned a companion, not a slave.

The imposition of the veil was not known among Arab women before Islám, and not only the story of 'Á'isha given above,[28] but other accounts by early writers show that the women resented this new restriction which hindered free intercourse with men, to which they had been accustomed.[29]

In the matter of religion, too, in the earliest days of Islám, women exercised a freedom in worship which in later days was withdrawn from them, though without doubt they had exercised it in the days of ignorance. Among the Traditions collected by Al-Suyúṭí we find an account of the wife of 'Umar, who used to be present at the morning and evening prayers among the men in the mosque. They said to her, "Why do you go outside (of the house) when you know that 'Umar hates it and is jealous?" She said, "What hinders him from forbidding me to do it?" They replied, "He is hindered by the saying of the Prophet, 'Do not prevent the handmaids of God from access to the places where He is worshipped'".

Another woman, 'Atíka bint Zayd b. 'Amr b. Nufayl, the wife of 'Umar b. al-Khiṭáb, used to ask his permission to go to the mosque and when he remained silent, she said, "I shall go until you prevent me".

Umm Ṣafiyya Khawla bint Qays used to say, "In the time of the Prophet and Abú Bakr, and at the beginning of the Caliphate of 'Umar, we used to be in the mosque, and the women used to mix with the men . . . and 'Umar said, 'I send you away, O freeborn women', and he sent us away, but we used to be present at the time of prayers".

Another Tradition concerning the above-mentioned wife of 'Umar relates that when she went out to prayer she was recognised, and they said to 'Umar, "Why did you not forbid her?" He said, "If I had not heard the Apostle of God say, 'Do not hinder the handmaids of God from going to the places where God is worshipped', I should have done so".

Again it is related that the women used to pray with the Apostle between daybreak and sunrise, then they went out, wrapped up in their garments.[30]

There is ample evidence, then, that at the beginning of the Islamic era women had much freedom in the choice of their husbands, that marriage was in many cases an equal partnership and that women could, and did, assert their right to an independent life. Social intercourse between women and men was not restricted to close relatives, but women might meet with strangers in society.[31] They went about freely and had the right, as we have seen, to go into the mosques at the time of prayer, to worship in common with the men. Moreover, those who were versed in jurisprudence expressly recognised the right of a wife on marriage to make a condition that there should be no second wife, nor even a concubine, and this right, as we have seen above, was frequently claimed. The woman, then, at the beginning of the Islamic period, had a dignity and independence not found later, and early Arabic literature reveals a feeling even of chivalrous reverence for womanhood.[32]

From the third century AH, this position of the women deteriorated. Even before the time of Muḥammad, the marriage of captive women with their captors and of female slaves with their masters, was in vogue, and we are told that the Muslim men preferred slaves as wives, because of the independent spirit of the free Arab women. A slave-wife was the chattel of her husband, who could therefore claim absolute authority over her. This led to the institution of the *ba'l* marriage or marriage of domination, clinched by the payment of a dowry in the case of freeborn women. The position of the wife approximated to that of a slave, and her husband claimed authority over her, an authority which became more and more despotic. A tradition of the Prophet related that he said that if it had been permissible for one human being to worship another, he would have liked to order women to worship their husbands.[33] Such a view of marriage, ascribed to the founder of Islám, could not fail to have its effect on his followers. The wife, in this type of marriage, went to her husband, instead of her husband coming to her, and the children were reckoned as belonging exclusively to him. "The effect of Muḥammed's legislation in favour of women was more than outweighed by the establishment of marriages of dominion as the one legitimate type, and by the gradual loosening of the principle that married women could count on their own kin to stand by them against their husbands".[34] Temporary marriages were common,[35] and men kept female slaves in addition to their legal wives. Polygamy, authorised by the Qur'án, with all its evil effects, was general, and the *ḥarím*-system, with its rigid seclusion of all but women of the poorest classes, together with the wearing of the veil, was sternly enforced.

Muḥammad's legislation concerning women was undoubtedly meant in the first place for their protection, *e.g.* his prohibition of female infanticide was an act of humanity, and his laws concerning marriage and seclusion may have tended towards ensuring the safety of women in lawless times. His laws also secured to women the right to property and inheritance, and he made some attempt to improve the loose moral standard prevailing among the Arabs of his time.

But when all this is admitted, the ultimate effect of his legislation was the degradation and enslavement of Muslim womanhood throughout the centuries up to the present time, simply because enactments which may have been suited to the times in which he lived, and others which were promulgated to suit his own temperament and his personal domestic circumstances, were given the force of Divine law and enshrined in a sacred book, believed to be uncreated, and fetters which should have been shaken off with the progress of time and civilisation were riveted on the necks of Muslim women, and have done more than anything else to hamper the progress of countries under Muslim rule.[36]

That Islám is responsible for the degradation of Muslim women is proved not only by the facts in regard to pre-Islamic and early Islamic times mentioned above, but also by the fact that in countries where, owing to natural circumstances or to the persistence of early customs among the people, the Muslim laws and customs regarding women have not been strictly enforced, women have enjoyed a much greater degree of freedom and respect than in more orthodox Muslim lands. Ibn Baṭṭúṭa speaks with great indignation of the women of the Maldives, because they did not cover their heads, not even their ruler, who was a woman. They wore a robe, which left half the body uncovered, and clad thus they went into the markets and elsewhere. Ibn Baṭṭúṭa, when appointed judge of these islands, endeavoured to remedy this state of things, but failed to get his way with the women. They were in the habit, a strange thing in his eyes, of going out to earn a living as servants, being engaged chiefly in spinning. The women refused to leave their country, and if a stranger married one of them he had to part from her it he left the islands. They did not allow any man to watch them eat.[37] Another strange thing to the traveller was the fact that these islanders were ruled by a woman, Khadíja, daughter of the Sulṭán Jalál al-Dín

'Umar. She was mentioned by the preacher in the mosque, in the Friday prayers and on other days in these terms: "O Lord, look upon Thy handmaid, whom Thou hast made pre-eminent in knowledge of the two worlds, and hast made her a means of mercy towards all the Muslims, that is, the Sulṭána Khadíja, daughter of the Sulṭán Jalál al-Dín; son of the Sulṭán Salah al-Dín".[38] The writer was further scandalised by finding that divorced women continued to live with the husbands who had divorced them until they re-married.[39] Obviously, these inhabitants of the Maldives were bad Muslims, but their failure to observe the laws of Islám reacted favourably on the position and liberty of their women.

Ibn Baṭṭúṭa, reporting on his visit to the Western Sudan, in regard to the district now inhabited by the Tuaregs, expresses his astonishment at the customs and manners of the people. He noted that the women were very beautiful and of more account than the men. The men were not inclined to jealousy on account of their wives. No man was called after his father, but counted his family to be that of his maternal uncle. What a man left at his death went to his sister's sons, not to his own. The writer notes that this custom prevailed elsewhere only among the Hindus and in Malabar. He goes on to say that the women of these Berber tribes felt no bashfulness in the presence of men and did not veil themselves, though they were zealous in the performance of their prayers. They would not leave the country with their husbands and even if they were willing, their families would prevent it. The women enjoyed friendship and companionship with men who were strangers and not relatives, and the husbands saw no objection to it.[40]

Ibn Baṭṭúṭa went one day to visit a man named Abú Muḥammad Yandakán, whom he found seated on a carpet, while nearby was his wife seated on a divan, conversing with a man who sat beside her. Ibn Baṭṭúṭa said to his host, "Who is this woman?" He replied that she was his wife. Ibn Baṭṭúṭa then inquired who was the man with her. He said, "A friend of hers". The traveller, much scandalised, said to him, "And are you content with this, you who have lived in our country and are acquainted with the sacred law?" His host rebuked him fittingly for his interference, in saying, "The association of women with men among us is a good custom and is carried on in a suitable manner. It arouses no suspicion and our women are not like those of your country." Ibn Baṭṭúṭa was highly offended and never again visited this man.[41]

The historian Ibn Khaldún, in his account of these Berber tribes of the Sahara, also gives a picture of the high position held by the women of the tribes. He says that, at the time of the Arab invasions, one of the most powerful of the Berber chiefs was the Jewish Káhina, queen of Mount Auras, whose real name was Dihya, daughter of Tabeta, son of Tífan. When Ḥasan, governor of Egypt, was ordered to march against the Berbers, he was informed that the Káhina was the most powerful ruler among them and he marched against her. She inflicted a signal defeat upon him and drove out his troops from her territory in AH 69. Five years later Ḥasan once more invaded North Africa and the Káhina thereupon destroyed all the towns and the farms in the country from Tripoli to Tangiers. The Berbers were indignant and submitted to Ḥasan, and the gallant Káhina was slain at Mount Auras, at a place called to this day Bír al-Káhina (the well of the priestess), and her subjects embraced Islám.[42]

The Tuaregs of Ibn Baṭṭúṭa's account and of modern times are the descendants of these Berbers, and the high position maintained by their women undoubtedly goes back to these pre-Islamic times. The modern Tuaregs trace their descent from a woman named Tin Hinane; inheritance is through the female line and the status of a man is in accordance with the status of his mother. The Tuareg woman displays her attractions in a manner quite unusual in Muslim countries. Her face is not veiled and she freely visits her relations. She has insisted on monogamy, and has male friends and visitors. She exercises control over her own property and her camels are branded with her own mark. She does not follow her husband to his home on marriage, but sets up her tent near her parents for a year after marriage. She can divorce her husband at her will and return to her own home. She is the undisputed mistress of the household. She is better educated than the men, she knows how to read and write and she is the one to teach the children to read.[43] The right of the *tobol*,[44] implying authority over the tribe, is transmitted through the women. The woman presides at the *ahal*, an assembly where gallantry is *de rigueur* and where men and women vie in wit and elegance.[45] It is noteworthy that the writer adds that the Tuaregs are not a religious people, and as they do not understand Arabic, they do not observe the ordinances imposed by the Qur'án, *e.g.* Ramaḍán is not generally observed.

In the Eastern Sudan also, in some respects, the women hold a higher position than is usual among Muslim women and no doubt the distinctive customs of these tribes go back to the days before they were converted to Islám. A modern writer – speaking of the Rubáṭáb in particular, but dealing with customs which he says are common to most of the tribes on the banks of the Nile in the provinces of Khartoum, Berber and Dongola – notes that the women do not veil themselves and that they enter one another's houses without asking permission. Both men and women pride themselves on powers of endurance, bearing flogging and branding with fire. They are fond of games and physical exercises and most of the women can swim. In the household the woman is supreme, its management is left entirely in her hands and the husband must consult her before disposing of any of his household goods. Further, he is expected to bear with all her caprices, and if she abuses him, he ought to laugh at it and will not be despised for doing so, as he would be if he submitted to abuse from a man. The husband is absolutely forbidden to use violence to his wife, whatever her offence.[46] The consent of a girl's mother is necessary for her marriage to anyone but her uncle's son. A man must show the utmost respect to his mother-in-law and all his wife's relatives.[47]

The tribesmen of the Shaigia, of Dongola, have long had a custom of being led into battle by a maiden. Azila, of the Amrab, led her tribe into battle about 1690 in the Shaigia war of independence. At the battle of Korti, 1820, the Shaigia were led by a virgin named Muhayra bint Abad of the Suareb, mounted in a litter on a camel, and her tribesmen rallied round her as a standard. A month later, at Jebel Dager, the Shaigia were again led by a woman, Ṣafia, daughter of Mek Sabil.[48]

Again, we find that primitive custom has been stronger than Islamic legislation in some respects among the Bedouin dwellers in the desert today. Doughty speaks of the comparative freedom of the Bedouin housewife and of how she may leave her husband at will, and custom will not allow him to prevent her from doing so.[49] He also speaks of a custom similar to that we have mentioned as prevailing in Dongola, by which, "at any general battle of the tribes, there is mounted some beautiful damsel of the shaykh's daughters, whose generous loud Alleluias for her people, in presence of their enemies, inflame her young kinsmen's hearts to leap in that martial dance to a multitude of deaths". "Such a maiden", he says, "is called an 'Atáyfa', and it would be infamous to kill such an one, but she may be in danger in the course of the battle."[50] Here we have a custom in accordance with the heroic spirit of a Nuṣayba, and it is evident that Islamic laws concerning the seclusion and incompetency of woman have failed to prevail; such martial training must produce a feminine type very different from the feeble captive of the *ḥarím*.

In all these cases we find that, though the country is nominally Muslim, the non-observance of Muslim laws and customs has enabled the women to retain some, or perhaps all, of their primitive freedom, which, in countries where Islamic ordinances have been rigidly enforced, has been lost, with consequent degradation to the womankind of those countries. It is to be noted that those Muslim countries which have determined to bring their civilisations into line with those of the modern West, have first of all found it necessary to abrogate the Islamic legislation concerning women.

On the other hand, we find in the history of the early centuries of Islám, in those countries where the new faith took firm root, sometimes through an unduly harsh interpretation of the precepts of the Qur'án, and still more through numerous Traditions which were brought to bear on the subject, the Muslim woman became more and more of a slave and chattel; and under the degrading and narrowing influence of the *ḥarím*, she lost that dignity and independence of character for which she had been noted in an earlier age. In the matter of religion, seclusion and the limitation of their freedom certainly hindered women in the exercise of their religious duties, and the almost complete lack of education which was the fate of most Muslim women up to very recent years, with a few notable exceptions, prevented them from having any intelligent conception of what was included in the doctrines of Islám.

Many Muslim writers speak with contempt of women's incapacity for religion and of their lack of intelligence and morals. An early writer says, "The majority of women are lacking in religion and virtue and that which prevails in them is ignorance and evil desires".[51]

Tradition states that the Prophet himself said, "I looked into Hell and I saw that the majority of its inhabitants were women, and I looked into Paradise and saw that but few of its inhabitants were women".[52] Another Tradition of the Prophet represents him as saying:

> Many men have been perfected, but of women only four; and the falling short of all other women was not due to their inherent nature, but because of their acquired qualities (*i.e.* that for which they were themselves morally responsible). They are to be described also as wanting in intelligence and religion, and the explanation of their lack of religion is their neglect of prayer and fasting due to pride. Their lack of religion is in truth nothing but their neglect of prayer and fasting and the faith of Islám. For the practice of Islám and

> faith in it are one and the same thing to the one who realises that good works come from faith.[53]

Taqí al-Dín al-Ḥisní (*ob.* AD 1426), writing with great bitterness of the women of his time, says, "The most double-faced (of mankind) are women, because of the weakness of their intellect and their religion and their convictions, and therefore their faith fails".[54]

Such statements, to which many more could be added, might well lead us to suppose that women would not be conspicuous among the religious leaders of Islám and would play but a small part in the development of Islám on the religious side. Western opinion has been liable to assume that woman, as such, was shut out from religious privileges and religious accountability and it has even been asserted that Islám does not allow a woman the possession of a soul. Dr Perron asserts that

> The path of holiness in Islám was seldom trodden by women and we find but few women on the same. It is too difficult for them, so at least think the men. These everywhere take the front place: all glory, all advantage, all authority, is for the men. They have made everything contribute to their advantage and pre-eminence; they have appropriated everything, monopolised everything, holiness and even Paradise, for themselves.[55]

Yet this does not give a complete picture of the real state of affairs. Woman in Islám was degraded almost as much by social tendencies as by the religious law, and woman as such was not excluded from the spiritual blessings which in Islám were intended to be available for all human beings. The Qur'án itself makes this plain:

> And God Most High said that for the Muslim men and the Muslim women (*i.e.* those who have surrendered

> themselves to His Will) and the believers, men and women, and those who pray, both men and women, and the sincere men and women and the patient men and women and the humble men and women and the charitable (who give the prescribed alms) and those who fast, both men and women, and the chaste and those, both men and women, who remember God often – God will recompense them with forgiveness and a great reward.[56]

Shu'ayb al-Ḥurayfísh (*ob.* AD 1398) quotes these verses and continues:

> So God, Glory be to Him, joined the mention of pious women with pious men, and in women are found the mystic states and ascetic devotion and good works and piety, as in men; and to women is given revelation, and for them are pilgrimages and the unveiling (of the Vision of God) and other things of the special favours which God Most High has assigned to them; also some of them are included in the first rank,

and he gives the names of several famous women saints.[57]

Also the writer already mentioned, Taqí al-Dín al-Ḥisní, bitter as were his denunciations of the women of his own time, admitted that there had been many good women, and set out to write a book dealing entirely with the lives of women, holy and of irreproachable faith; in his introduction he says:

> Praise be to God, Who created the earth and the heavens and provided them with the things created and made that a sign of His Unity – and gathered together the believers, men and women, and established the sacred law, chosen for Himself, and sent His Prophet

> and through him sent down His book of clear signs, and the people of happiness obeyed Him and did His work, from among the dutiful men and women . . . and when He exhorted the creatures to be obedient, He did not single out the men, but spoke of the Muslims, men and women, and the believers of both sexes and those who observed the law, men and women, and the verses dealing with this are many and are not secret.[58]

So he justifies himself for choosing to write about women and shows that to them also God has granted the highest favours and has chosen some of them to be saints and to receive His revelations.

We see, therefore, that in spite of some ecclesiastical restrictions and in spite of the general contempt for her sex, the Muslim woman was, theoretically at least, on a spiritual equality with man and was held to be of equal worth in the sight of God, and that, as a matter of fact, no obstacle was erected great enough to prevent her from rising to that full experience of the inner spiritual life and to that devoted exercise of faith, which was possible for the man and proved to be equally possible for her.

1 Robertson Smith, *Kinship and Marriage in Early Arabia*, pp. 65, 172.
2 Cf. Wellhausen, *Die Ehe bei den Arabern*, pp. 474 ff.
3 Súra LXXVIII, 31–34; LXVI, 34–35; LII, 20; XXXVII, 40–47.
4 *Kitáb al-Aghání*, XIV, p. 134.
5 *Op. cit.* XIV, pp. 134, 135.
6 Her poems have been published as the *Diwán of al-Khansa*, ed. L. Cheikko, Beyrout, 1895. For specimens translated into English see R. A. Nicholson, *Eastern Poetry and Prose*, pp. 18, 19.
7 *Al-Aghání*, IX, p. 11.
8 Al-Shanfará of Azd, *Mufaḍḍalíyát*, II, p. 69, tr. C. J. Lyall.
9 *Al-Aghání*, IX, pp. 149-51.
10 See p. 145 ff.
11 *Op. cit.* XIII, pp. 65, 66.

12 *Op. cit.* XV, p. 96.
13 *Op. cit.* XIII, p. 124.
14 *Op. cit.* XIV, p. 124.
15 *Op. cit.* XVIII, p. 72.
16 *Op. cit.* X, pp. 54 ff. Taghribardí, *al-Nujúm al-Záhira*, I, p. 321.
17 Cf. R. Briffault, *The Mothers*, I, p. 154.
18 Al-Baládhurí, *Futúḥ al-Buldán*, pp. 92, 93. Ibn Ḥajar, *Isába*, IV, p. 807.
19 Al-Baládhurí, *op. cit.* p. 125.
20 Caussin de Perceval, *L'Histoire des Arabes*, III, pp. 158, 159.
21 Al-Ṭabarí, *Annales*, I, p. 1911.
22 *Op. cit.* I, p. 1912.
23 *Op. cit.* I, pp. 1913 ff. Caussin de Perceval, *op. cit.* III, p. 157.
24 *Mathnawí*, I, ll. 2427, 2431.
25 See also the account of modern Bedouin women given by Doughty, quoted here, p. 160.
26 Cf. R. A. Nicholson, *Literary History of the Arabs*, pp. 87–91.
27 Abú Tammám, *Diwán al-Ḥamása*, Cairo, 1913, p. 374.
28 See p. 150.
29 Cf. Kalábádhí, "Ma'ání al-Akhbár", fol. 172 b.
30 Al-Suyúṭí, *Kanz al-'Ummál*, p. 262.
31 *Al-Aghání*, XIX, p. 161.
32 Cf. Lyall, *Translations of Ancient Arabian Poetry*, Introd. pp. xxxi ff. and Von Kremer, *Culturgeschichte des Orients*, p.102. Cf. also R. Briffault, *The Mothers*, I, p. 375.
33 Abú Dáwúd, *Sunan*, I, p. 212.
34 W. Robertson Smith, *Kinship and Marriage in Early Arabia*, p. 104.
35 Ibn Khallikán, *op. cit.* tr. de Slane, II, p. 210.
36 Cf. Palmer, *Al-Qur'án*, I, p. lxxv.
37 Ibn Baṭṭúṭa, *Tuḥfa al-Nuzzar*, IV, pp. 122 ff.
38 *Op. cit.* IV, pp. 130 ff.
39 *Op. cit.* p. 151.
40 *Op. cit.* pp. 387 ff.
41 *Op. cit.* p. 390.

42 Ibn Khaldún, *Histoire des Berbères*, tr. de Slane, pp. 213, 214.
43 Benhazera, *Six mois chez les Touareg du Ahaggar*, pp. 11, 12.
44 Originally a tambourine by means of which the chief summoned the tribesmen.
45 Benhazera, *op. cit.* p. 51. See also R. Briffault, *op. cit.* I, p. 286.
46 J . W . Crowfoot, *Sudan Notes and Records*, pp. 120, 121.
47 *Op. cit.* pp. 124, 128.
48 A. E. Robinson, *Journal of the African Society*, Oct. 1925, pp. 51, 53.
49 *Travels in Arabia Deserta*, p. 238. Cf. also C. R. Conder, *Palestine Exploration Fund*, 1889, p. 324.
50 Doughty, *op. cit.* p. 61.
51 Abú Ṭálib, *Qút al-Qulúb*, II, p. 238.
52 *Op. cit.* II, p. 252.
53 Kalábádhí, "Kitáb al-Ta'arruf", fol. 20 a.
54 "Siyar al-Ṣáliḥát", fol. 67 b.
55 *Femmes arabes avant et depuis l'islamisme*, p. 350.
56 The Qur'án, XXXIII, 35.
57 *Rawḍ al-Fá'iq*, p. 212.
58 "Siyar al-Ṣáliḥát", fol. I b.

CHAPTER XII

The Position Attained by the Woman Saint

We have already noted[1] the high position attained by the woman saint among the followers of Islám, and we find that writers on religion hold up the woman saint as an example not only to other women, but to men as well. So al-Ghazálí says by way of exhortation to his male readers:

> Consider the state of the God-fearing women and say (to your own soul), "O my soul, be not content to be less than a woman, for a man is contemptible if he comes short of a woman, in respect of her religion, and (her relation) to this world". So we will now mention something of the (spiritual) states of the women who have devoted themselves to the service of God,[2]

and he proceeds to hold up before his readers the example of several well-known women saints and to show the degree in the spiritual life to which they attained.

Rábi'a al-'Adawiyya was undoubtedly the greatest of the women mystics of Islám and made the greatest contribution of any woman towards the development of Ṣúfism, but there were other women of her time, and many after her, who were revered as saints and had some contribution to make. Before Ṣúfism arose, women were recognised as saints, such as Amína, the mother of the Prophet, and Fáṭima, his daughter, who enjoy the veneration of all Muslims because of their relationship to Muḥammad. Apart from these, the earliest Muslim woman saint of whom we have a record is Umm Ḥarám, whose tomb is to be found near Larnaka in Cyprus.[3] This saint was a historic personage and is mentioned by several of the early Arab writers. She was the daughter of Milḥán, and of the kindred of Muḥammad. Her husband was 'Ubayda b. al-Ṣámit. Her name is given variously as Rumayṣa, Rawla and Sahla, while others say that her own name was unknown. A full account of her is given in a Turkish manuscript dated about AD 1800 by Sh. Ibráhím b. Muṣṭafá, who had collected information from earlier sources.[4] This biographer writes in glowing terms of the virtues of this lady, saying:

> Lauds without number are most meet to be ascribed to the Majesty of Him, the Self-Existent, Who, having distinguished with perfect honour the noble companions and venerable female friends of Muḥammad . . . favoured them with perfect grace and made them the source of many virtues. . . . He (the Prophet) especially delighted the taste and quickened the noble heart of Umm Harám with the pleasing announcement, "Thou art of the first".[5]

Again he speaks of

> that exalted lady, the intercessor interceded for, who (through the mercy of the Lord of the worlds and the guidance of the prince of the apostles) was made a manifestation of wonders and of sanctity, a source of chastity and purity of life.[6]

Umm Ḥarám, being anxious to take her share in the holy war, after a dream by the Prophet, was declared by him to be of the first of the troop which was to war at sea, and was allowed to go. In AH 27 permission was given by 'Uthman to wage war by sea, and 'Ubayda b. al-Ṣámit, with his wife Umm Ḥarám and several of the Companions, started from Medína and entered Damascus and then Jerusalem. By way of Ramla they went to Tripoli in Syria and thence embarked for Cyprus.[7] This was in the year AH 28 or 29.

When they landed, Umm Ḥarám set out with her husband, but was thrown by her mule and killed.[8] According to her biographer, "they were attacked by Genoese infidels, and falling from her beast, she broke her pellucid neck, and yielded up her victorious soul, and in that fragrant spot was at once buried". Baládhurí adds that her grave is called "The grave of the holy woman".[9] By her death while engaged in the holy war, Umm Ḥarám attained to martyrdom.[10] Like other saints, she was credited with miracles. Her biography includes, among the miracles of that exalted lady, this story:

> On her journey from Jerusalem to Ramla, she alighted on her way as a guest at the house of a Christian monk. She beheld in the house three huge stones like columns, and to show a marvel and display saintship, she desired to buy the said stones from the monk. The monk, fully persuaded of the impossibility of transporting the stones and carrying them away, gave them as a present to the exalted lady. She accepted them, and said, "Let them remain by way of trust; in due time they will be taken away", and departed. And on the evening of her burial the said stones, by the might of the Lord of the worlds, moved from their place and, walking in the sea – a wonderful sight – appeared in this fragrant place; and one of them set itself at her sacred head, one at her holy feet and the other stone, as though suspended over them, rested there by the power of God. And now, if we look to be instructed, the elevation and juxtaposition with other stones of a stone so huge, must be deemed an impossibility. It is therefore clear and manifest that the stone is suspended. These marvels are of the number of prodigies and saintly works of that source of wonders, and of the signs of her high rank. And even now many holy marvels of hers are seen, and those witnessed by pilgrims

> who seek her trustfully and by the servants who live about her pleasant shrine, are such as none may number and count. May God be pleased with her and benefit us through her intercession. We pray Thee, O God, for uprightness in her service and to exalt us under her banner, through the favour of the chief of the apostles.[11]

Another early saint was Rábi'a bint Ismá'íl of Syria, whose name is sometimes spelt Ráiy'a (with the *yá* instead of *bá*) by some writers.[12] She was early confused with her greater namesake, Rábi'a al-'Adawiyya, but since she was a married woman and lived and died in Syria, and also is said to have died fifty years before Rábi'a of Baṣra, her history is sufficiently distinctive to have made confusion unnecessary.

The husband of Rábi'a of Syria was Aḥmad b. Abí al-Ḥawwárí,[13] himself a well-known ascetic and a servant of Abú Sulaymán, another ascetic. When he became betrothed to Rábi'a, then a widow, he told her that he did not trouble himself about women, being too much occupied with his own spiritual state, to which she replied that she was more concerned with her spiritual condition than he was with his, and that she had no inclination towards men, but she had inherited from her late husband 300,000 *dínárs*, lawfully earned, and these she wished to bestow upon Aḥmad and his brothers, knowing them to be pious men, and this money, she thought, might prove to be a way to God Most High.[14]

Her betrothed sought out his master, Abú Sulaymán, and reported what Rábi'a had said (Abú Sulaymán having warned Aḥmad, as a Ṣúfí, against marriage, saying: "Not one of our friends has married without changing – for the worse"), and he relates: "Abú Sulaymán put his head under his garment and was silent for a while, then he lifted up his head and said, 'O Aḥmad, marry her, for this woman is one of the saints of God, and this is the speech of those who are sincere (in their faith)'".[14] So Aḥmad married her, but their relations seem to have remained Platonic. We are told elsewhere that she said to him, "I do not love thee with the love of a wife, I love thee with the love of a sister, and my desire towards thee is only to serve thee".[15] Certainly she acted generously towards him, for he tells how he married three other wives (not having taken to heart the advice of his master, it would seem) and Rábi'a used to cook good things for him and treat him well and say, "Go with your food and your cheerful company to your wives".[16] At the time when she was cooking the food, she would say to her husband, "Eat from this food, for none of it was cooked apart from praise (*i.e.* I was praising God all the time I was cooking)"[17] – a story which calls to mind Brother Lawrence.

She was noted for her prayers and her fasts. She used to spend the whole night in prayer, and wore herself out with ascetic practices, so that her husband and her friends were distressed at the effect upon her.[18]

Among the sayings attributed to her is one pointing to the exclusive claim of God to the service of His chosen: "If the servant is obedient, God makes him look beyond his work and he occupies himself with Him to the exclusion of His creatures".[19]

She is reported to have said:

> I never hear the call to prayer, without remembering the trumpet-call of the Day of Resurrection, and I never see the snow without remembering the fluttering of the records (*i.e.* the record of their deeds given into the hands of those who are to be judged),[20] and I never see a swarm of locusts without remembering the Assembly (for the Last Judgement).[21]

It is said that she used to see the Jinns and the houris quite plainly, and she would say "I saw the houris (the heavenly spouses awarded to good Muslims in Paradise) and they used to veil themselves from me with their garments".[22]

She was famed for her attainment of the mystic states (*aḥwál*). Sometimes passionate desire and love took possession of her, sometimes intimacy[23] (with the Divine) and sometimes fear.

When the state of love took possession of her, she used to say:

> My Beloved – there is none like unto Him, and
> none shares my heart with Him,
> My Beloved is absent from my sight and my person,
> but He is not absent from my heart.

Her husband related that when she was under the influence of fear he heard her saying:

> My provision is small, I do not see it to be
> sufficient for me,
> But do I weep for that, or because Thou art so far from me?
> Wilt Thou burn me with fire, O Goal of my desire?
> This is my hope from Thee, this is what makes me fear.[24]

One day her husband called to her and she did not answer him; then, after a while, she answered him and said, "What prevented me from answering you, was that my heart was filled with joy in God, and I was unable to answer you".[25]

Among her miracles, such as the majority of Muslim saints are credited with, her husband relates that one day there was a bowl before her and she said, "Take away this basin, for I see written on it that the Commander of the Faithful, Hárún al-Rashíd, is dead". Inquiries were made; on that same day Harún al-Rashíd had died.[26]

Rábi'a bint Ismá'íl was held in high respect among the Ṣúfís of her time and they used to consult her and to seek information from her about the mystic states.[27] She may claim to be one of the earliest of Muslim mystics, since, as we have noted above,[28] asceticism rather than mysticism was the characteristic of the Ṣúfís of this early period.

Rábi'a of Syria is said to have died in AH 135, and she was buried at the top of Mount Tor near Jerusalem. It is said that she was the first to be buried there, and Ibn Khallikán says that her tomb was an object of pilgrimage in the Middle Ages.[29]

Of this Rábi'a, Abú Ṭálib says that her position among the people of Syria was comparable to that of Rábi'a al-'Adawiyya among the people of Baṣra.[30]

Another famous woman ascetic of the early period was Mu'ádha al-'Adawiyya, who was contemporary with Rábi'a al-'Adawiyya, and among her associates. She was the daughter of 'Abdallah al-'Adawí and was surnamed Umm al-Ṣahbá, and was among the devotees of Baṣra. Jámí says of her that, from humility, for forty years she never lifted up her face to the sky. She never ate anything by day, nor did she sleep by night. Her friends said to her, "Will you not do much harm to yourself?" But she said, "No harm will come to me; I have transferred the sleep of the night to the day, and eating from the day to the night".[31] It was related of her by Muḥammad b. Fuḍayl that when day broke, Mu'ádha used to say, "This is the day in which I shall die", and she did not sleep until evening, and when night fell, she said, "This is the night in which I shall die", and she did not sleep until morning came. When the cold weather came, she used to dress in thin garments so that the cold should prevent her from sleeping. Her woman-servant related that Mu'ádha used to pass the night in prayer and if sleep overcame her, she rose and walked about in her court-yard, saying, "O my soul, sleep is before thee. If thou hadst died, how long would have been thy sleep in the tomb!" And she would be thus until the morning came.

She used to pray six hundred *rak'as* each day and night and she used to say: "I wonder at the eye which sleeps, knowing the length of the sleep in the grave".

Mu'ádha was no celibate, but had a son and a husband, who both went out on a military expedition, and the father said to his son, "O my son, go forward and fight, that I may be content with thee", and he flung himself on the unbelievers and fought until he was killed. Then his father advanced and did likewise.

The women came together to his wife Mu'ádha (to console her), and she said, "Welcome, if you have come to congratulate me and if you have come with any other purpose, you may return whence you came".[32] From which we may gather that Mu'ádha was of the same Spartan type as the daughter of Abú Bakr, who would not suffer her son 'Abdallah to wear a shirt of mail when fighting in the cause of righteousness.

Of Mu'ádha we are told that after her husband's death she carried self-mortification so far that she never rested her head upon a bed until the day of her death.[33]

Mu'ádha is a faithful representative of the school of Ḥasan al-Baṣrí, concerned with asceticism rather than mysticism, and believing that the mortifying of the flesh in this world offered the greatest hope of salvation in the next. Hers would seem to have been the same grim faith as that of Ḥasan, living always under the shadow of fear of the wrath to come, and her acquaintance with Rábi'a al-'Adawiyya does not seem to have led her to seek the way to God through love, or to find that joy in the service of the Beloved characteristic of both Rábi'a of Syria and Rábi'a of Baṣra.

An ascetic who was famed chiefly for her godly sorrow was Sha'wána, of whom Jámí writes:

> She was a Persian and dwelt in Ubulla. She had a beautiful voice and used to discourse in melodious tones, also she used to recite many things to the ascetics and disciples and Ṣúfís who came to listen in her assembly (*i.e.* the gathering of the Ṣúfís together round a well-known *pír* or teacher, such as Sha'wána evidently was).
>
> She was among the women zealous in service, who feared God, who wept and made others to weep. Her friends used to say to her, "We are afraid that you will

> lose the sight of your eyes from much weeping", but she said, "Verily to be blind in this world through much weeping is better, to my mind, than to be blind in the next through the fires of Hell".[34]

One of her associates, Yaḥyá b. Bustam, says:

> I used to be present at Sha'wána's assembly and I used to see what she did in the matter of lamentation and weeping, and I said to a friend of mine, "Suppose we come to her when she ceases and tell her to have pity on herself", and he said, "You are right", and we came to her and said, "If only you would have pity on yourself and abate this weeping somewhat, and then you would have more strength to do what you want". She wept, then she said, "I would that I might weep till the fount of my tears were dried up; then would I weep blood till there should remain no drop of blood in my members. I must weep, I must weep," and she did not cease weeping until she lost consciousness.

And he goes on to say, "We rose up and parted from her and we left her in that state, and she was crying out, 'O ye dead, sons of the dead, and brethren of the dead'".[35]

She used to say, "Let the one who is not able to weep pity those who weep, for the one who weeps, weeps only because he knows himself and his sins and that towards which he is going".

Again, she used to say that "the eyes which are prevented from beholding the Beloved, and yet are desirous of looking upon Him, cannot be fit (for that Vision) without weeping", and her friends said that this sorrow overcame her to such an extent that she neglected prayer and worship.

In a dream there appeared to her one who said:

Shed tears when you are sorrowful: for your sorrow
will heal those in grief.
Be diligent and arise and fast continually, wasting
away (with emaciation),
For emaciation is one of the works of the obedient.

She returned to obedience and used to intone these verses, weeping, and the women weeping with her.[36]

Among her prayers is the following: "O my God, Thou knowest that the one thirsting for Thy love is never satisfied",[37] and al-Ghazálí tells how Sha'wána in her prayers used to say:

> O my God, how great is my desire to meet with Thee and how great is my hope of Thy reward. Thou art gracious, there is no disappointment from Thee, the Hope of all who hope; there is no frustration with Thee, Thou Desire of all who yearn. O my God, if I am unworthy of Thee and my works do not bring me near unto Thee, yet my weakness has made confession of my sins, and if Thou dost forgive – Who has more power (to forgive) than Thyself, and if Thou dost punish – Who is more just to perform it than Thyself? O my Lord, my tears have flowed for my soul in looking upon her, but there remains for her the beauty of looking upon Thee, and woe be to my soul if she rejoices not therein. O my God, let not faith fail me all the days of my life, nor cut off from me Thy benevolence after my death. I have hoped that He Whose goodness has followed me all the days of my life will be near me with His pardon at the hour of death. O my Lord, how should I despair of the beauty of the Vision of Thyself after my death, when Thou hast bestowed upon me nought but good in my lifetime? O God, if my sins have made me afraid, verily my love to Thee has pro-

> tected me (or brought me near unto Thee). O my Lord, if it were not for the sins I have committed, I would not have feared Thy chastisement, and if I had not known Thy grace, I should not have hoped for Thy reward.[38]

One who served her said, "From the time my eyes fell upon Sha'wána, I never turned towards the world, because of her blessed influence, and I never despised one of the faithful".[39]

It is said that in her old age Fuḍayl b. 'Iyáḍ used to visit her and discuss with her, and once when he asked for her prayers on his behalf, she said to him: "O Fuḍayl, is there anything between you and God, so that if I pray, that will be the cause of an answer?" *i.e.* is there any hindrance to your approaching God directly, that you ask for a mediator?

Fuḍayl, when he heard her reply, burst out sobbing and then fainted away.[40]

Sha'wána may certainly claim a place among the mystics as well as among the ascetics, for her prayers quoted above show plainly that she followed the way of love, like Rábi'a, and that her eyes were not only blinded by tears of penitence, but dazzled by the radiant glory of the Beloved, and that what she looked for after this life was the vision of her Lord in His perfect beauty. Her prayer shows also that in her life she was in conscious communion with her Friend, feeling herself to be in His personal presence, a relationship to which the Ṣúfís of the earliest ascetic school hardly dared to aspire.

It was undoubtedly the recognition that she was possessed of the mystic gnosis, and truly walked with God, that made her an acknowledged teacher and spiritual guide to the Ṣúfís of her day.

Another great saint, but of a different type from these early mystics, was Nafísa, great-granddaughter of Ḥasan, son of the Khalifa 'Alí, who was born at Mecca in the year AH 145 and brought up at Medína, to a life spent in good works and the worship of God. She married Isháq, son of the Imám Ja'far al-Ṣádiq, and bore him two children, al-Qásim and Umm Kulthúm.[41] After her marriage, she went to Egypt with her cousin Sakína al-Madfúna, and settled down to live not far from the Khalifa's palace in Cairo. Like the other ascetics of Islám, she used to fast all day and spend the night in prayer.

She was reputed to know the Qur'án and the commentaries by heart and was so versed in religious knowledge that even her great contemporary, the Imám al-Sháfi'í, used to come and listen to her discourses and enter into discussions with her; the degree of his respect for the scholarship of this saintly woman and for her sanctity also, may be judged from the fact that he used to pray with her the special prayers for Ramaḍán.[42]

She was famed throughout Egypt and wherever she went her reputation followed her and she gained the full approbation of all, both individuals and the people generally, who revered her for her good works, her frequent pilgrimages, her lengthy fasts and her nights spent in prayer.[43] She died in Cairo in the month of Ramaḍán, in the year AH 208.

One of her biographers relates that when she was at the point of death, and, as usual, fasting, those with her tried to compel her to break her fast, but she refused, saying, "This would seem a strange thing to me. For thirty years I have been asking God that I should meet with Him when I was fasting, and shall I break my fast now? This shall not be." Then she repeated the Súra al-An'ám and when she reached the part where God said, "For them is an abode of peace with their Lord",[44] she passed away.[45]

The same writer tells us that during her lifetime she had dug her grave with her own hands and had descended into it and prayed and there repeated the whole Qur'án six thousand times. When Nafísa died, the people assembled from all the villages and towns in the neighbourhood and lighted candles that night and the sound of the wailing for the dead was heard from every house in Cairo, and they prayed over her body, while many bore witness that they had seen none like her. Then she was buried in the grave which she had dug in her own house. Up to the time of the writer, and even to the present time, her shrine has been a place of pilgrimage for travellers from afar.[46] Her husband, indeed, wished to convey her body to Medína, for burial in the sacred city, but the people of Cairo begged that she should be buried among them.[47]

Many miracles, showing her charity towards others, were attributed to Nafísa. The story is told of how one year the Nile failed to rise in flood at the usual time, and the people were in great distress, fearing that for lack of water for their crops they would perish from famine, and in this extremity they came to the saint, appealing for her help. She gave them her veil and bade them cast it into the river, and when they had done so, immediately the river rose in an unusually high flood and the people were saved.

Another miraculous story related of the Lady Nafísa tells how, in a neighbour's house, there was a poor Jewish girl, completely crippled by arthritis. One day her parents, having to leave her to go to the market, asked their saintly neighbour to take charge of the invalid. Nafísa came and prayed beside her and through the saint's prayer the sick girl regained the use of her limbs, and both she and her parents hastened to embrace the religion of their benefactress.

The biographer of Abú Sa'íd b. Abí al-Khayr gives an account of a woman saint contemporary with the Shaykh, named Íshí Nílí, who lived in Níshápúr. He says: "She was very devout and an ascetic, and members of the great families and the worthies of Níshápúr used to come and visit her and to gain blessing from her. For a period of forty years she had not gone out of her house nor gone to the warm baths. She had a nurse who always waited upon her and when Shaykh Abú Sa'íd came to Níshápúr, and the fame of him was spread about the city, to the effect that a Shaykh had come from Mayhana, whose miracles were evident, who was speaking in the assembly and who had an answer to give to anyone amongst the congregation who had some problem on his mind, Íshí said one day to this nurse: 'Rise up and go to the assembly of the Shaykh and take note of what he says, so that when you return, you may repeat it to me.' The nurse came into the Shaykh's congregation while the Shaykh was preaching, and she could not remember the words of his discourse, but the Shaykh recited these verses:

I have a *dáng*[48] and a half almost; I have bought two
bottles (of wine) – not quite full,
On my lute there remains neither treble string nor bass,
To whom (except me) should you talk of
Kalandar-ship and ecstasy?

"When the nurse returned, Íshí asked what the Shaykh had said; she remembered only these verses and repeated them. Íshí said, 'Go and wash your mouth (because you have told a lie). Are these words of the kind that ascetics and wise men use?' The nurse went and washed her mouth.

"Now this Ishí was accustomed to make eye-salve for the people and to give it away to them. That night, while asleep, she saw something horrible in a dream; she sprang up and both of her eyes felt painful, and although she used salve, they did not recover. She had recourse to all the physicians, but could find no cure. For twenty days and nights she was complaining of this pain.

"One night in a dream she saw (one who said), 'If you wish your eyes to be cured, go and seek to satisfy the Shaykh of Mayhana and gain his precious favour'. So the next day Íshí took a thousand *dirhams* and put them in her purse and gave them to her nurse and said, 'Go to the Shaykh and when he has finished his discourse, give them to him'.

"When the Shaykh was free, the nurse came to him and greeted him, and placed the silver before him. It was the custom of the Shaykh, when the assembly was over, to have a novice bring him a piece of dry bread and a toothpick. The Shaykh used to eat that bread and use the toothpick. The Shaykh was using the toothpick when the nurse gave him that money. When she wished to return (to her mistress), the Shaykh said, 'O nurse, come hither and take this toothpick and give it to your mistress and tell her to stir it in water and wash her eyes with that water, so that her outward eyes may be cured and tell her to put out of her heart contempt and enmity towards this sect, so that her inward eye may also be healed'. The nurse came and told Íshí, who followed the advice of the Shaykh and washed the toothpick in water and with that water bathed her eyes and immediately they were cured.

"The next day she rose up and took all she possessed in the way of jewels and ornaments and raiment and came to the Shaykh and said, 'O Shaykh, I have repented, and cast out contempt and enmity from my breast'. The Shaykh said, 'May it be blessed (to you)', and bade them take her to the mother of Abú Ṭáhir, that she might be invested with the patched robe (of the Dervishes) and the Shaykh bade her choose the service of this order that she might be esteemed in this world and the next. Íshí went to carry out the Shaykh's behest and donned the patched robe and occupied herself in the service of the devout women of that order and all that she had – ornaments and property and all else – she gave away and reached a high degree in the Way and became a leader among the Ṣúfís."[49]

Other saintly women there were, famous for their good deeds and their charity, or for their wisdom or their writings, some devoting themselves to religious learning and known as Shaykhas.

Such was the famous Shuḥda, daughter of Abú Naṣr Aḥmad Ibn Al-Faraj b. 'Umar al-Ibarí, who is frequently mentioned by biographers of the saints. Ibn Khallikán gives an account of her in his *Biographical Dictionary*.[50] Her family belonged to Dínawar in Persia, but she herself was born and died in Baghdád. She was surnamed Fakhr al-Nisá' (the Glory of Women) and al-Kátiba (the woman scribe). By her learning she gained a great reputation and was considered one of the first scholars of the age; she wrote a beautiful hand[51] and gave instruction to large numbers of students in the Traditions, which she herself had learnt from the highest authorities; thus she formed a link between the traditionists of the rising generation and those of the past.

She died in 1178, aged upwards of ninety years, and was buried outside the Abraz Gate of Baghdád.

Another of these Shaykhas, or religious teachers, was Zaynab, daughter of Abú al-Qásim 'Abd al-Raḥmán al-Shárí, the Ṣúfí. She was born at Naisapúr in AD 1130 and died there in AD 1218–19. She was esteemed as a woman of great learning who had studied under the best scholars of her time and from them she obtained certificates authorising her to teach these subjects, especially the knowledge of the Traditions, which she had studied under their tuition. Among these masters was Abú al-Qásim, the Qur'án reader, and 'Abd al-Mun'im al-Qushayrí. She was granted licences to teach also from the *ḥáfiz* 'Abd al-Gháfir al-Fárisí and the commentator al-Zamakhsharí (*ob.* 1143–4), the learned author of the Kashsháf. In her turn she granted licences to her pupils, among whom was her biographer, Ibn Khallikán.[52]

Ibn Baṭṭúṭa gives several references to Shaykhas of this type, who were accepted as teachers and whose opinion was sought by the scholars of their time. When he was travelling in Syria, he was given a licence and permission to teach in Damascus by the pious Shaykha, Umm Muḥammad 'Á'isha bint Muḥammad b. Muslim b. Saláma al-Hawání, and the virtuous Shaykha Ruḥla al-Dunya (the goal of everyone's journey), Zaynab bint Kamál al-Dín Aḥmad b. 'Abd al-Raḥím b. 'Abd al-Wáḥid b. Aḥmad, of Jerusalem. This was in AD 1326.[53] In June of the following year, Ibn Baṭṭúṭa was in Baghdád, where he listened to the Imám Siráj al-Dín, explaining the *Musnad* of Abú Muḥammad 'Abd Alláh b. 'Abd al-Raḥmán, and in his explanation the Shaykh said, "We have been instructed in it by the virtuous Shaykha, of recognised authority, the mistress of kings, Fáṭima, daughter of the upright Táj al-Dín, Abú al-Ḥasan 'Alí b. 'Alí b. Abí al-Badr". She related the chain of witnesses through whom the tradition had been transmitted.[54]

At a much later period, we find a very interesting figure, among the women saints of Islám, of a type distinct from those already mentioned, an Indian princess who lived in the seventeenth century of our era. This was Fáṭima, best known as Jahán-Árá,[55] the favourite daughter of the Mughal emperor Sháh Jahán and his empress Mumtáz Maḥall (to whose memory her devoted husband erected the famous Táj Maḥall). Her brother was Dárá Shakúh (who wrote a biography of the saints, called the *Ship of the Saints*) and the two appear to have been bound together not only by the tie of strong affection, but also by a common seeking after God and a desire for union with Him. Dárá Shakúh became a novice in the Ṣúfí Way under the spiritual direction of the famous teacher and saint, Mullá Sháh,[56] and impressed by her brother's account of him, the princess also desired to be admitted as a novice. An account of Mullá Sháh's relations with the princess is given by his biographer, Tawakkul Beg,[57] himself a disciple of the saint.

The princess wrote to the master several letters expressing her desire to renounce the world and enter upon the mystic Way: he read them all, but left them unanswered for a time. Being convinced at last that she was sincere and determined, he decided to give her his support and consented to her initiation, though he had not even seen her.[58] The princess herself wrote an account of her initiation in a work entitled, "Risála-i ṣáḥibiyya", from which Tawakkul Beg quotes. She describes how she had offered her faith to Mullá Sháh and had begged him to be her spiritual guide, and how he had consented to her initiation according to the rule of his fraternity. She tells of the deep impression made upon her by her first sight of the blessed form of the master, from her hiding-place behind the *purdah*, when Mullá Sháh paid a visit to her father, then staying in Kashmír. She says that her faith in him became a thousand times more fervent than it had been, and ecstasy filled her soul. The following day her brother, acting for the saint, initiated her into the Way, which required the recital of the formula of the Qádír dervishes and of the order of Mullá Sháh. She goes on to tell how afterwards she repaired to the chapel of her palace and remained there until midnight praying, and then went back to her apartments and became absorbed in contemplation. There she had a vision, as she believed, of the Prophet and the saints, and, filled with gratitude at this sign of the Divine favour, when she came to herself, she prostrated herself before the throne of Absolute Being. There she poured out her soul in thankfulness to God for the "immeasurable happiness" He had vouchsafed to a "weak and unworthy woman".[59] She offers thanks for having been allowed to conceive of the Absolute Being in the way which she had always desired. Those who do not attain to the knowledge of God are not worthy to rank as human beings, they are still brutish. The one who attains to this knowledge represents the perfection of created things. His personal and individual existence is absorbed into the absolute existence; he becomes as a drop in the ocean, a mote in the sunbeams, a part (swallowed up) in the whole.

The saint, raised to this state of exaltation, whether man or woman, is always the most perfect of beings. God can grant this grace to whom He will.

The princess became a true mystic and we are told that she reached such a degree of perfection that she attained to pure union with God and to the gnosis which comes from the vision of God.[60]

Mullá Sháh had a great affection for all his pupils, but he felt a special attachment to the princess and even said that her degree of mystic knowledge was so great that she would be worthy to act on his behalf as his deputy.

We hear of a woman mystic of the same ecstatic type, and of much the same period, who was well known in Morocco, Umm 'Abd Allah 'Á'isha bint M. b. 'Abd Allah, to whom the Divine revelation was vouchsafed, through the guidance of her brother, Sayyid Aḥmad, in the year 1655–6. She was the first of his followers to receive this blessing. She was seized by an overwhelming illumination, and a mighty ecstasy took possession of her and deprived her of her senses. It is said that she gave permission to her husband to marry (another) and gave him the choice between that or having patience with her present state, and she begged him to excuse her (for this action). She spent all her fortune and gave it as alms for the sake of God, and divided it all among her relatives, until nothing remained. Her husband complained of her action to the Sayyid Qásim and said to him: "What am I to do with her? She is like one who is on fire and the fire catches her garments and she begins to throw them from her without discrimination." What he wished to say was that the fire of (the Divine) love had consumed the ties which attached her to this world, as the fire consumes the clothing which clings to the body of the one it overtakes, and he has to throw them off so that they are scattered without discrimination on his part.

She had an inclination towards solitude, and when she sat among other women, God cast her into a trance-like state so that she did not know what was said. She had a strong affection for her brother, Sayyid Aḥmad, and was unable to refrain from looking at him. Her husband, Abú 'Abd Allah Sayyid M. 'Ásim al-Andalusí, at first was unable to attain to the degree of sanctity which he beheld in her, and the reserve she showed towards him as well as to the attractions of the world, but one day an ecstasy seized him and he grew faint and lost consciousness. He was carried away, by the order of Sayyid Aḥmad, and brought in to her, and she thanked God fervently that he had attained to the same state as herself, and so her mind was at rest concerning him.

She died in 1660 and was buried the same day under the dome of her father's tomb.[61]

The Turks have produced several poetesses of note and among them a Ṣúfí poetess, Sidqí, daughter of Qamr Muḥammad, one of the learned men of Constantinople in the reign of Sulṭan Muḥammad IV. Sidqí appears to have lived the celibate life; she died in 1703 and is buried beside her father near the Adrianople Gate, near the convent of Amír Bukhárá. Her poetry is full of mysticism and of the pantheism of the later Ṣúfís.[62] She wrote two mystical poems called *The Treasury of Lights* and *The Collection of Information*, and among her poems is the following Gazel:

He who union with the Lord gains, more delight
desireth not!
He who looks on charms of fair one, other sight
desireth not.
Pang of love is lover's solace, eagerly he seeks therefor,
Joys he in it, balm or salve for yonder blight, desireth not.
Paradise he longs not after, nor doth aught
beside regard;
Bower and Garden, Mead, and Youth, and Húrí bright,
desireth not.
From the hand of Power Unbounded draineth he the
Wine of Life,
Aye inebriate with Knowledge, learning's light,
desireth not.
He who loves the Lord is monarch of an empire, such
that he –
King of Inward Mysteries – Sulymán's might,
desireth not.
Thou art Sulṭan of my heart, aye, Soul of my soul e'en
art Thou;
Thou art Soul enow, and Sidqí other plight
desireth not.[63]

Latest in point of time, but with an equal claim to a place among the women saints of Islám, is Zarrín-Táj, known as Qurrat al-'Ayn, the Bábí teacher and poetess, who was martyred in AD 1852. Though Bábíism, in its full development, diverged so widely from orthodox Islám that its adherents could hardly be reckoned as Muslims at all, yet it originated in the Shí'a quest for the hidden Imám, the Manifestation of God in the flesh, whom Mirza Muḥammad 'Alí, the Báb, declared himself to be, and the position of the Báb, before this declaration, corresponded to that of the Ṣúfí Shaykh or Pír. With regard to the relationship between Bábíism and Ṣúfism, it is stated by an authoritative writer that "Ṣúfís and mystics regard

Bábíism as a systematised and organised Ṣúfism, essential in its doctrines with their own pantheistic beliefs; and consider its fundamental teaching to be the divine spark latent in man, by the cultivation of which he can attain to the degree of *faná fi'allah* or 'Annihilation in God', wherein he may cry out, like Manṣúr-i-Ḥalláj, *'Ana'l-Haqq'*, 'I am the Truth', or 'I am God'".[64]

In her fearless proclamation of her faith, as in the heroic witness of her death, Qurrat al-'Ayn showed herself a worthy successor of the great Ṣúfí martyr. She was the daughter of Ḥájí Mullá Ṣáliḥ, known as the sage of Qazrín, the erudite doctor.

> She, according to what is related, was skilled in diverse arts, amazed the understandings and thoughts of the most eminent masters by her eloquent dissertations on the exegesis and tradition of the Perspicuous Book, and was a mighty sign in the doctrines of the glorious Shaykh of Aḥsá.[65] At the Supreme Shrines (*i.e.* Kerbela and Nejef), she borrowed light on matters divine from the lamp of Káẓim (*i.e.* Ḥájí Sayyid Káẓim of Resht, spiritual director of the Báb) and freely sacrificed her life in the way of the Báb. She discussed and disputed with the doctors and sages, loosing her tongue to establish her doctrine. Such fame did she acquire that most people who were scholars or mystics sought to hear her speech and were eager to become acquainted with her powers of speculation and deduction. She had a brain full of tumultuous ideas, and thoughts vehement and restless. In many places she triumphed over the contentious, expounding the most subtle questions. . . . In short, in elocution she was the calamity of the age, and in ratiocination the trouble of the world. Of fear or timidity there was no trace in her heart, nor had the admonitions of the kindly-disposed any profit or fruit for her. Although she was of (such as are) damsels

> (meet) for the bridal bower, yet she wrested pre-eminence from stalwart men, and continued to strain the feet of steadfastness until she yielded up her life at the sentence of the mighty doctors in Teherán.[66]

During the lifetime of Ḥájí Sayyid Káẓim of Resht (mentioned above), Qurrat al-'Ayn visited Kerbela, where she became acquainted not only with Sayyid Káẓim himself, but with many of his chief followers, including Mullá Ḥusayn of Bushraweyh, and to him she wrote begging that he would inform her if he should succeed in finding the spiritual guide whom they were expecting. Ḥusayn, on his conversion to Bábíism, handed this letter to the Báb, who recognised the rare qualities of the writer and included her among the eighteen Letters of the Living (*Ḥurúfát ḥayy)* who made up the "First Unity" of the Bábí hierarchy.

Qurrat al-'Ayn continued for some time at Kerbela, where, seated behind a curtain, a precaution made desirable by her marvellous beauty, she used to lecture and preach to the disciples of the late Sayyid Káẓim. The governor sought to arrest her, and she went to Baghdád and there defended her creed and conduct before the chief Muftí with great ability. The question of whether she was to be allowed to continue her teaching was submitted first to the Pasha of Baghdád and then to the central Government, and she was ordered to leave Turkish territory. On her journey from Baghdád to Kirmansháh and Hamadán, she continued to preach and made several converts to Bábíism. Some Bábís disapproved and asked the Báb if it was seemly for a woman to preach publicly to men. The Báb not only sanctioned her preaching and applauded her zeal, but gave her the title of Janáb-i-Ṭáhira, and her high position in the Bábí church became uncontested.[67]

She was present at the first assembly of the Bábís as a distinct party, held at Badasht, accompanied by a bodyguard of disciples, the most zealous of all the Bábís present, over whom she exercised absolute authority. She was given the task of encouraging the faithful and stirring up the lukewarm, and preached from an extempore pulpit, with her followers around her. She declared that the time had come when the doctrine of the Báb should cover the face of the earth, and God should be worshipped in accordance with this doctrine. A new light had arisen, a new law was to be born, a new book was to replace the old. Such great things could not be accomplished without suffering and sacrifice on the part of the generation charged with achievement, and it was not too much that women themselves, sharing the labours of their husbands and brothers, should accept all their perils. It was no longer the time for them to be shut up in the depth of the *ḥarím* and await passively what their menfolk might be able to accomplish. Leaving on one side social rules, the modesty of peaceful times, even their duties, and their native weakness, and above all the timidity so natural to their souls, they ought to show themselves, in the most absolute sense, the companions of men, to follow them and fall with them on the field of martyrdom.

Her hearers were moved to tears and cried out: "Ay jahán" (O my life), "Ay ṭáhira" (O pure one), in beating their breasts. Orthodox Muslims who were present, drawn by curiosity, became Bábís. This discourse not only produced a great effect at the time, but it was repeated and commented upon by all who heard it and so reached others.[68] At the time of the Mázandarán insurrection in 1849, Qurrat al-'Ayn was given up to the Government authorities and sent to Teherán, where she was placed in custody and remained a prisoner till her death. Her gaoler, Maḥmúd Khán, came completely under the power of her eloquence and zeal and, hoping to secure her release, he begged her to deny her faith, but instead, she foretold both his death and her own, saying:

> Do not hope that I shall deny my faith, even in appearance for one moment, for an aim so childish as that of conserving for a few days more a transient form which has no value. No, if I am questioned, and I shall be, I

> shall have the happiness of giving my life for God. Listen, Maḥmúd Khán, now, to what I am going to tell you, and tomorrow my death will serve as a sign that I am not deceiving you. The master whom you serve will not reward you for your zeal; on the contrary, you will perish cruelly, by his order. Before you die, try to have raised your soul to the knowledge of the truth.

This prophecy, the utterance of which is well authenticated, was fulfilled in both cases. Qurrat al-'Ayn was asked, and refused to abjure her faith, and met a cruel and lingering death with superhuman fortitude.[69]

She was famed as a poetess, though little of her work is surviving, at least under her own name, and Prof. Browne ascribes this to the fact that she was too well known as a Bábí for her poems to bear her name, though he was told that many verses written by her were actually among the favourite songs of the people. A *Ghazal* which is definitely attributed to Qurrat al-'Ayn is written in the spirit of the Ṣúfís who preceded her. It runs as follows:

The thralls of yearning love constrain in the bands of pain and calamity
These broken-hearted lovers of Thine to yield their lives in their zeal for Thee.
Though with sword in hand my Darling stand with intent to slay, though I sinless be,
If it pleases Him, this tyrant's whim, I am well content with His tyranny.
As in sleep I lay at the dawn of day that cruel Charmer came to me,
And in the grace of His form and face the dawn of the morn I seemed to see.
The musk of Cathay might perfume gain from the scent those fragrant tresses rain,

While his eyes demolish a faith in vain attacked by the
pagans of Tartary.
With you, who contemn both love and wine for the
hermit's cell and the zealot's shrine,
What can I do? For our faith divine you hold as a thing
of infamy.
The tangled curls of thy darling's hair, and thy saddle
and steed are thine only care;
In thy heart the Infinite hath no share, nor the thought
of the poor man's poverty.
Sikandar's pomp and display be thine, the Kalendar's
habit and way be mine;
That, if it please thee, I resign, while this, though bad,
is enough for me.
The country of "I" and "We" forsake; thy home in
Annihilation make,
Since fearing not this step to take, thou shalt gain the
highest felicity.[70]

Here is the complete surrender of the lover to the will of the Beloved, the renunciation of this world and of the self, and finally the absorption in the Divine and the abiding life in Him, characteristic of the teaching of the Ṣúfís from Rábi'a onwards.

Such women as these whom we have mentioned who, by the holiness of their lives and their intimate communion with the Divine, can rightly claim a place among the saints, as well as those whose religious enthusiasm took the form of studying and teaching the sacred lore of Islám, must be reckoned among the religious leaders of their time, and had their definite contribution to make towards the development and the vitality of the religion of Islám.

1 Part One, Chapter I.
2 *Iḥyá*, IV, p. 353.
3 See Part Three, Chapter XIV, pp. 212–13.

4 Translated by C. D. Cobham in *Exerpta Cypria*, pp. 374 ff. Cf. also *J.R.A.S.* Jan. 1897, "Story of Umm Ḥarám".

5 Referring to her journey to Cyprus in the holy war and her death there, whereby she was awarded the crown of martyrdom.

6 *Excerpta Cypria*, p. 374.

7 *Op. cit.* pp. 375, 376.

8 Baládhurí, *Kitáb al-Futúḥ*, ed. de Goeje, p. 153.

9 *Op. cit.* p. 377.

10 Abú al-Maḥásin, *al-Nujúm al-Záhira*, ed. Juynboll, I, p. 95.

11 *Excerpta Cypria*, p. 377.

12 Yáfi'í, *Rawḍ al-Ríyáḥín*, p. 140. Ibn al-Jawzí, "Ṣafwa al-Ṣafwa", fol. 142 b.

13 Aḥmad b. Abí al-Ḥawwárí was born in AH 164 and died in AH 246, and could not therefore have been the husband of this Rábi'a if she died in AH 135. But as he is stated by all the Ṣúfí writers to have been her husband, it is possible that the date of her death is incorrect.

14 Abú Ṭálib, *op. cit.* II, p. 247.

15 "Siyar al-Ṣáliḥát", fol. 39 a.

16 Abú Ṭálib, *op. cit.* p. 247.

17 Jámí, *Nafaḥát al-Uns*, p. 719.

18 Ibn al-Jawzí, *op. cit.* fol. 143 b.

19 Munáwí, "Kawákib", fol. 52.

20 See above, Part One, Chapter II, p. 30.

21 Sha'rání, *Al-Ṭabaqát al-Kubrá*, p. 87. Attributed also to Rábi'a of Baṣra.

22 Munáwí, *op. cit.* fol. 52.

23 See above, Part Two, pp. 116 ff.

24 Jámí, *op. cit.* p. 720.

25 Munáwí, *op. cit.* fol. 52.

26 Jámí, *op. cit.*, *loc. cit.* As Hárún reigned AD 786–809 this would put the date of Rábi'a bint Ismá'íl considerably later than the one usually given, and make it possible for her to be the wife of Aḥmad.

27 Abú Ṭálib, *op. cit.* II, p. 247.
28 Part Two, p. 100.
29 Cf. later, pp. 213–14.
30 *Qút al-Qulúb*, II, p. 247.
31 Jámí, *op. cit.* p. 718.
32 "Siyar al-Ṣáliḥát", fol. 24.
33 Sha'rání, *op. cit.* p. 86.
34 Jámí, *op. cit.* p. 718. Munáwí, *op. cit.* fol. 32 b.
35 Al-Ghazálí, *Iḥyá*, IV, p. 353. Munáwí, *op. cit.* fol. 32 b.
36 Jámí, *op. cit.* p. 718.
37 Sha'rání, *op. cit.* p. 88.
38 *Iḥyá*, IV, p. 355.
39 Sha'rání, *op. cit.*, *loc. cit.*
40 Jámí, *op. cit.* p. 718.
41 Sha'rání, *op. cit.* p. 88.
42 Ibn Khallikán, p. 90, No. 777. Sha'rání, *op. cit.*, *loc. cit.*
43 Munáwí, *op. cit.* fol. 136 b.
44 Súra VI, 127.
45 Munáwí, *op. cit.*, *loc. cit.*
46 *Op. cit.* fol. 136.
47 Maqrízí, *Al-Khiṭaṭ*, p. 441. Taghribardi, *al-Nujúm al-Záhira*, I, p. 599.
48 A small silver coin, worth one-sixth of a *dirham*.
49 *Asrár al-Tawḥíd*, pp. 91, 92.
50 Tr. De Slane, I, p. 625.
51 Arabic handwriting is a fine art, and to this day is taught in schools by *shaykhs*, and even in girls' schools the teaching of it is rarely entrusted to a woman. A man who is highly skilled in the art may become a Professor of Calligraphy.
52 *Biographical Dictionary*, tr. De Slane, I, p. 551.
53 Ibn Baṭṭúṭa, *Tuhfa al-Nuzzár*, I, p. 253.
54 *Op. cit.* II, p. 110. Cf. Majdí Pasha, *Bulletin de l'Institut Egyptien*, 5th Series, tome X, 1916, pp. 327–58, where he gives an account of nineteen of these Muslim Shaykhas.

55 *Dabistán*, p. 329.
56 Died at Lahore, 1661. Cf. Latíf, *History of Lahore*, p. 59.
57 In the "Neskhah-i Aḥwál Sháhí".
58 Tawakkul Beg, *op. cit.* fols. 41 a, 41 b.
59 *Op. cit.* fols. 42 a, 42 b.
60 *Op. cit.* fol. 43 b. For a description of her tomb, cf. *Archaeological Survey of India* (1862–5), vol. I, pp. 230, 231, and *A.S.* (1902–3), p. 27.
61 M. b. al-Ṭayyib al-Qádirí, *Nashr al-Mathání*, Fez, AH 1310, I, p. 227.
62 Garnett, *Women of Turkey*, p. 538. Gibb, *Ottoman Poems*, p. 212.
63 Tr. Gibb, *op. cit.* p. 111.
64 E. G. Browne, *J.R.A.S.* 1889, p. 504.
65 Founder of the Shaykhí school of theology, with which in its origin the Bábí movement was closely connected; its headquarters are at Kirmán.
66 *A Traveller's Narrative of the Episode of the Báb*, tr. and ed. by E. G. Browne, pp. 30–32.
67 E. G. Browne, *op. cit.* pp. 310, 311.
68 Gobineau, *Les Religions et les Philosophies dans l'Asie Centrale*, pp. 180–4.
69 E. G. Browne, *op. cit.* pp. 310 ff. Gobineau, *op. cit.* pp. 293 ff.
70 Translated from the Persian by E. G. Browne in A *Persian Anthology*, pp. 70, 71.

CHAPTER XIII

Celibacy and the Monastic Life

It is probable that the example set by their Christian sisters in the religious life first caused the women saints of Islám to realise the value of celibacy and the cloistered life for those who desired to follow the mystic Way and aspired to the Ṣúfí's goal of union with the Divine.

There was considerable opposition on the part of orthodox Islám to the ideal of asceticism and most of all to the doctrine of celibacy. In the Qur'án "monasticism" is condemned as being an innovation introduced by the Christians themselves, and not a Divine ordinance[1], and Abú Dáwúd, an uncompromising opponent of the Ṣúfí teachings, says that the Prophet declared, "There is no celibacy in Islám".[2] In the well-known Tradition related of 'Akkáf al-Hilálí, who was asked by the Prophet if he was married and said he was not, the Prophet said to him, "Then you are one of the followers of Satan, or one of the Christian monks. It so, go to them, but if you are one of us, then do as we do, for our *Sunna* includes marriage. The most wicked among you are your celibates and the most ignoble among your dead are your celibates. Woe be to you, 'Akkáf, (I adjure you) marry."[3]

In the same sense the Prophet is reported to have said, "The man who has no wife is very unfortunate", and, "The man who does not marry is none of mine".[4]

Another Tradition of the Prophet relating to this subject reports that he said, "One *rak'a* from a married man is better than seventy from the celibate".[5] Again, the Prophet is related to have said, "The curse of God be upon those men who live in celibacy and who say, 'We will not marry'. The curse of God be upon those women who remain unwed and say, 'We will not marry'."[6]

Al-Dhahabí records a Tradition dealing prophetically with this subject, according to which Muḥammad is reputed to have said,

"When three hundred and eighty years shall have passed over my community, then celibacy and the monastic life upon the tops of the mountains shall be lawful for them".[7] The Christian monks appear to have had a distinct preference for lofty situations for their monasteries, presumably because this made for solitude, and today in Syria almost every hill-top is occupied by a *Dayr* or convent. This preference evidently goes back to the time of the Prophet.[8]

A later Muslim writer, also opposed to asceticism, accuses women of choosing the celibate life for their own convenience and comfort, and being tempted thereto by Satan, who says to the religious-minded woman, "You are a woman devout and occupied with God, and if you do not marry you will be relieved from the matter of children and (be free) to go abroad, and your property will increase steadily, and your worship will be your sustenance", and the writer adds that such a woman is helped by other devout worshippers of God like herself, whom Satan has corrupted.[9]

On the other hand, Abú Ṭálib mentions that celibacy was favoured after the second century AH, apparently in order to avoid the responsibilities of marriage, for he says:

> Celibacy was approved and remaining unmarried was preferred in this nation at the end of this period, and it is reported that after AH 200, the one who had the least burden (the light-backed) was he who had no wife or child. In another tradition it is said that there came upon the people a period when a man was ruined by the hands of his wife and parents and children, who upbraided him with his poverty and put upon him what he was not able to bear and (so) he had recourse to the places which led him into debt and he was ruined.[10]

The Ṣúfís realised the advantage of celibacy for the mystic, and the same writer, giving his own views on celibacy and marriage, says:

> The best thing for the novice [*i.e.* the one who aspires to sainthood] in such times as these of ours, is to renounce marriage, in order to be safe against seduction, if he has been trained in virtue and if his soul does not urge him on to disobedience, and desire for women does not take possession of his heart, so as to distract his mind, or prevent him from continuous service, through the wandering of his thoughts and the distraction of his mind through the matter of women.[11]

Again, he expresses the view that if the disciple is inclined towards celibacy and can be satisfied with solitude, the peace which it brings is much to be desired, but if the disciple craves for marriage and is not safe from the claims of desire, then let him marry.[12] The Ṣúfí, Abú Sulaymán al-Daráni, expressed the same view when, in answer to an inquiry about the desirability of marriage, he said, "To be able to do without them [*i.e.* women] is better than to bear with them, but to bear with them is better than to endure the fire of Hell".[13]

This same Ṣúfí teacher used to say that marriage was good for those who had patience to surmount its difficulties, but "the solitary one will find in the sweetness of work and in freedom of mind, what the married man does not find". He said further, "I have not seen one of our friends who married and remained in his former rank (as a Ṣúfí)", and again, "There are three things which indicate a longing for the world in the man who seeks them: he who seeks a livelihood, he who marries, and he who writes traditions".[14]

Al-Hujwírí holds that the Dervish (*i.e.* the Ṣúfí) must consider in his mind the respective evils of celibacy and marriage, in order to choose the lesser evil for himself. The evils of celibacy consist in neglecting the ordinance of the Prophet and in the danger of falling into unlawful ways, while marriage involves the evils of the distraction of the mind with other than God, and the concern of the body with sensual pleasure. Marriage therefore is best for the sociable, and celibacy for the solitary.[15]

He states his own view that celibacy is the better way, and concludes, "Ṣúfism was founded on celibacy; the introduction of marriage brought about a change" (not for the better), and he says that desire can be removed by self-restraint, but still better by the force of a rival love (the love of God) which extends its empire over the whole body and its senses. The celibate must guard his eyes and his thoughts from temptation and keep his heart from the distractions of this material world – in short, he must guard himself from the temptations of the world, the flesh and the devil, and so "he will be approved in Ṣúfism".[16]

Bishr al-Ḥáfí (the Barefooted, who died AD 841–2), used to say, "He who has no need of women, relies upon God Almighty", and when he was asked why he did not marry, in accordance with the *Sunna*, he replied, "I am occupied with duties other than those of the Law, that is, with the duty of keeping my soul zealous and free from the evil in creation".[17]

Málik b. Dínár is related to have said, "No man attains to the degree of assured certainty (in the heavenly gnosis) unless he leaves his wife as if she were a widow".[18]

Suhrawardí, discussing this subject, says that the Ṣúfí, if he marries, marries for God's sake, and equally, if he remains solitary, it is for the sake of God. In either case, his choice is deliberate and the sincere man knows which to choose, for the natural desires (ungovernable in others) in the Ṣúfí are bridled with the bridle of knowledge. Whether or not celibacy seems good to him, at least he will not let nature hurry him into marriage, though he will not prefer celibacy to marriage unless it seems good to him.[19] A Dervish was asked why he did not marry, and he replied, "A wife is suitable for a man, and I have not yet attained to true manhood, and how should I marry?"[20]

Another Dervish, when advised to marry, said, "I have greater need of divorcing my Self than of marrying a wife".[21] A similar answer was given by Málik b. Dínár, when he was asked, "Are you not going to marry?" and he said, "If I could divorce my carnal Self,

I would have divorced her",[22] *i.e.* "I have more need to get rid of the ties I have, than to make fresh ones, to hinder me in my Quest".

Closely connected with the idea of celibacy is that of retirement and solitude, to which the Ṣúfís attached great value, and much was written on separation (*tajríd*), retreat (*khalwa*) and isolation (*uzla*). Al-Kalábádhí, a very early writer on Ṣúfism,[23] writing on the subject, says that the real meaning of "separation" is to be separated outwardly from property and inwardly from all that is unreal. Again, he says that isolation (*tafríd*), that is, setting oneself apart for God, means to get away from the phenomenal world and be alone in the mystic states, and that one's actions should all be in relation to God; there should be no vision of the self, no pleasure in the creatures and no seeking after rewards.[24]

Al-Qushayrí also speaks of the value of retirement and solitude for the seeker after God. To go into retreat is fitting for God's elect and retirement is essential for those who seek union. It is also essential for the novice at the beginning of the Way. He quotes al-Junayd as saying, "The man who seeks peace from his religion must give rest to his body and heart and withdraw from the society of men, and the wise man is he who seeks solitude for himself".[25]

The celibate ideal and the life of retirement were then realised as invaluable for all who sought to follow the mystic Way, and what was an advantage to the man Ṣúfí, because it freed him from the distractions of this world, was of still greater advantage, indeed almost a necessity, for the woman Ṣúfí, if she was to pursue her quest without hindrance. So, unexpected as it might seem, we find Muslim women recluses living the life of retirement in much the same way as the Christian nuns.

This desire to withdraw from the world naturally led to the establishment of religious houses. These are heard of very early in the history of Islám, and the history of the earliest of such foundations proves incidentally the prevalence of celibacy among certain of the followers of the Prophet. Al-Ṭabarí refers to "the house of Sa'd b. Khaythama, who was a celibate, without family, and there were celibates among the followers of the Apostle from among those who fled to him and therefore this house of Sa'd b. Khaythama was called the house of the celibates".[26]

Ibn Baṭṭúṭa also says that "On the bank of the moat dug by the Apostle of God, when he met with the assembly of the confederates (not far from Medína) is a ruined dwelling, known as the abode of the celibates, and it is said that 'Umar built it for the celibates of Islám".[27] As the Ṣúfí doctrine spread and its adherents increased, it became necessary to provide monasteries for those who wished to live apart. Jámí says that the first monastery (*khánaqáh*) for Ṣúfís was the one built at Ramla in Syria, and the cause of its being built was that one day a Christian prince had gone out hunting and on the road he saw two persons of this sect (the Ṣúfís) who had met together and were embracing one another. They then sat down in that same spot, and, spreading out what food they had, they ate together. His business brought the Christian Amír there, and their affection to one another pleased him, and he called one of them and asked him who the other was. He replied, "I do not know". The Amír said, "What (relation) is he to you?" The man answered, "None at all". The Amír asked, "From what place has he come?" He said, "I do not know". The prince said, "Then whence came this affection which you showed to one another?" The Dervish replied, "He belongs to my Way". The prince asked, "Have you any place where you meet together?" and when the man said they had not, the Amír said, "I will build you a place where you may meet together", and so he built that monastery in Ramla.[28]

Maqrízí, the historian, speaks of the word *khánaqáh* as being Persian and adopted into Islám at the end of the fourth century. He says that the rise of Ṣúfism made it necessary to have religious establishments for the devotees and that the first to set aside a house for devotion was Zayd b. Ṣawḥán b. Ṣabra, and his aim was to provide for the men of Baṣra who had given themselves up to devotion and who had no worldly occupation and no means, and therefore he built them a house and established them in it and gave them what their calling required in the way of food and drink and clothing, and so on. One day he went to visit them and found they had been invited to a feast by 'Abd Allah b. 'Amr, governor of Baṣra, who wished to do them honour. But Zayd realised that his devotees could not serve God and Mammon, nor be tempted by the things of this world and give their full attention to the affairs of the next, and he sent them back to their monastery.[29]

The same writer speaks of the derivation of the Arabic name for a monastery, *ribáṭ*, which he says is "a place wherein dwell the people of the Way". He says that the name was originally taken from the tying up of horses, each separately, but later became the name of the religious house of the Ṣúfís, who had one abode common to all and in this respect were like the homeless. The inhabitants of the *ribáṭ* had one purpose and aim and lived in the condition which befitted their calling.[30] Though the greater number of these monasteries were for men, yet we find also convents for women from an early period. Several convents for women existed in Mecca and are mentioned by the writers of the *Chronicles of Mecca*. We are told of two near a place called al-Durayba, one of them known by the inhabitants as the convent of Ibn al-Sawda, and "over the door", says the historian, "is a stone with an inscription stating that Umm Khalíl Khadíja and Umm 'Ísá Mariam, the two daughters of the Qá'id Abú Tamr al-Mubárak, that is 'Abd Allah al-Qásimí, founded it for women Ṣúfís desiring to lead a celibate life, who belonged to the Sháfi'rite, in the year AH 590, and it is also called the convent of the Hurrísh".[31]

Another Meccan convent was known as the convent of Bint al-Táj, and over the door was a stone stating that it was founded for pious Ṣúfí women of that neighbourhood about AH 619.[32] Yet another convent in Mecca was called the convent of Al-Dúrí for women, and was in existence in the second half of the seventh century AH.[33]

Among the convents for women in Egypt the most famous was the one known as the Hostel of the Baghdádís, which was at the entrance of the Asfar road, leading into the lane of Baybars at the

Place of Sacrifice (in Cairo).[34]

This convent was built by the noble lady Sitt Jalíla Tadhharíya, daughter of the king Al-Záhir Baybars,[35] in the year AH 684, for the holy Shaykha Zaynab, daughter of Abú'al-l-Barakát, known as the daughter of the Baghdádí, and the princess sent the Shaykha with her pious women down to it, and this place was well known up to the time of Maqrízí the historian,[36] from the reputation of the holy women who were its inhabitants. Maqrízí writes of it thus:

> They have always a Shaykha to advise the women and remind them (of their religious duties) and instruct them in the science of religion. The last (Superior) whom we know of (by name) there, was the noble Shaykha, preeminent among the women of her time, Umm Zaynab Fáṭima, daughter of 'Abbás, a Baghdádí, who died in the year AH 714, when she had exceeded the age of eighty. She was acquainted with jurisprudence, of great learning, an ascetic, content with little, God-fearing, exhorting others, zealous in what was profitable, and in religious exercises tending to salvation and holy fear. The place was ruled with kindness, and many women of Damascus and Cairo profited by her teaching, and she possessed outstanding ability, and power to influence souls. After her time it came about that each woman who assumed the headship of this convent was called "The Baghdádí", and we hear of another noble Shaykha, the Baghdádí, who remained there for many years, living the holiest of lives, until she died in the year AH 796. We know that this house was a place of reception for women who were divorced or deserted, who could use it as a retreat until they re-married or returned to their husbands; since there was strict discipline maintained in it and the greatest care and assiduity in religious obser-

> vances, so that . . . whoever broke a rule was punished.
>
> Then when hard times came, through the events which occurred after the year AH 806,[37] the affairs of the convent suffered, and the proximity to it of a prison for women prevented it from being used, but its good reputation has lasted. A *Qádí* of the Hanífites had the supervision over it.[38]

Maqrízí mentions also the convent of Sitt Kalíla Dawla, daughter of 'Abd Allah al-Tataniya and wife of 'Amr Sayf al-Dín al-Barlí, which she founded in AH 694.[38]

In addition to those in Egypt, there were also Muslim nuns to be found in other parts of North Africa.[39]

Women appear also to have been prominent as founders of monasteries for men. One of these in Mecca was called the monastery of The Lady (*al-Khátún*) and was founded in AH 577 for Ṣúfí men, both Arab and Persian, by Fáṭima, daughter of the Amír Abú Layla M. b. Anúshirwán.[40]

Another foundress of a monastery for Ṣúfís was the Lady Ṭagháyí al-Khanda al-Kubrá; this was known as the convent of Umm Anúk and was outside the Barqujya gate of Cairo, in the desert. She was Turkish, the wife of the sultan Malik al-Násír M. b. Qalawún and the mother of the Amír Anúk. She was much given to good works and charity and her monastery was well endowed. On her death in AH 749 she was buried within the precincts of the convent, which was still in existence in Maqrízí's time.[41]

So we see that in spite of opposition the women saints of Islám, by the sanctity of their lives, by their religious zeal and by their learning, were able to reach a high rank in the religious life, and thereby also to improve their social status, while the adoption of the celibate life gave them an independence and freedom in the exercise of the religious life which was quite alien to the ideal of orthodox Islám.[42]

1 Qur'án, Súra LVII, 27.
2 Abú Dáwúd, *Al-Sunan*, I, p. 173.
3 M. Al-Shaybání, *Usd al-Ghába*, IV, p. 3.
4 Ibn Ḥajar, *Iṣába*, IV, p. 370.
5 Suhrawardí, *'Awárif al-Ma'árif*, margin *Iḥyá*, II, p. 177.
6 Abú Ṭálib, *Qút al-Qulúb*, II, p. 243.
7 Al-Dhahabí, *Mizán al-I'tidál*, I, p. 377.
8 Cf. the tradition that Muḥammad visited the convent of St Katharine in Sinai, built on a mountain peak (H. J. Beadnell, *The Wilderness of Sinai*, p. 168).
9 Taqí al-Dín al-Ḥisní, "Siyar al-Ṣáliḥát", fol. 60.
10 Abú Ṭálib, *op. cit.* II, p. 239.
11 *Op. cit.* II, p. 238.
12 *Op. cit.* II, p. 244.
13 Munáwí, "Al-Kawákib al-Durríya", fol. 126 b.
14 Abú Ṭálib, *op. cit.* II, p. 247.
15 Al-Hujwírí, *Kashf al-Maḥjúb*, tr. Nicholson, pp. 360, 361.
16 *Op. cit.* pp. 364, 366.
17 Al-Sha'rání, *Al-Ṭabaqát al-Kubrá*, p. 96. Suhrawardí, *'Awárif al-Ma'árif*, margin *Iḥyá*, II, p. 167.
18 Abú Nu'aym, "Ḥilya al-Abrár", Leyden MS.
19 Suhrawardí, *op. cit.* II, pp. 161, 162.
20 *Op. cit.* II, p.163.
21 *Op. cit.* II, p. 167.
22 Munáwí, *op. cit.* fol. 74 b.
23 Ob. AD 990 or 1000.
24 "Kitáb al-Ta'arruf", fol. 31 a.
25 *Risála*, pp. 66, 67. Cf. Ramón Lull: "'Say, O Fool, what is solitude?' He answered, 'It is solace and companionship between lover and Beloved'. 'And what are solace and companionship?' 'Solitude in the lover's heart, when he remembers nought save his Beloved'." (*op. cit.* p. 76).
26 *Annales*, I, p. 1243.
27 Ibn Baṭṭúṭa, *op. cit.* I, pp. 289, 290.

28 Jámí, *Nafaḥát al-Uns*, p. 34.

29 Maqrízí, *Al-Khiṭaṭ*, II, p. 414, where he gives Abú Nu'aym as his authority.

30 Maqrízí, *op. cit.* p. 427.

31 *Chron. Mekka*, II, p. 115.

32 *Op. cit.* II, p. 113.

33 *Op. cit.* II, p. 114.

34 'Alí Básha al-Mubárak, *Al-Khiṭaṭ al-Jadída*, VI, p. 53.

35 Reigned over Egypt AD 1260–77.

36 Maqrízí lived AD 1364–1442.

37 The disorders which followed the war with Tímúr (Tamerlane).

38 Maqrízí, *op. cit.* II, p. 428.

39 Yáqút, *Mu'jam al-Buldán*, IV, p. 661.

40 *Chron. Mekka*, p. 109.

41 Maqrízí, *op. cit.* II, p. 425.

42 For the whole question of Asceticism and Monasticism in Islám cf. R. A. Nicholson on "Asceticism (Muslim)" in the *Encyclopaedia of Religion and Ethics*; also Goldziher, *Revue de l'histoire des Religions*, XXXVII, pp. 314 ff.; and M. Horten, "Mönchtum und Mönchsleben in Islám" (*Beiträge zur Kenntnis des Orients*, XII, Bd. 1915).

CHAPTER XIV

THE COMMUNION OF SAINTS

It is clear from the foregoing that women saints received much veneration during their lifetime, and they shared the worship bestowed on Muslim saints after their death. To them prayers were offered directly and intercession was made to God in their name, while their tombs and the shrines erected to their memory were the object of pilgrimages from different parts, whence came worshippers to seek a blessing through their mediation with God. There is every evidence that the cult of the Saints was accepted and developed by the Muslim mystics, and not by the mystics only, with as ardent a faith as by the Catholic Church itself, and indeed the belief in the Communion of Saints and their intercessory power may have been derived, like much else in Islamic mysticism, from the early Christian Church. It is noteworthy that the Ṣúfí writers honour Our Lady Mariam, the spotless Mother of Jesus,[1] above all women, above men too, and acknowledge that she reached perfection.[2] The Saints were God's chosen – the elect of the elect – and therefore between them existed a spiritual bond which could not be severed in this life or the next. The author of the "Siyar al-Ṣáliḥát" tells of a woman saint who addressed Dhú al-Nún al-Miṣrí by name, and when he inquired how she knew him, she said, "God created the spirits two thousand years before their bodies, then He set them around His throne. Those who recognised one another became intimate and those who had nothing to do with each other, did not become friends. My spirit recognised your spirit in that beginning of things."[3]

Abú Sa'íd b. Abí al-Khayr also says that

> God created the souls four thousand years before He created their bodies and placed them near to Himself and there He shed His light upon them. He knew how

> much each soul received as its share from that light and He bestowed His favour on the souls in proportion to the share received; so that they remained tranquil in that light and became nourished thereby. Those who in this world live in fellowship and agreement with one another must have been on terms of intimacy there. Here they have friendship with one another and are called the friends of God and they are in that state because they love one another for the sake of God. . . . If one be in the East and one in the West, they find fellowship and comfort in conversing with one another and although one belong to an early age and another to a later, yet (the latter) finds benefit and comfort only by the speech of the former.[4]

This clearly involves the doctrine of immortality, including the survival of personality, and the Communion of Saints, who belong not only to the church visible, but to the church invisible, and here again, of course, there can be no distinction of sex. The saints on earth are still in fellowship with those "whose course is run". These appear in dreams and visions to their brethren still in this world and relate their experiences in that new life beyond the grave and give counsel and reproof to those left behind.[5]

It is related that 'Abda bint Abí Shuwál, the servant of Rábi'a al-'Adawiyya, a year or so after the saint's death saw her in a dream and asked her concerning the state in heaven of other saints, especially 'Ubayda bint Abí Kiláb, described as one of the greatest and noblest and most fearless of the saints, of whom 'Abd al-Wáḥid b. Zayd[6] said: "I have seen saints old and young, men and women, and I have seen neither woman nor man nobler or with better intellectual gifts than her." She said to Málik b. Dínár, whom we have already mentioned as being one of Rábi'a's associates, "O Abú Yaḥya, when will the God-fearing servant reach the highest degree of all?" He replied, "Oh, 'Ubayda, when the servant reaches that stage than which there is none higher, there will be nothing to hinder him from arriving at God Himself", and 'Ubayda gave a loud cry and fell down unconscious.[7] In the above-mentioned vision, 'Abda questioned Rábi'a about this saint's station in heaven, and she replied, "Indeed, she has gone beyond us to a high degree". 'Abda said, "Why is that, when you were esteemed among the people (while on earth) more than she?" Rábi'a said, "Because she paid no attention to any state, whether it were morning in this world or evening". Then 'Abda asked concerning Abú Málik, another Ṣúfí, and Rábi'a said: "He visits God when he chooses." 'Abda asked, "What is Bashr b. Manṣúr doing?" Rábi'a said, "Oh, he was given more indeed than he asked for".

'Abda then said, "Show me a means by which I may approach nearer to Almighty God", and Rábi'a said, "Think on Him often, and so you may speedily be given that which shall bring you rest".[8]

Another story already related[9] shows that Rábi'a's followers believed that her personality survived after death and that she had passed into the heavens, and there are countless similar stories of the saints, after their deaths, appearing in dreams to those still in this world and revealing to them something of the wonders and the joys awaiting them there.

One of the Ṣúfís relates: "I was invoking Rábi'a al-'Adawiyya in prayer, and I saw her in a vision, and she said, 'Your offerings are presented to us on trays of light covered with veils of light'."[10]

Another story of a God-fearing woman tells how, in her sleep, she entered Paradise and saw all the Blessed standing at the gates of Paradise, and she asked, "Why are the people of Paradise waiting?" and she was told, "They have come to behold this woman by whose approach Paradise itself is honoured", and the dreamer asked, "Who is this woman?" and she was told, "Umm Sawdá, called Sha'wána",[11] who was the woman's sister. The dreamer goes on:

> While I was thus (astonished), behold she was taken by an angelic being who flew with her into the air, and

> when I saw her, I cried out, "O my sister, do you not see where I am, from where you are? If it be allowed, let me join you", then she smiled at me and said, "You may not approach me now, but I bid you remember two things, your need of sorrow in your heart and your need to let the love of God conquer your desires so that they may hurt you no more till death".[12]

•

We find that the reverence felt for the saints of Islám was extended, very early in its history, to their last resting-places, and, later, costly shrines were erected and frequently mosques built to their memory. Naturally the graves of the Prophet's family were the first to be so honoured.

Chief among these was the reputed tomb of Fáṭima, the Prophet's daughter, at Medína,[13] still visited by Muslim pilgrims from all over the world, and Burton relates that the following prayer is offered at her grave:

> Peace be upon thee, daughter of the Apostle of Allah! Peace be upon thee, daughter of the Prophet of Allah! Peace be upon thee, thou daughter of Mustafa! Peace be upon thee, thou mother of the Shurafá.[14] Peace be upon thee, O Fifth of the People, of the Garment.[15] Peace be upon thee, O Pure Virgin. Peace be upon thee, O daughter of the Apostle. Peace be upon thee, O spouse of our lord 'Alí al-Mustáza. Peace be upon thee, O mother of Ḥasan and Ḥusayn, the two Moons, the two Lights, the two Pearls, the two Princes of the Youth of Heaven and Coolness of the Eyes (*i.e.* joy and gladness) of true Believers! Peace be upon thee and upon thy sire, al-Musṭafa, and thy husband, our lord 'Alí! Allah honour his face and thy face and thy father's face in Paradise, and thy two sons, the Ḥasanayn! And the mercy of Allah and His blessings![16]

'Ali Mubárak gives an account of some of the shrines of women accounted as saints, to be found in Cairo, including that of Sayyida Ruqayya, presumably the daughter of Muḥammad, who married first 'Utbal and then 'Uthmán, of which he says:

> The sanctuary of Sayyida Ruqayya is to be found near the gateway which leads to the shrine of the Lady Nafísa, near to the mosque of Shajarat al-Durr (The Spray of Pearls)[17] on the right of the road from the shrine of Sayyida Sakína,[18] looking on to the memorial of Nafísa. It contains a hostel for Ṣúfís and a place for prayer and taps of water and many trees and a number of graves, among them the tomb of Sayyida Ruqayya, and over this is a canopy of wood, ornamented with ivory and mother-of-pearl, and above it a dome has been built and every year a Mawlid[19] is celebrated for her and visitors come every week and verses are recited, telling of her fame. The yearly revenue of this shrine is over thirteen thousand piastres.[20]

The tomb of Umm Kulthúm, daughter of 'Alí and Fáṭima, is described by Ibn Baṭṭúṭa as being near Damascus, and he says:

> Her name was Zaynab and . . . the Prophet gave her the name of Umm Kulthúm, because of her likeness to her aunt, Umm Kulthúm, his own daughter. Near the tomb is a noble mosque, around which are dwelling-houses, and it is endowed and the people of Damascus call it the shrine of the Lady Umm Kulthúm.[21]

The same writer, in describing his visit to Hebron, says:

> Near the Mosque called Al-Masjid al-Yaqín, is a cave in which is the tomb of Fáṭima, daughter of Ḥusayn b.

> 'Alí, and on the upper part of the tomb and the lower, are two tablets of marble, on one of which is written, engraved in excellent script, "In the Name of God, the Compassionate, the Merciful. To Him be glory and everlasting (dominion). To Him belong what He has created and produced. Upon His creatures He has imposed mortality: in the Apostle of God is an exemplar. This is the tomb of Umm Salma, Fáṭima, daughter of Ḥusayn, son of 'Alí."
>
> On the second tablet is inscribed: "M. b. Abí Sahl the sculptor, in Cairo", and under that these verses:
>
> "Thou hast made to dwell the one, whose dwelling-
> place was my heart,
> In spite of me, between the earth and the stone,
> O tomb of Fáṭima, daughter of the son of Fáṭima,
> Daughter of the Imáms, daughter of the glittering stars.
> O tomb, how much lies within thee of religion and piety,
> Of chastity, of reserve and of modesty."[22]

The Lady Nafísa, already mentioned[23] as famous for her good works and her miracles, is one whose intercession is much sought after. Her grave is one of the privileged places where those who desire can go to pray with the sure expectation of being heard: "That saintly woman, who, so long as she lived, never denied the exercise of her power before the Throne of God, to the unfortunate and oppressed, does not refuse their petitions, now that she has passed away, and God leaves no request unheard, for the fulfilling of which the holy Nafísa lends her intercession".[24] Her shrine is in Cairo and is mentioned by Ibn Baṭṭúṭa, who says that in the necropolis of Qaráfa at Old Cairo is the mausoleum of the Lady Nafísa, daughter of Zayd b. 'Alí b. Ḥusayn b. 'Alí,[25] one whose prayers were answered and who was zealous in her devotion. This mausoleum is very well built and brightly adorned. Near it is a monastery much frequented.[26]

'Alí Básha al-Mubárak also describes this sanctuary and says that the memorial of the Lady Nafísa was originally a school known as Umm al-Sulṭán, but it was destroyed with everything around it. This destruction, and the fact that Nafísa's shrine was moved in consequence, is mentioned also by Ibn Khallikán.[27] The first to build over the grave of the Lady Nafísa was the Amír of Egypt, 'Ubayd Allah b. al-Sirrí, and this was written on the marble tablet over the gateway of her tomb. The dome over the tomb was renewed by the Khalifa al-Háfiz in AH 532 and he also gave orders for the marble work in the *miḥráb*.[28] About the year AH 1280 a building was erected there and dwellings built for the dervishes, and there they had lived in the writer's time.[29] This place had been planted out with a number of trees and the cost of erecting the building had been met by pious endowments (*awqáf*).[30] Nafísa's shrine is near the mosque of Ibn Túlún.[31]

Other shrines sacred to women of the Prophet's family mentioned by 'Alí Básha al-Mubárak are the mosque of Sayyida Zaynab, daughter of the Imám 'Alí and granddaughter of the Prophet, after whom a whole district in Cairo is named, and the shrines of 'Á'isha, daughter of Ja'far al-Sádiq, and of Umm Kulthúm, his great-granddaughter. Another very sacred mosque is that of the Lady Sakína, mentioned above, who was the daughter of the Imám Ḥusayn.

These women owed their reputation for sanctity, in part at least, to their membership of the sacred family of the Prophet, but the shrines of others were equally venerated.

In connection with that early Muslim saint, Umm Ḥarám,[32] her biographer writes:

> It is by the perfect Divine favour of the Giver of all gifts in the other world that the beloved of God and the honoured Prophet has given life to the hearts of the believers by saying: "If any of the male companions or

female disciples be buried in a holy place, they will intercede for such dwellers in that place as are worthy of their intercession." So likewise in this life it is by the grace of God that – as it is said by the Imám Munáwí in his comment on Jámi' al-Ṣaghír – whenever the people of Damascus are sorely tried by the droughts and other troubles, and with full trust appeal to that honoured lady, asking from the Giver of all good and munificence, rain and rest and deliverance from trouble and attack – the Dispeller of all cares and sorrows, God Most High, out of respect to that honoured lady, dispels their anxieties and troubles and grants them His rain and grace. And especially there is no doubt that for those who with earnest endeavour and in full faith make the customary and acceptable visitation to the honoured tomb and revered shrine which contain her sacred body, the Giver of blessings in unequalled wisdom, satisfies all their needs. It is the perfect favour and grace of God Most High, that He has made the aunt of that most glorious of created beings,[33] an intercessor for the inhabitants of this island and the visitors who earnestly appeal to her, so that when we confide in her exalted person we attain all our desires and aims in this world and the next.[34]

Rábi'a bint Ismá'íl[35] was buried outside Jerusalem, to the east on the Mount of Tor, according to Ibn Khallikán (who confuses her with Rábi'a of Baṣra), near the mosque of the Ascension. This is evidently the same tomb as that mentioned by Ibn Baṭṭúṭa, among shrines which he visited in Jerusalem, as being that of Rábi'a al-Badawiyya, belonging to the Bedouins, who, he says, is not to be confused with the celebrated Rábi'a al-'Adawiyya, of Baṣra.[36] This tomb was an object of pilgrimage in the Middle Ages,[37] and is still reverenced in the grotto sacred also to St Pelagia and the prophetess Hulda.

Another interesting shrine in Syria is a *walí*[38] near Damascus, on an ancient platform surrounded by a grove of oak trees, which is known as Umm Shaqaqíf (the Mother of Pieces). The saint in whose honour the shrine is held sacred was one of four maidens each under the protection of a particular saint. She was called Fáṭima, according to one version of the legend, and 'Arjá (the lame) according to another. She was lame, blind in one eye, bald, poor and in rags. She went with her companions to draw water at a spring, at which the four patron saints were seated. The other three girls drew their water and departed. 'Arjá, when she drew up her jar, found only the handles, her saint had shattered it. When urged to desert him, she refused, and, touched by her devotion, he first restored the jar, then, at her request, healed her lameness, cured her blindness, gave her flowing hair, clothed her decently and bestowed wealth upon her. So she returned to her home, became an object of worship, and, when she died, was buried on this spot. Such is the legend connected with this shrine, which is still accounted a place of blessing. The women of the neighbourhood come and break jars in fulfilment of their vows, because 'Arjá's jar was broken.[39]

The tomb of Rábi'a al-'Adawiyya was at Baṣra and is mentioned among the Ṣúfí shrines to be found there by Maqdísí, who wrote in AD 985.[40] Her grave was visited as a place of pilgrimage.[41]

An Indian shrine mentioned by Ibn Baṭṭúṭa is of great interest, and, from the fact that it bestows sanctity on those who visit it, we may assume that its inmate was reckoned a saint after her death, if not before. This is the tomb of Raḍiyya, daughter of the sultan Shams al-Dín of Delhi. We are told by the historian Firishta that

> this princess was adorned with every qualification required in the ablest kings and the strictest scrutineers of her actions could find in her no fault but that she was a woman. In the time of her father, she entered deeply into the affairs of government, which disposition he encouraged, finding she had a remarkable tal-

> ent in politics. In that year in which he took the fort of Gwalior, he appointed her regent in his absence. When he was asked by the *Umará* why he appointed his daughter to such an office in preference to so many of his sons, he replied that he saw his sons gave themselves up to wine, women, gaming and the worship of the wind (flattery); that therefore he thought the government too weighty for their shoulders to bear and that Raḍiyya, though a woman, had a man's head and heart and was better than twenty such sons.

After her father's death, Raḍiyya denounced one of her brothers, who had murdered another, and was supported by the populace, who put the murderer to death and accepted Raḍiyya as their sultan in AD 1236. Sulṭána Raḍiyya, upon her accession, changing her apparel, assumed the imperial robes, and every day gave public audience from the throne, revising and confirming the laws of her father, which had been abrogated in the last reign, and distributing justice with an equal hand.[42] Ibn Baṭṭúṭa tells us that she ruled with absolute authority for four years. She rode on horseback, armed, and after the manner of men, and never veiled her face. Finally, she was overthrown in favour of a younger brother, and married one of her relatives. Raḍiyya and her husband took up arms against the new sultan, but were defeated, and Raḍiyya took to flight and was murdered for the sake of her costly clothing. She was buried in the marshes where she had been murdered and over her tomb was built a dome. At the time of Ibn Baṭṭúṭa's visit, her tomb was visited and was a place where blessing could be gained. It was on the bank of the great river known as al-Jown, at a distance of three miles from Delhi.[43]

Other more modern shrines of women saints to be found in India include that of Haro Ana, which is to be found four miles from Chauter (Baluchistán). A few flags and a wooden shed mark the place. She was a Tehánrí woman, famed for her virtue, who lived a virgin all her life. In her lifetime she was credited with miraculous powers and given lands by the Wanéchis.[44] On her death-bed she told her relations to bury her body on a spot by which the enemies of the Wanéchis had to pass, assuring them that the enemies would either not come that way or, if they did, would suffer for it. So she was buried at the west end of Wani, since called the Haro Ana Pérai. When, in the nineteenth century, the Wanéchis were raided, they prayed at Haro Ana's shrine, recovered their cattle and defeated the enemy.[45]

In the Punjáb, in Multán, is to be found the tomb of Mai Sapuran, a woman who was a Nunarí by caste and became one of the disciples of the saint 'Abd al-Ḥakím (who died in AD 1732). Her shrine is in the village called by her name. She was reputed to be able to spread out her prayer-carpet on the waters of the Rárí and to kneel for prayer upon it,[46] and both she and her descendants had the power to cure the bites of mad dogs.[47]

Among these shrines also is that of Bíbí Náhzan, to be found near Kalát, who sank into the earth together with her maid when they were persecuted by some infidels, and this shrine also is visited by persons who have been bitten by mad dogs, while those who pay a fixed contribution to the shrine believe that they secure immunity from cholera. Another shrine in Kalát is that of Bíbí Naní, who guards the water-supply and who is said to have been a daughter of Ya 'Alí. Probably she was originally a goddess of the old Persians and Bachíns.[48]

There is the tomb of a girl saint to be found at Elbasan, in Central Albania, where both Christians and Muslims worship at the shrine. This saint is supposed to have come from Khorasán. Her father tried to compel her to marry and betrothed her to a young man. She lay down to sleep, died and was buried on the spot. There is a wooden sarcophagus, with a stone pillar at the head, but without any date or name. The saint's blessing is sought by the childless, and for the sick, and an elaborate ritual is gone through. The water of a pitcher left in the tomb all night is drunk by those who seek the saint's favour and hope for the blessing of children. Candles are also brought to the tomb and lighted on Thursday evenings.[49]

The shrine of a famous woman saint among the Kabyles is that of Lalla Imma Tifellút, in the mountainous region inhabited by the Barí Ṣalaḥ.[50] The time at which she lived is unknown, but details of her history have been handed down. She was the most beautiful maiden of the mountain, a model of purity and chastity in her youth. When a too-ardent admirer abducted her as she came down one evening to draw water as usual, and carried her off upon his mule, at the end of the journey, when he drew aside the curtains of the palanquin, he found that a dove had taken the place of his captive. Then this maiden, who had shown herself so averse to marriage and the attentions of men, in later life became a kind of feminine demon, a Circe whose love was said to mean death, so that her tribe were doubtful whether she was to be regarded as a daughter of Satan or as an angel. But one day she left her dwelling for the summit of the mountain and there went into retreat. Clothed in wool, with a hempen girdle, she spent her days and nights in prayer and communion with God – a Magdalene reclaimed from her sins. She took staff in hand and went among the Kabyle tribes seeking to revive the Muslim faith among the lukewarm, but with little success. At last her asceticism and her constant prayers had their reward and she received the gift of prophecy and the power to work miracles, and she was now accepted by all as a saint and all the good fortune which came to the Bení Ṣalaḥ was attributed to her. When she died, she was buried with great pomp at the foot of the cedar where she had lived, in accordance with her own wish. Her tomb was enclosed in a chapel of stone and a small dome indicates the spot where her much venerated remains rest. The shrine is surrounded by cedar trees, which are accounted too sacred ever to be cut down or damaged. Even the eggs and the nestlings of the birds belonging to the grove enjoy the protection of the saint.[51]

Other shrines of women saints among the Kabyles include that of an unknown saint whom the Bení Ṣalaḥ call Lalla Tawrirt, the

Lady of the Hill; the *ḥawítha*[52] of Lalla Imma Mr'ita, in the midst of a cemetery; that of Lalla Imma Wacháa on the left side of the valley of al-Guethran; and the oak shrine of Lalla Imma Mimen, on the right side of the valley Bení-Azza. All these saints, who were holy women during their earthly existence and who died in the odour of sanctity, have their day of pilgrimage and their annual festival. They have also their religious *serviteurs*, who are usually people of the same district as those who erected either the chapel in which repose the mortal remains of these saints, or the shrine which recalls the place where they prayed or had their dwelling-place.[53]

All these shrines of women saints have been venerated by Muslims, in some cases for centuries past, and are still the object of veneration today. Of the festivals held at the shrines of women saints, and the part which these sanctuaries occupy in popular Islám today, more will be said in the next chapter.

1 'Aṭṭár, *Tadhkirat al-Awliyá*, I, p. 59.
2 M. al-'Abdárí, *Madkhal al-Shari' al-Sharíf*, II, p. 19.
3 Taqí al-Dín al-Ḥisní, "Siyar al-Ṣáliḥát", fol. 45.
4 Al-Munawwar, *Asrár al-Tawḥíd*, p. 399.
5 Cf. R. A. Nicholson, *The Idea of Personality in Ṣúfism*, p. 72.
6 See p. 29.
7 Munáwí, "Kawákib", fol. 69 b.
8 Ṣibt Ibn al-Jawzí, "Mir'át al-Zamán", fol. 257 a. See also Ibn Khallikán, tr. de Slane, p. 517.
9 See p. 66.
10 Al-Qushayrí, *Risála*, p. 234.
11 See p. 174.
12 Al-Ghazálí, *op. cit.* IV, p. 354.
13 It must be noted that the exact place of Fáṭima's tomb is doubtful. Maqdísí mentions two sites (*Bibl. Geog. Arab.* III, p. 46), and al-Ṭabarí gives a site in the Buqi' (*Annales*, III, p. 2436).
14 Descendants of the Prophet.
15 According to a tradition, Muḥammad once threw his cloak

around Fáṭima, her husband 'Ali and her two sons, and so made of them a group apart.

16 R. F. Burton, *A Pilgrimage to Mecca*, I, pp. 327, 328.

17 Queen of Egypt, AD 1250–7.

18 Ibn Baṭṭúṭa places Sakína's tomb near to the tomb of Umm Kulthúm, close to Damascus (*op. cit.* I, p. 236).

19 A feast in celebration of the birthday of a saint.

20 'Alí Básha al-Mubárak, *Al-Khitat al-Jadída*, VI, p. 5.

21 Ibn Baṭṭúṭa, *op. cit.* I, pp. 225, 226.

22 *Op. cit.* I, pp. 118, 119.

23 See pp. 177 ff.

24 Maqrízí, *Al-Khiṭaṭ*, II, p. 441.

25 This ought to be, bint Ḥasan b. Zayd b. Ḥasan b. 'Alí.

26 Ibn Baṭṭúṭa, *op. cit.* I, p. 75.

27 *Wafayát al-A'yán*, No. 777.

28 Maqrízí, *op. cit.* II, p. 442.

29 'Alí Mubárak, *op cit.* VI, p. 5.

30 The modern Government of Egypt includes a Ministry of Waqfs to deal with pious foundations and their endowments.

31 Governor of Egypt AD 868 to AD 884. This mosque was restored in the thirteenth century AD.

32 See pp. 167 ff. Her tomb was in Cyprus.

33 Umm Ḥarám was of the kindred of the Prophet.

34 Sh. Ibráhím b. Muṣṭafá, *Excerpta Cypria*, p. 377.

35 See pp. 170 ff.

36 Ibn Baṭṭúṭa, *op. cit.* I, p. 124.

37 Ibn Khallikán, tr. de Slane, p. 516.

38 In Syria the word *walí* is commonly used for the shrine of a saint.

39 S. I. Curtiss, *Primitive Semitic Religion Today*, pp. 82, 83.

40 *Bibl. Geog. Arab.* III, p. 130.

41 'Aṭṭár, *op. cit.* p. 73.

42 *History of Hindustán*, tr. A. Dow, I, p. 183.

43 Ibn Baṭṭúṭa, *op. cit.* III, pp. 166–8.

44 A section of one of the Afghan tribes.

45 *Baluchistán District Gazetteer*, vol. II, pp. 123, 124.

46 See pp. 56 ff.

47 *Multán District Gazetteer*, 1902, p. 122.

48 *Baluchistán District Gazetteer*, vol. IV, p. 37.

49 From information supplied by Mrs Margaret Hasluck.

50 Near Blida.

51 Trumelet, *Les Saints de l'Islám*, pp. 306–25.

52 A name used in N. Africa for a pyramid of stones, in the form of a circle or horse-shoe, adorned with rags or frayed scraps, which is erected over the tombs of marabouts, whose reputation for sanctity is not great enough to justify their devotees in going to the expense of erecting a cupola. Cf. also T. Canaan, *Mohammedan Saints and Sanctuaries in Palestine*, pp. 60 ff.

53 Trumelet, *op. cit*. p. 308.

CHAPTER XV

The Cult of Women Saints in Modern Islám

It remains to consider the effect of the development of a mystical faith and the cult of the saints upon popular Islám today. Throughout the Muslim world, the dervishes are the modern exponents of Islamic mysticism, but while the Ṣúfí, as we have seen in the foregoing pages, developed a philosophic doctrine concerning God and His relation to His saints, the dervish is contented rather with a particular manner of life.

The foundation of religious orders goes back to a very early date in the history of Islám, and some of the early Ṣúfí teachers were reputed to have been responsible for the founding of such orders, but probably this was due to the desire of later Ṣúfís to derive their spiritual descent from such great teachers. Among these was Ibráhím b. Adham, who died in AH 161 (AD 777) and who was accepted by such great leaders as 'Abd al-Qádir and Sídí Sanússí as their spiritual ancestor.[1] Another leader claimed as founder of an order was the great Ṣúfí teacher and poet Abú Sa'íd b. Abí al-Khayr,[1] but there is no historic evidence for the statement. The number of orders now in existence is very great and it is possible to mention only a few of the most important here.

The most widespread of all, with adherents over almost the whole of the Islamic world, is that of the Qádiriyya, founded by Shaykh 'Abd al-Qádir al-Jiláni, who is considered the patron saint of Baghdád, where he died in AH 561 (AD 1166). He had forty-nine sons, who carried on his work after his death. His most devoted followers went so far as to ascribe to him powers almost divine. This order has separate *záwiyas* (cloisters), and a central institution in Baghdád. These dervishes are known for their philanthropic principles and mystical exaltation, but, in spite of this, the Mahdí and his troops belonged to this order. The main order of the Qádiriyya has produced many subsidiary branches and dervishes of this school are to be found spread over Islám from Morocco to Malaysia.[2]

Among the orders which, while not world-wide, cover a considerable part of the Muslim world, is that founded by Aḥmad al-Rifá'í, who lived near Baṣra and died in AH 570 (AD 1182). He carried asceticism to an extreme degree and was a great lover of animal life. He was said to have great power over venomous snakes and his followers claim the same power. He was noted for his humility and his love for his enemies. He has been called the St Francis of the dervishes, and by his followers he was made almost into an emanation of the Divine.[3]

Members of this order are found throughout the Arabic-speaking Near East, and in Turkey.

An order of considerable importance found mainly in the east of the Islamic world is that of the Khalwatiyya, who derive their name from their practice of going into retreat. This practice was undoubtedly derived from the Christian recluses, and was adopted by the leaders of the mystic orders for themselves and their disciples as being more adapted than any other means for realising complete sanctification in this life, and the absorption of the individuality of man in the Essence of God.[4] Junayd, who died at Baghdád in AH 298 (AD 910–11), is said to have founded an order on these lines, but the real founder of the existent order was one 'Umar al-Khalwatí, also a Persian, who died AH 800 (AD 1397). The adherents of this order are ascetics and mystics, practising retreats and great austerities. They have spread beyond Persia into Asia Minor, European Turkey, the Hijáz and the Indies.[5]

Another order, of limited extent, is that of the Suhrawardiyya, founded by Shiháb al-Din Suhrawardí, a Persian by birth, and well known as a writer on Ṣúfism, who died in AH 632 (AD 1234–5). He represents the pantheistic development of Ṣúfism, and his teachings are purely mystical. The adherents of this school are found chiefly in Persia and India.[6]

An order which had its origin in Asia Minor is that of the

Mevlevis, founded by the great Ṣúfí poet Jalál al-Dín Rúmí, born in Balkh, who died at Konia in AH 672 (AD 1273). They are known as the "Brethren of Love", because the whole principle of the order has been the love of God.[7] The headship of the Mevlevi Order is still in the family of Jalál al-Dín and it still has its headquarters at Konia.[8]

Certain orders have remained purely local. Such is that founded by Sídí Aḥmad al-Bedawí, who is said to have been a wild youth, fond of horsemanship, and then to have suddenly become a recluse. After visiting the tombs of 'Abd al-Qádir and al-Rifá'í he went to Tanta (Lower Egypt), where he died in AH 675 (AD 1276). His order was based originally on the union of the true believers in the "holy war" against Louis XI. His disciples are called Aḥmadiyya locally, and are found all over Egypt. To him especially was ascribed the power of giving children to the barren and this may account, to some extent, for the excesses which mar the celebrations of the saint's Mawlids around his tomb, but it is probable too that in him were crystallised the old Egyptian beliefs in the sun-mysteries, since the dates of his festivals appear to coincide with the old feasts. The saint is widely venerated and prayers are addressed to him all over the country, while there are numbers of shrines bearing his name.[9]

A Spanish Muslim, Abú Madian,[10] born in Seville, was the first to bring the doctrines of Ṣúfism into Morocco and was responsible for their spread throughout Algeria. He was a mystic of a high order and one who practised great humility in his outward life. His followers are called Madawiyya and they represent rather a philosophic school of Ṣúfism than the popular religion of most of the modern orders, and they are found only in small numbers. The characteristics of this school are the constant invocation of God, renunciation of the world, vigorous piety, the practice of the contemplative life and research into mysticism.[11]

An order limited to India is that of the Chishtí, founded by Mu'ín al-Dín Chishtí, who died at Ajmir in AD 1236. It is a Ṣúfí brotherhood and is widely disseminated in India.

A modern order, also local, but of great importance, is that of the

Sanússí, founded in 1835 by Sídi Sanússí. Its adherents profess the Ṣúfí doctrines and a return to the Qur'án and the Ṣúfism of the early centuries of Islám. They maintain the necessity of the Imámate, and they uphold the superlative excellence of the contemplative and devoted life. They are strongly represented in Tripoli. Like the Wahhabites, though primarily religious reformers, they have had a considerable effect upon political events.

All of these orders have their *silsila*, or chain of links, showing how they were founded, and this chain is of two kinds, one[12] showing the series of saints from whom the founder of the order received instruction, and this chain usually claims to go back to Abú Bakr or 'Alí, this derivation being due to a desire to link up extra-canonical foundations with orthodox Islám and to give to associations which in many respects resemble Trade Guilds, a definitely religious sanction. The other chain[13] shows the series of Shaykhs who have held the headship of the order and through whom the *baraka*, or blessed influence, of the original founder has been passed on.

Each of these orders has at its head a Shaykh, under whom are his Khalifas or Ná'ibs, and under these again are those known variously as *muqaddam* in North Africa, *murshid* in Persia, *'am* or *shaykh* in Egypt, and in the Sudan simply *shaykh*. These latter are the heads of the various local groups and engage in the work of propaganda and management, enrol new members and initiate them. The members are known variously as *khouán*, *fuqará'*, *aṣḥáb* or dervishes. There are regular meetings at stated intervals called *ḥaḍras*, and in some parts simply *dhikrs*. From an early period the orders have established convents for themselves, sometimes a *ribáṭ*, for communal life, or the *záwiya* for the secluded life; in Persia this is called a *khanáqáh*, and in Turkey a *tekye*. It may be only a place of residence and a meeting-place for the order, but it sometimes includes a mosque and not infrequently the tomb of a saint.

Initiation is administered to the *muríd* or novice, usually by the *muqaddam*, who has himself received his investiture from the Shaykh. The orders have their own special liturgies, and mysticism is an essential part of the religious faith of the votaries.[14]

Among the dervishes are to be found "walís" or saints, usually credited with miraculous powers, and there are also wandering *faqírs,* like the friars of the Middle Ages, who travel through the villages, preaching the doctrine of repentance and urging their hearers to renounce their sins.

In addition to the regular adherents there are tertiaries or lay members, who continue to follow their trade and to lead a normal life as members of the community. The great mass of the peasants and artisans in Islamic countries are members of one of the dervish orders.

The Muslim child, taught in the village school, most probably receives his instruction from a dervish, who first leads his pupils towards the Way. The apprentice learns still more from the journeyman in his trade, and very often the head of a trade is the spiritual director of those who work in it, while all may learn from the travelling teachers already mentioned.

Most of what has been said applies to women as well as men.

There are large numbers of women dervishes, the majority of whom are lay-members. These are sometimes received into the order by the local leader, a man, but are frequently instructed and trained by women and almost always hold *dhikrs* by themselves. These women dervishes in North Africa are called *Khiwát* (sisters) if they are adepts, accept the duties and practices of the order and in some cases, though these are rare, are present at gatherings with the men, keeping themselves a little apart. The most intelligent among them can attain to the degree of *muqaddama,* and in this case have the work of initiating the new women adepts and presiding at their gatherings or assisting the *muqaddam,* when he presides. If there is no *muqaddama,* the *muqaddam* initiates the women who ask for it in the presence of the other sisters, and, more rarely, in the gathering of the men.[15]

Among the orders which admit women are the Qádiriyya, which has between two and three thousand women members in

Africa, the Raḥmaniyya, with thirteen thousand women members, the Khalwatiyya, the Tidjania, the Heddáwa, and the A'íssawiyya.[16] A writer on modern Turkey says that societies of pious women affiliated to dervish orders are found, and that these were called "Sisters of Rúm" by Hajji Bektásh.[17] She tells of the widow of a Shaykh of Cavalla, a woman of great intelligence who, after her husband's death, presided over a society of female devotees, holding their meetings at her residence.

Another Turkish lady, who was also a poetess, was known as the Dervísh Hánum, but she proved unwilling to give information as to the Sisterhood of Mystics of which she was a member. A number of Turkish women of good education have entered on the Mystic Path and such are distinguished by the title of "Ṣúfí Hánum".[18]

The practices of the dervishes include renunciation of the world, the retreat or sometimes a solitary life, vigils, fasting and the *dhikr*, or remembrance of God.[19]

The latter devotional exercise frequently consists simply of the repetition of the sacred name "Allah, Allah, Allah", but whatever form it takes, its main purpose is to produce a state of mystic ecstasy. The dervishes usually hold a *dhikr*, under their local leader, once a week, and also on special occasions such as marriages, births and circumcisions both of boys and girls, and herein the women play their part. There are also *dhikrs* at the Mawlids.

These Mawlids, held in honour of the birthday of a saint, occur almost nightly in such a great Muslim city as Cairo; they include the Mawlids of women saints also. The most famous of these is the Mawlid of Sayyida Zaynab, who is greatly revered in Cairo, and the festival is celebrated near her mosque there. Women visitors are allowed on this occasion into the enclosure round the saint's resting-place, and others may make the circuit outside. There is music, reciting and dancing, at all these Mawlids, and in Syria, under Turkish rule, there was much firing of guns, with fatal results at almost every festival. The chief ceremony, in the mosque at such a

Mawlid as that of Sayyida Zaynab, is the performing of *dhikrs* by bands of dervishes.[20]

The Mawlid of Lalla Imma Tifellút[21] is celebrated in the spring, when the whole tribe of the Bení Ṣalaḥ, men, women and children, go in pilgrimage to the saint's tomb. Thirty or forty goats and a number of calves are provided for the feast and what is not needed is sold by auction, the proceeds of which go to the guardian of the tomb. The poor of the district crowd to these free feasts. Weekly visits are also paid to the shrine by those who desire to pray there. The saint's blessing upon her tribe is still to be had for those who seek it. If a Kabyle loses a goat, he promises a kid to the saint if she will restore it to him. When the goat is found, the goat-herd selects a kid, rears it and when it has become a buck, he presents it to the saint, or rather to her Wakíl, the guardian of the shrine. If the owner of a herd of goats wishes to preserve them against the attacks of jackals, he presents a he-goat to the saint and for the next year his herd will be safe from marauders. The Bení Ṣalaḥ relate that in 1840 when the Amír 'Abd al-Qádir was encamped with his troops in their country, he went to pray at the tomb of Lalla Imma Tifellút, and there had a dream in which an angel made known to him that it was the last time he would pray in the country of the Bení Ṣalaḥ. "It is written", said the angel, "that the day of the French has come, and God, Who gives the earth to whom He will, Who sometimes bestows His gifts in unstinted measure where He wills and sometimes limits them, God, I say, has decided that they (the French) shall be masters of the country."

However that might be, it was as a matter of fact the last time that the Amír made his appearance in the country of the Bení Ṣalaḥ.[22]

We have dealt already, in the preceding section, with the tombs of the great saints of the past, and have noted the veneration accorded to them by all pious Muslims. To these are added the shrines and tombs of modern Walís and Waliyyas, which are to be found everywhere, not only in the great cities, but in every village, and all receive their tribute of respect and to all come petitioners, seeking the intercession of the saint, man or woman as it may be.

These shrines are of many types and are called by different names, but the modern saints are not honoured with the pretentious buildings and costly mausoleums dedicated to the greater saints, which are venerated all over the land and visited by thousands at the annual festivals. The modern tombs take the form of the *maqám*,[23] which is usually a square building with a *qubba* or dome, generally shaded by a tree, which is itself sacred. In North Africa this title is given to a heap of stones arranged in a pyramid or circle, commemorating the sojourn in that spot of some revered marabout.[24] The *walí* is so called in Syria and represents a more sacred class of shrine, a spot where miracles have been wrought, and this is usually under the care of a Shaykh. Its area is considered holy and may afford a refuge for those fleeing from the avenger of blood.[25] The *ḥawítha*, found in North Africa and already described,[26] is often no more than a heap of stones. The saints in whose honour such shrines are erected are not canonised by any superior authority of the Muslim community, their sanctity is rather the result of the *vox populi*, which in its choice acts freely and without constraint, hence the vast number and popularity of such shrines.[27] All of them show visible signs of the extent to which the aid of those they commemorate is sought. Nails are hammered into doors, with the prayer that the suffering to be relieved may remain where the nail is; an extracted tooth is left with the saint that the pain may not return to the owner. A shrine may be seen surrounded by small sticks thrust into the ground, to which are tied fluttering bits of cloth, taken from the garments of those who make their petition, or those on whose behalf the petition is made, and the faith of the petitioner is the same, whether she or he comes to the Báb al-Zuwayla in Cairo – behind which it is believed that the *Quṭb*,[28] the spiritual head of all the saints, has his abode – or whether it be to the tomb of the unknown saint who lies buried in the desert near the great mosque of Khartoum. From the Walí or the Waliyya, it would seem that these humble seekers after favour have more hope of response than from God Himself.[29]

Of the cult of the saints, women and men, in Baluchistán today, a modern observer writes:

> Saints or *Pírs* are invested with all the attributes of God. It is the saint who can avert calamity, cure disease, procure children for the childless, bless the efforts of the hunter or even improve the circumstances of the dead. The underlying feeling seems to be that man is too sinful to approach God direct, and therefore the intervention of someone more worthy must be sought. Anyone visiting a shrine will observe stones, carved pieces of wood, bunches of hair tied to trees, remnants of clothes, horns of wild animals, bells and various other articles of paltry value. They are placed at the shrines by devotees in the performance of vows. The mother who is blessed with a child will bring it to the shrine, where she will shave it and offer the hair and the baby's clothes in performance of the vows made during the course of her pregnancy. The object is that the local saint may be induced to interest himself or herself in the welfare of the little one. The hunter brings the horns of the deer which he has slain, in the hope of further good sport; whilst those who are suffering from disease pass the stone or carved pieces of wood over the part affected, trusting that by this means the ill from which they are suffering will be removed.[30]

Not only the tombs of saints have this power, but in many parts of the Muslim world there are trees sacred to saints which have a similar virtue. This belief in the sanctity of tree-shrines no doubt goes back to primitive and animistic religion, in which a definite cult of trees is found.[31] M. Clermont Ganneau considers that most of the popular Muslim shrines in Palestine, with the trees near by, represent the hill sanctuaries and shady groves of the Canaanites and that their pagan origin has been concealed by placing them under the protection of Muslim saints, who are represented as giving their own names to the place, this close connection of names and places being characteristic of the Phoenician and Canaanite mythology. The fact that so many modern Muslim *qubbas* are consecrated to women, he thinks, is a remnant of the worship of female divinities among the Canaanites. The modern Walí is often venerated along with a Waliyya, who is considered as his sister or daughter, the original conjugal relationship having been changed by the Muslims into one of consanguinity.[32]

The Arabs also had sacred trees. Al-Tabarí speaks of the sacred date-palm at Najrán, which was worshipped by the Arabs at an annual festival, and upon which they hung beautiful garments offered as gifts, and ornaments; then they used to go out and devote themselves to it by day, and prayed to it.[33] Yáqút also speaks of sacred trees, one near Mecca, and another at Hudaybiyya, mentioned in the Qur'án,[34] to which many people resorted and found a blessing thereby. Lest it should become an object of worship like Al-Lát and 'Uzzá, it was cut down and destroyed, and when the people arose in the morning, there was no trace of it.[35]

Still in popular Islám we find traces of this cult. The favourite shrines of the Yunihs, of Asia Minor, are sacred trees growing by the side of the mountain paths, on which they hang as votive offerings bits of coloured rag, wooden spoons and other small articles.[36]

Formerly, it may be that the tree acquired sanctity because the local god or spirits were supposed to dwell in it and give it of their life, now it is associated with some Muslim saint.

At Aḥmadábád, near the tomb of an Indian Muslim saint – one Músá Suhág, who dressed in woman's clothes as a symbol that he was devoted to God as a wife to her husband, and whose followers still dress like women and live as celibates – is a sacred tree, the branches of which are covered with glass bangles, thrown by persons who pay their vows to the saint; if the bangles stay in the tree, they believe that their petitions will be granted.[37]

In Syria, in the oak-groves above the village of Bárúk, in the Lebanon mountains, can be found a sacred tree named Sitt (Lady) Sára, owing its sanctity to Sarah the wife of Abraham, whose footprint, that of a veritable daughter of the giants, is still pointed out on the rock below the tree.

To this shrine are brought rags torn from the clothing of sick persons, which are tied on to the branches of the tree, with a prayer to Sitt Sára for healing, for it is only on behalf of the sick that her mediation is sought. In the course of time these shreds have accumulated to such an extent that they literally hid the tree itself, and of recent years a daughter-tree dedicated to Sitt Rufka (Rebecca) has been adopted by those who desire favours for their sick ones, and prayers are offered now to Sitt Rufka for the same purpose, and the stream of worshippers never fails. It is hardly necessary to state that Abraham and his household are claimed by Muḥammadans as good Muslims, Abraham being known to them as Khalíl, the Friend of God, and his reputed tomb at Hebron is a jealously guarded shrine. So, as to the women of the Prophet's family, to the womenfolk of the "friend of God" also, is given the dignity of sainthood.

As a modern writer on Islám says with truth, "Practically, the conception of the mystical, saintly life and the organization of dervish fraternities cover all Islám, and are the stimulants and vehicles of Muslim piety. The religious institutions tend to foster this. Above all comes the pilgrimage to Mecca and the many imitation pilgrimages all over the Muslim lands, to the tombs of celebrated saints." He goes on to speak of the tremendous effect of the pilgrimage ceremonial on the pilgrim to Mecca and adds, "the same scenes are being repeated at saintly shrines over the Muslim world".[38]

In conclusion, then, Mysticism, together with the worship of the Saints, living and dead, is still a real part, indeed the most real part, of religious life, to the men and women of present-day Islám and in so far as it leads the Muslim to seek for a direct experience of God, to shake off the formalism and traditionalism of orthodox Islám, and to strive instead after the deepening of the spiritual life, and to seek to do the Will of God in love to Him and service to His creatures, so far its influence must be an inspiring and uplifting force. In so far, too, as the worship of the saints leads modern Muslims to look up to those who, like Rábi'a of Baṣra, were true saints of God, as their ideal and to seek to follow in their steps, this must mean progress in the religious life.

The women saints, a great host, out of whom it has been possible to mention only a few of the most outstanding in the foregoing pages, certainly represent the greatest height to which Muslim womanhood has attained, and in the reverence accorded them by Muslim men and the example which they offer to Muslim women, lies a real hope for the attainment of a higher standard, religious and social, for Muslim women of today.

The Path of the saint, whether Christian or Muslim, lies through renunciation of self and communion with the Unseen, and the saint is impelled along the Way by the consuming flame of his love to God. He holds the faith that:

> That which thou lovest, O man, that too become thou must,
> God if thou lovest God, dust if thou lovest dust.

The modern Muslim woman, even more than man, is outgrowing orthodox Islám. The tendency is, on the one hand, towards religious indifference, on the other towards mysticism, which offers a living religion. It may be that the real grounds of hope for the future, for those who are of the House of Islám, lie in this latter tendency.

1 L. Rinn, *Marabouts et Khouan*, p. 28.

2 Margoliouth, *Encyclopaedia of Islám*, Art. "'Abd al-Qádir". Montet, *Encyc. of Religion and Ethics*, Art. "Religious Orders (Muslim)".

Depont and Coppolani, *Les Confréries Religieuses Musulmanes*, p. 154.

3 Cf. Le Chatelier, *Les Confréries Musulmanes*, p. 202. For a further account of the Rifá'í ritual see J. P. Brown, *The Dervishes*, pp. 113–24. Cf. T. Canaan, *Mohammedan Saints and Sanctuaries in Palestine*, pp. 119 ff.

4 Cf. Le Chatelier, *op. cit.* p. 48.

5 Cf. also Montet, *op. cit.* "Religious Orders (Muslim)", sect. Khalwatiyya, and Depont and Coppolani, *op. cit.* chap. IX.

6 Cf. L. Rinn, *op. cit.* pp. 211 ff. Depont and Coppolani, *op. cit.* pp. 166 ff.

7 Cf. J. P. Brown, *The Dervishes*, chap. X.

8 E. J. W. Gibb, *History of Ottoman Poetry*, I, p. 151, note 3.

9 Cf. Depont and Coppolani, *op. cit.* p. 333, 334. Also Vollers, *Encyclopaedia of Islám*, Art. "Aḥmad al-Badawí".

10 Ob. AH 594 (AD 1197–8).

11 Cf. L. Rinn, *op. cit.* pp. 211 ff. Depont and Coppolani, *op. cit.* pp. 166 ff.

12 *Silsilat al-ward.*

13 *Silsilat al-baraka.*

14 Montet, "Religious Orders (Muslim)", *Encyclopaedia of Religion and Ethics.*

15 L. Rinn, *Marabouts et Khouan*, p. 88.

16 Montet, *op cit., loc. cit.* L. Rinn, *op. cit., loc. cit.*

17 Garnett, *Mysticism and Magic in Turkey*, p. 175; *Women of Turkey*, p. 507. Cf. J. P. Brown, *The Dervishes*, p. 165.

18 Garnett, *op. cit.* pp. 176, 177.

19 Qur'án, Súra XXIX, 44; XXXIII, 41; XVII, 28.

20 Cf. Lane, *Modern Egyptians*, II, pp. 220–2.

21 See pp. 217–18.

22 Trumelet, *op. cit.* pp. 326–8.

23 Ganneau identifies this with the *makóm* of Deuteronomy, the "high places" against which the prophets preached in vain. See *Arabs in Palestine*, p. 209. Cf. T. Canaan, *Mohammedan Saints and Sanctuaries in Palestine*, pp. 47 ff.

24 Trumelet, *op. cit.* p. 159.
25 Masterman, "Saints and Martyrs (Syrian)", *E. R. and E.*
26 See p. 218.
27 Cf. Goldziher, *Le culte des saints chez les Musulmans*, p. 268.
28 See p. 20.
29 Cf. T. Canaan, *Mohammedan Saints and Sanctuaries in Palestine*, pp. 132, 263.
30 R. Hughes-Buller, *Census of India*, Baluchistán, 1901.
31 Cf. Robertson Smith, *Religion of the Semites*, pp. 185–193.
32 Clermont Ganneau, *The Arabs in Palestine*, p. 209.
33 Al-Tabarí, *Annales*, I, p. 922, ed. de Goeje.
34 Súra XLVIII, 18.
35 Yáqút, *Mu'jam al-Buldán*, ed. Wüstenfeld, III, p. 261.
36 Garnett, *Women of Turkey* (*Muslim*), p. 212.
37 T. W. Arnold, "Saints and Martyrs (Indian)", *E. R. and E.*
38 D. B. Macdonald, *The Religious Attitude and Life in Islám*, pp. 215, 218.

LIST OF AUTHORS QUOTED

ARABIC AUTHORS

M. b. M. al-'Abdárí. *Madkhal al-Shari' al-Sharíf*. Alexandria, AH 1293.

Dáwúd al-Antákí. *Tazyín al-Aswaq*. Bulaq, AH 1291.

M. b. Ḥusayn Baha al-Dín. *Al-Kashkúl*. Bulaq, AH 1288.

A. b. Yaḥyá al-Baládhurí. *Kitáb al-Futúḥ al-Buldán*. Leyden, AD 1863–6.

Ibn Baṭṭúṭa. *Tuḥfa al-Nuẓẓár*. Paris, AD 1893; edited by C. Defrémeny and B. R. Sanguinetti.

Dabistán-i-Mazáhib. Bombay, AD 1846.

Abú Dáwúd. *Al-Sunan*. Cairo, AH 1280.

Al-Dhahabí. *Mizán al-I'tidál*. Lucknow, AD 1884.

M. b. Isháq al-Fakihi. *Akhbár Makka*. Leipzig, AD 1858.

Abú al Faraj al-Isfahání. *Kitáb al-Aghání*. Bulaq, AH 1280.

M. b. M. al-Ghazálí. *Iḥyá 'Ulúm al-Dín*. Cairo, AH 1272.

Ibn Ḥajar. *Iṣába fí tamyíz al-Ṣaḥába*. Calcutta, AD 1873.

Taqí al-Dín al-Ḥisní. "Siyar al-Ṣáliḥát." MS. Paris 2042.

Shu'ayb b. 'Abd al-'Azíz al-Ḥurayfísh. *Al-Rawḍ al-Fá'iq*. Cairo, AH 1279.

'Alí b. Ḥusám al-Dín. *Kanz al-'Ummál* (al-Suyuṭi's works). Haidarabad, AD 1894–7.

M. b. Ḥasan Imád al-Dín. "*Ḥayát al-Qulúb*" (on margin of *Qút al-Qulúb*). Cairo, AH 1310.

'Amr b. Bahr al-Jáḥiẓ. *Kitáb al-Ḥayawán*. Cairo, AH 1324.

Bayán wa al-Tabyín. Cairo, AH 1332.

Jamál al-Dín b. 'Alí al-Jawzí. "Ṣafwa al-Ṣafwa." MS. Brit. Museum. Or. 3048.

Ṣibt Ibn al-Jawzí. "Ta'ríkh Mir'át al-Zamán." MS. Brit. Museum. Add. 23,277.

M. b. I. b. I. al-Kalábádhí. "Kitáb al-Ta'arruf." MS. Collection Prof. Nicholson.

"Ma'ání al-Akhbár." MS. School of Oriental Studies, No. 200.

Ibn Khaldún. *Muqaddima*. Beyrout, 1900.

Histoire des Berbères, tr. de Slane. Paris, 1925.

Ibn Khallikán. *Wafayát al-A'yán*. Göttingen, AD 1835–50.

Biographical Dictionary, tr, de Slane. Paris, AD 1842.

Abú Ṭálib al-Makkí. *Qút al-Qulúb*. Cairo, AH 1310.

Al-Maqdísí. See *Bibliotheca Geographorum Arabicorum*, tom. III. Leyden, AD 1906.

Ghánim al-Maqdísí. "Kashf al-Asrár." MS. Berlin. We. 1653.

M. b. 'Ali al-Maqrízí. *Al-Khiṭaṭ*. Cairo, AD 1922.

'Alí Básha al-Mubárak. *Al-Khiṭaṭ al-Tawfikiyya al-Jadída*. Bulaq, AD 1889.

Mufaḍḍal b. M. al-Dabbí. *Mufaḍḍalíyát* (ed. C. J. Lyall). Oxford, 1918.

'Abd al-Rá' úf al-Munáwí. "Al-Kawákib al-Durríya." MS. Brit. Museum. Add. 23,369.

Abú al Qásim al-Ḥasan b. M. al-Nisábúrí. *'Uqalá' al-Majánín*. Cairo, AD 1924.

Abú al-Qásim al-Qushayrí. *Risála*. Bulaq, AD 1867.

Ibn Sa'd. *Kitáb al-Ṭabaqát al-Kabír*. Leyden, AD 1904.

Abú Naṣr al-Sarráj. *Kitáb al-Luma'*. London, AD 1914 (ed. Nicholson, Gibb Series).

Al-Sarráj al-Qárí. *Maṣári' al-Ushsháq*. Constantinople, AH 1301.

M. b. 'Abd al-Kárim al-Shahrastání. *Kitáb al-Milal wa al-Niḥal*. London, AD 1842.

'Abdal-Wahhábal-Sha'rání. *Al-Ṭabaqát al-Kubrá*. Cairo, AH 1299.

M. b. al-Aṭir al-Shaybání. *Usd al-Ghába fí ma'rifa al-Saḥába*. Cairo, AH 1280.

Al-Suhrawardí. "*'Awárif al-Ma'árif*" (on margin of al-Ghazálí's *Iḥyá*). Cairo, AH 1272.

'Abd al-Raḥmán al-Sulamí. "Ṭabaqát al-Ṣúfiyya." MS. Brit. Mus. Add. 18,520.

Abú Ja'far M. b. Jarír al-Ṭabarí. *Annales*. Leyden, AD 1879.

Abú al-Maḥásin b. Taghribardí. *Al-Nujúm al-Záhira*. Leyden, AD 1855–61.

Abú Tammám. *Diwán al-Ḥamása*. Cairo, 1913.

M. b. al-Tayyib al-Qádirí. *Nashr al-matháni fí a'yán al-qarn al-thamáni*. Fez, AH 1310.

Wüstenfeld (editor). *Die Chroniken der Stadt Mekka*. Arabic Text. Leipzig, AD 1858.

Yáfi'í al-Sháfi'í. *Rawḍ al-Riyáḥín*. Cairo, AH 1297.

Yáqút b. 'Abd Allah. *Kitáb Mu'jam al-Buldán*. Leipzig, AD 1866.

PERSIAN AUTHORS

Shams al-Dín A. Aflákí. "Manáqib al-'Árifín." MS. India Office. No. 1670.

Faríd al-Dín 'Aṭṭár. *Tadhkirat al-Awliyá*. Ed. Nicholson. London, AD 1905. Uyghur version, tr. de Courteille. Paris, AD 1889.

Firishta. *History of Hindustán*. Tr. A. Dow. London, AD 1768.

'Alí b. 'Uthmán al-Hujwírí. *Kashf al-Maḥjúb*. Tr. R. A. Nicholson. London, AD 1911.

'Abd al-Raḥmán b. al-Jámí. *Nafaḥát al-Uns*. Calcutta, AD 1859.

Al-Munawwar. *Asrár al-Tawḥíd*. Petrograd, AD 1899.

Jalál al-Dín Rúmí. *Mathnawí*. Bks I and II. Ed. R. A. Nicholson. London, AD 1925.

Maḥmúd Shabistarí. *Gulshan-i Ráz*. Ed. Whinfield. London, AD 1880.

Tawakkul Beg Kulálí. "Neskhah-i Aḥwál Sháhí." MS. Brit. Mus. Or. 3203.

URDU AUTHOR

M. 'Abbás. *Mashâhír Niswán*. Lahore, 1902.

TURKISH AUTHOR

M. Zihní. *Meshâhír al-Nisá*. Constantinople.

EUROPEAN AUTHORS

T. W. Arnold. "Saints and Martyrs (Indian)", *Encyclopaedia of Religion and Ethics*. Edinburgh, 1908.

H. J. Ll. Beadnell. *The Wilderness of Sinai*. London, 1927.

M. Benhazera. *Six mois chez les Touareg du Ahaggar*. Alger, 1908.

St Bernard. *The Love of God*. Tr. M. C. and Coventry Patmore. London, 1884.

R. Briffault. *The Mothers*. London, 1927.

J. P. Brown. *The Dervishes*. London, 1927.

E. G. Browne. "Ṣúfism." *Religious Systems of the World*. London, 1876.

A Traveller's Narrative of the Episode of the Báb. Cambridge, 1891.

A Persian Anthology. London, 1927.

R. Burton. *Personal Narrative of a Pilgrimage to Mecca*. London, 1893.

T. Canaan. *Mohammedan Saints and Sanctuaries in Palestine*. London, 1927.

Le Chatelier. *Les Confréries Musulmanes*. Paris, 1887.

C. D. Cobham. *Excerpta Cypria*. Nicosia, 1895.

John Cordelier. *The Spiral Way*. London, 1922.

S. I. Curtiss. *Primitive Semitic Religion Today*. London, 1902.

O. Depont and Coppolani. *Les Confréries Religieuses Musulmanes*. Alger, 1897.

R. Dozy. *Histoire de l'Islamisme*. Tr. Chauvin. Leyden, 1879.

C. Doughty. *Travels in Arabia Deserta*. London, 1926.

St Francis. *Little Flowers of St Francis*. Tr. T. W. Arnold. London, 1908.

Clermont Ganneau. *Palestine Quarterly Survey*. 1875.

L. M. J. Garnett. *Mysticism and Magic in Turkey*. London, 1912.

The Women of Turkey and Their Folk-lore. London, 1891.

E. J. W. Gibb. *Ottoman Poems*. London, 1882.

History of Ottoman Poetry. London, 1900.
A. J. de Gobineau. *Les Religions et les Philosophies dans l'Asie Centrale*. Paris, 1900.
I. Goldziher. *Muhammedanische Studien*. Halle, 1889.
"Culte des saints." *Revue de l'histoire des Religions*. 1880.
"De l'Ascétisme aux premiers temps de l'Islám." *Revue de l'histoire des Religions*. 1898.
Mme de la Motte Guyon. *Poems*. Tr. W. Cowper. London, 1811.
F. von Hügel. *The Mystical Element of Religion*. London, 1909.
R. Hughes-Buller. *Census of India*. Baluchistán, 1901.
St John of the Cross. *Ascent of Mount Carmel*. Tr. Lewis. London, 1889.
Spiritual Canticle. Tr. Lewis. London, 1909.
Rufus Jones. *Studies in Mystical Religion*. London, 1909.
A. von Kremer. *Culturgeschichte des Orients*. Leipzig, 1873.
E. W. Lane. *Manners and Customs of the Modern Egyptians*. London, 1836.
Ramón Lull. *The Lover and the Beloved*. London, 1923.
C. J. Lyall. *Translations of Ancient Arabian Poetry*. London, 1885.
D. B. Macdonald. *The Religious Attitude and Life in Islam*. Chicago, 1909.
P. S. Margoliouth. *The Early Development of Mohammedanism*. London, 1914.
L. Massignon. *Lexique Technique de la Mystique Musulmane*. Paris, 1922.
Textes Inédits Relatifs à la Mystique Musulmane.
M. de Molinos. *The Spiritual Guide*. England, 1688.
E. Montet. *Le culte des saints musulmans dans l'Afrique du Nord*. Geneva, 1909.
R. A. Nicholson. *Selected Poems from the Diwán-i Shamsí Tabríz*. Cambridge, 1898.
Literary History of the Arabs. London, 1907.
Studies in Islamic Mysticism. Cambridge, 1921.
Translations of Eastern Poetry and Prose. Cambridge, 1922.
The Idea of Personality in Ṣúfism. Cambridge, 1923.
"Asceticism (Muslim)." *Encyclopaedia of Religion and Ethics*. Edinburgh, 1908.
E. H. Palmer. *The Desert of the Exodus*. Cambridge, 1871.
Caussin de Perceval. *L'Histoire des Arabes*. Paris, 1902.
A. Perron. *Femmes arabes avant et depuis l'islamisme*. Paris, 1858.
Plotinus. *Enneads*. Tr. S. McKenna. London, 1917.
L. Rinn. *Marabouts et Khouan*. Alger, 1884.

John of Ruysbroeck. *Book of the Sparkling Stone*. Tr. C. A. Wynschenk Dom. London, 1916.

W. Robertson Smith. *Kinship and Marriage in Early Arabia*. Cambridge, 1885.

Religion of the Semites. London, 1894.

F. Thompson. *Works of Francis Thompson*. London, 1913.

C. Trumelet. *Les Saints de l'Islam*. Paris, 1881.

Evelyn Underhill. *Mysticism*. London, 1912.

Man and the Supernatural. London, 1927.

Carra de Vaux. *Penseurs de l'Islam*. Paris, 1923.

J. Wellhausen. *Die Ehe bei den Arabern*. Göttingen, 1893.

INDEX I

Proper Names and Titles (Titles of books, etc., in italics)

INDEX II

SUBJECTS

INDEX III

Technical Terms